Competitive Intelligence and Senior Management

Competitive Intelligence and Senior Management

"The best solution to where to place the office of competitive intelligence is on a par with functions that report directly to the Board"

Josèph H.A.M. Rodenberg RM

Eburon Delft
2007

Printed on acid-free paper

ISBN 978-90-5972-192-0

Eburon Academic Publishers
P.O. Box 2867
2601 CW Delft
The Netherlands
tel.: +31 (0) 15 - 2131484 / fax: +31 (0) 15 - 2146888
info@eburon.nl / www.eburon.nl

Cover design: Studio Hermkens, Amsterdam
Graphic design: Textcetera, The Hague

Table of Contents

PART III
Epilogue

Acknowledgements

For many years I have been privileged to occupy a position as a management consultant in intelligence-based marketing and management solutions, and have run my own consultancy firm since 1985.

Many clients have placed their faith in me by sharing their in-depth information and knowledge about their organisations as well as their personal feelings, expertise and experiences. This trust has been the basis of our well-reputed consultancy practices in the Benelux countries and throughout Europe, the Americas and the Far East. Working with so many successful national and international companies has been, and continues to be, a great honour.

I should like to extend my personal thanks to all the managers and business leaders with whom I and our firm, Rodenberg Tillman and Associates, have enjoyed this co-operation.

This book is the 3rd in a series which makes intelligence applicable in the business world.

In 2000, I published my first book entitled "Business and Competitive Intelligence, management discipline in the 21st Century". In 2004 my second book followed; this was entitled "Enterprise Intelligence, creating the intelligent and alert company".

As with my previous books, I should like to express my heartfelt thanks to Enyta and my loving children Constantijn, Veronique and Stéphanie.

In addition, I should like to thank my son Constantijn for his great help with the fine-tuning of the text and layout, and with the design of all the diagrams in this book.

Josèph H.A.M. Rodenberg RM
Houten/Barcelona, February 2007

PART I

Aspects of Competitive Intelligence

I

Preface

"Any company that cannot imagine the future won't be around to enjoy it".
(Hamel and Prahalad)

We live in a world of dramatic changes that increasingly involve processes such as globalisation, internationalisation, privatisation, deregulation, disruptive technologies, outsourcing, off-shoring, near shoring, protectionism and the phenomenon of such upcoming nations as the BRIC countries, Brazil, Russia, India and China. At present, the G8 countries consist of the US, Japan, Germany, France, the United Kingdom, Canada, Italy and Russia; in 2020-2030 the leading industrial countries will consist of China, the US, India, Russia, Brazil and Japan. This transformation will change the world, especially the future position of Europe. Peter Drucker, who died in November 2005, stated that sixty percent of innovation comes from outside your industry boundaries. Gary Hamel states: "if a company is interested in finding the future, most of what it needs to learn is to learn from outside the industrial sector".

European companies, whether they are multinational, international, national, regional or local, will face tremendous competitive pressure in the future. Every company will face this competitive pressure in their own backyard. Although I am writing about the "future", we should never forget that the future is not next year. The future is today and it already started years ago. The aim of management is to be successful in the near future. However, success in the future does not depend on a study of the future but on the future success of decisions taken today.

For many hundreds of years, military victories have been won by smartness and cleverness or, in other words, intelligence. As the famous Chinese general Sun Tzu (c. 544-496 BC), author of *The Art of War,* stated: "Know your enemies and know yourself and in a hundred battles you will never be in danger." In business most companies do not have an intelligence capability in place. Only large organisations in the US, Europe and the Far East have an intelligence regime in place with the aim of strengthening the competitive position called "competitive intelligence". However, competitive intelligence in these large organisations is not always as professional as it should be. Every employee in an organisation deals with information. He or she spends almost 30 percent of his/her time gathering information and knowledge to do a proper job. Departments of strategy, marketing, marketing research, business development, research and development and many others try daily to acquire the applicable information. Much of this information is usually neither available nor structured and most of the time it is difficult to access. Most of the various departments are busily trying to put together the pieces of the puzzle, a process that is hampered by the fact that there is little sharing of information and knowledge in most organisations. The key challenge is to put together all the bits and pieces of the necessary information so you and management are able to see the big picture, to really see the changes in the competitive arena, to have the right insights into the changes on the marketplace, to foresee disruptive technologies in time and to be aware in time of new competitors who are already active beyond our horizon.

The most difficult thing in business today is to take the right decisions. Napoleon once said, "Nothing is more difficult, and therefore more precious, than to be able to decide." On average, management takes decisions based on about thirty to forty percent of the available information and knowledge in combination with a certain 'gut feeling' and intuitions. In addition, many assumptions have proved incorrect. US humorist and showman Will Rogers (1879-1935) explained this as "It's not what we don't know that gives us trouble, it's what we know isn't so." Most organisations still struggle with how to deal with information. Information is useless if you don't know what to do with it. Knowledge that is a few years old is purely experiential and has little practical use today. The challenge to management is to obtain better insights and foresights of information and knowledge, not by means of yet more information technology, but with improved information management and knowledge management creating intelligence.

Yet we continue to spend hundreds of millions on IT in the hope of better structuring data and information and making them more accessible. Many IT companies offer business intelligence solutions intended to identify, structure and render accessible the internal streams of data and information. Nevertheless, many organisations still face huge problems in getting good results from these efforts since many of them still lack the right business insights into their internal data and information. The ultimate objective is to use the correct business insights to finally get control of the business. However, management is drowning in data and information, lacks actual business insights and, even worse, commercial foresights.

In addition, many companies have introduced supportive tools such as Performance Management, Balance Score Cards and others driven by KPIs, Key Performance Indicators. As a result, there has been increasing pressure on people within organisations that are managed by these kinds of supportive tools aimed at obtaining better control of the organisation's performance.

Finally we have the financial facts and figures that give a clear indication about the performance of the organisation. Earnings, profitability and cash flow determine the short- term value for shareholders value. But these performance indicators chiefly explain what happened in the past and are not relevant for the future success of the company; despite methods such as DCF, discount cash flow, and extrapolation, these performance indicators explain a company's success in the past rather than in the future. Although these methods give us some insights into what might happen, we should not place undue reliance upon them. All of this describes how strong the internal focus of many organisations still is. But how about the outside world? Of course, we develop our strategies to make choices and to position the company against our rivals on the markets. But how well have we formulated our strategies? Are those strategies really "evidence-based"? Have we used accurate and current data, information and knowledge from the business environment, based on continuous and consistent efforts throughout the year? Or was it merely an exercise of a couple of weeks aimed at getting the strategic, business or marketing plan done in order to make next year's budgets? Was it the result of a calendar-driven activity, a remote strategy development process or did it involve gathering data and information from markets, customers, competitors, R and D and so on and of trying to piece the puzzle together? The key question I regularly ask at clients' assignments is: "Will your market look the same in six to twelve months?" Everyone says no.

What is on the agenda of top management in 2006-2008? In a study conducted among 1400 Chief Information Officers (CIOs), the Gartner Research Group asked them what the business priorities for the near future would be. Of these 1400 CIOs, 400 were from the EMEA regions (Europe, Middle East and Africa).

According to Gartner, business priorities in 2006 and beyond are: Improving business processes
1. Controlling the operating costs of the enterprise
2. Attracting and expanding customer relationships
3. Improving the competitive lead
4. Improving competitiveness
5. Using intelligence in products and services
6. Security breaches and disruptions
7. Revenue growth
8. Faster innovation
9. Faster innovation and cycle times

Six out of these ten priorities have to do with building improved sustainable competitive edges: attracting and expanding customer relationships, improving the competitive lead, improving competitiveness in general, the growth of revenues and faster innovation. Building a sustainable competitive lead implies having a continuous in-depth understanding of what is really happening on markets, with customers and the competition, in technologies and legislation. If management strives to compete, they must have insights and foresights on how they themselves perform against the competition. Only if they have real competitive insights and foresights in the competitive arena, management will be able to outmanoeuvre and outperform the competition.

"Bad decisions can often be traced back to the way decisions were made. The alternatives were not clearly defined, the right information was not collected, and the cost and benefits were not accurately weighted: there was a lack of intelligence. But sometimes the fault doesn't lie in the decision-making process but rather in the mind of the decision maker. The way the human brain works can sabotage the choices we make."

But why does management in most organisations benefit too little from the changes, dynamics and opportunities in the external business environment? If companies don't keep a continuous watch on the outside by having a monitoring system, a watchtower or radar in place, they will always struggle to benefit from the changes and opportunities in the outside world. They will always be surprised by crucial developments in the competitive landscape, they will always be too late to seize business opportunities and incapable of changing business threats into business opportunities. How is it possible to compete unless one maintains a constant eye on current and potential competitors? The most important decisions are taken not inside but outside the organisation.

This book will help management in organisations to better understand the factors of future success. This doesn't entail projecting information into the future, but rather creating better business insights and business foresights for today and beyond. The basis of our philosophy is the statement made by Peter Drucker many years ago that "the future can't be predicted, but future events can." By managing the flow of internal and external information and knowledge more efficiently, and transforming these into competitive intelligence, management is able to achieve improved business insights and foresights. Competitive intelligence is not about databases, so no explanation will be given about the success or failure of information technology.

I will describe the management discipline of competitive intelligence as a precondition for a company's existence, and show how it can help departments of strategy, marketing, sales, business development, innovation, research and development and others to perform better and how it can support senior management, executive teams and supervisory boards in taking the right decisions.

The current emphasis on risks has put considerable pressure on senior management. Everyone realises that even an innocent scenario can become a nightmare if not properly managed. Senior management has no choice but to lead the implementation of competitive intelligence, driving intelligence awareness through every level of the organisation. The real danger is that senior managers are not up to this new challenge.

"The best solution to where to place the office of competitive intelligence is on a par with functions that report directly to the Board"

"The key doesn't lie in better information, but in turning information into information that cannot be ignored".
(Jim Collins in *Good to Great*)

This statement by the American business consultant Jim Collins is about the life-blood of organisations: information. However, we have too much data and information flowing throughout our organisations. The great challenge for management is to transform this information into intelligence for better decisions.

According to Tom Peters, one of the authors of In *Search of Excellence*, "big organisations are starving to death because they are over-controlled and far too bureaucratic. This is easy and transparent; however, as managers we aren't paid to have it easy. Bear in mind that creativity is never the result of regulations, procedures or data research."[1]

Today one of the most important tasks of management is to be in control of the business. But tasks are not the same as challenges. In order to ensure control of the business, heavy investments have been made in information technology, business intelligence solutions, risk management and management information systems. In addition, companies have created tools to monitor employees by installing balance scorecards and performance management systems. Nowadays the key performance indicators seem essential for the successful performance of most companies. There are also the financial indicators such as revenues, Earnings Before Interest and Taxes (EBIT), net profit and cash flow, to list just the most important resulting in the almighty indicator "shareholders value". Of course, we should not forget the increasing role of the supervisory boards, accountants, lawyers, audit committees and, recently, the pressure from private equity firms. All these aspects focus on control of the current business but the focus is directed inward, not outward.

---

1   In his seminar on December 19 2006 at Nyenrode University.

What remains of human entrepreneurship and creativity? What has happened to information and knowledge management as the lifeblood of an organisation?

What about a consistent approach to looking at the outside world, to deciding how to benefit from unfulfilled customer demand, how to identify real opportunities in markets, among customers and in technologies for future success? How can companies compete unless management maintains a constant reconnaissance of the competitive landscape? Why are so many companies always lagging behind and overtaken by unforeseen events? Of course the future cannot be predicted, but future events can. Why do some seventy to eighty percent of all mergers and acquisitions worldwide fail? All these mergers and acquisitions are not beneficial to the economy; they hardly lead to the improved competitiveness of the merged companies. In most cases, mergers and acquisitions benefit top management alone. When the former Vice President of Goldman Sachs, Leon Cooperman, was asked if even one merger had ever produced in the expected results, his reaction was, "There might be success stories; however, I can't think of one right now."

Some years ago, Business Week published a clear message about how matters might be improved: "Do your homework. It's amazing how many companies don't. Lazy, complacent or simply unaware. Thousands of executives routinely take critical business decisions based on incomplete information about the changes and dynamics in the competitive landscapes."

Most executives are still unaware of how vital competitive intelligence can be for companies in decision-making. If generals are unable to take decisions without good intelligence, what makes CEOs think they can? I hope to succeed in convincing senior management to adopt competitive intelligence as the management discipline that ensures future success.

Entrepreneurship in Europe is disappearing. Within major organisations and companies, there are increasing numbers of managers who are given targets and who finish the job in 2-3 years. The main focus is control and, as a result, there is neither the time nor the initiative to innovate. The focus within the business world is moving from entrepreneurship towards management and control. After all, managers come and go, they don't innovate. Their main activities in the period between 2001-2006 were cost-cutting and restructuring. As a result, in Europe we have developed a mentality of risk-avoidance.

Europeans are resigned to the fact that there will be no growth in prosperity over the next decennia. The result of this is a climate of satisfaction, a resting on the laurels of past achievements and human well-being. If Europe hopes to regain its competitive edge, we shall all have to work more hours, keep older workers on board until the age of seventy, and revive a spirit of personal drive and passion to make things happen again. None of this can be brought about without some essential action on the part of the various governments in Europe.

Europeans are open to the notion of increasing the number of weekly working hours, but they are not motivated to do it because of the extremely high level of income taxes. Nobel Prize-winning economist Edward C. Prescott explained in 2004 that it is not true that Europeans work less because they enjoy life more. In his article "Why do Americans work more than Europeans?" Prescott explained that the tax burden in the 1970s in the US and Europe was comparable, as was the number of working hours year round. In the 1990s the tax burden was increased in Europe and decreased in the US, and Europeans worked fifty percent less than Americans. If the European and US tax burdens had been equal, the same would have been true of the labour market. Prescott concluded that the governments in Europe punish the working class with higher taxes. And do Europeans enjoy the extra leisure time governments force them to have? Europeans spend most of their leisure time cleaning, doing odd jobs, cooking and performing other domestic tasks. Because of the high tax burden in Europe, in contrast to the US, it is too expensive to hire people to do this kind of work.

If Europe wants to regain its competitive edge, both politics and business should take action by stimulating entrepreneurship and innovation, increasing the number of working hours and decreasing the tax burden, investing in research and development as well as in education, focussing less upon management and control in organisations and more on personal initiative, drive, passion, leading to "freedom of action, personal and professional development".

Success in business today is no guarantee of success in the future. Successful managers and business leaders need people around them with their feet on the ground. Success also creates blind spots, making criticism from colleagues and discussion even more necessary. Management control is good, but trust is even better. I have listed five recommendations:

1. Management should have people around them who act as the critical "watchdog"
2. Communicate that disagreement on key issues is welcome to the "watchdog"
3. Formulate teams of people able to look beyond the various disciplines towards the whole company's current and future competitive landscape
4. Be tolerant of people who think differently and don't "kill" the messenger who brings the unfavourable or unexpected analysis
5. Ensure transparency so all managers have access to all pieces of the complete information puzzle.

These five recommendations can be realised by establishing a professional competitive intelligence team capable of protecting management from "corporate dyslexia".

> *"If we think that highly valuable information can be generated almost for free, we do the wrong things. Everything that is free degenerates".*
> (Theo Bouwman, CEO of PCM Publishers)

My message to CEOs, Executive Committees, Boards of Directors, Members of Supervisory Boards and Audit Committees is the following:

You have a wide range of tools in your organisations but you still lack sound business foresights, two-thirds of your mergers and acquisitions still fail, and you are regularly taken by surprise by unexpected developments in your business environment. Often, your company strategy fails to achieve the hoped-for results. The most frequent explanation for such failures is the change in market conditions. How long are you going to go on accepting these major disasters? Of course, you don't worry because, on average, the usual time top management stays in position dropped during the 1990s from seven years to a mere three years. That is even less than the corporate governance management-based contracts of four years. So you ask yourself, why should I worry? You get a high salary, pension arrangements, options or shares, bonuses and, in most cases, a handy premium should you be forced to leave the company.

These are the most commonly-used management tools in your organisation: good management reporting on finance and control performance management based on numerous indicators, various ICT-tools focused on internal data and information flows balance score cards:

▶ accountancy and control
▶ legal advisory teams
▶ risk management
▶ corporate governance

In addition, you have your members of the supervisory board, the audit committee and, now under construction in the Netherlands, the so-called "in-control letter". However, you are still not in a comfortable position. Members of supervisory boards have become very cautious because of increased personal responsibilities and the Public Company Accounting Reform and Investor Protection Act of 2002, also called the Sarbanes-Oxly Act. This has made financial reporting more transparent and easier to evaluate objectively, which makes financial reporting almost fully in control of risks.

> *"Management spend over sixty-five percent of their time and resources on the management of internal uncertainty. It doesn't leave much time to focus on the complex change in their industrial sectors and the broader scope".*
> (Wharton Business School)

The opposite is the case with the operational risks, which are much more subjective and rely on personal estimates, experiences and intuition. We should also take into account the attitude toward the management of successes in the past, complacency and blind spots. In many cases certain individuals and external forces are blamed for failure, which enables management to avoid redefining their basic assumptions. Potential failures are seen as the evidence of a faulty implementation of strategies rather than as proof that the wrong decisions have been made. On the other hand, the scope of management limits success in business and influences behaviour.

Which management tools have management not yet installed to fulfil their needs? Valuable, useful and relevant advice beyond what management already knows; timely and significant future insights where knowledge and useful conclusions are reached by a sifting of conflicting and unrelated information and facts; early warnings, including the options for solving and benefiting from these; the ability to understand the pattern of future events and problems; supporting evidence through the behaviour of their peers.

These needs can be answered by establishing a competitive intelligence capability, preferably in those functions that report directly to the CEO. The aim of competitive intelligence is to gather, interpret and analyse disaggregated data, information and knowledge from all relevant competitive aspects in the external environment and transform this into strategic intelligence for improved decision-making. Competitive intelligence makes it possible to stay ahead of the competition. Competitive intelligence may be compared to a game of chess: it allows you to think many moves ahead of your opponents. It enables management to identify competitors' weaknesses and make it possible to benefit from the identification of future opportunities.

I have listed ten objectives which management can achieve with competitive intelligence:

1. the avoidance of surprises in the fast-changing dynamics of external international markets;
2. the timely identification of threats and opportunities;
3. the structured and consistent feeding of strategic management processes;
4. the prevention of complacency and arrogance about past successes on the part of management;
5. the ongoing identification of weak areas in competitors' strategies as well as the gaps in one's own strategies;
6. the pro-active monitoring of developments in both one's own sector and contiguous sectors;
7. the establishment of the early warning signals necessary for the consistent improvement of performance in markets and with customers, so as to remain ahead of the competition;
8. the creation of consistent good performance, because intelligence focuses on the five key drivers for change: markets, customers, competition, technology and legislation;
9. improved decision-making in respect of the role of watchdog for senior management;

10. the ability to react pro-actively and intelligently to opportunities in the market place and market space.

In his book *Good to Great*, Jim Collins has undertaken in-depth research in order to discover where the difference lies between good and great companies. To make a company great, a primary task is the creation of a culture in which people have ample opportunity to be heard and, ultimately, for the truth to be heard. This is identical to the practice of competitive intelligence: "telling senior management the brutal truth". Collins defines four practices:

- ▶ Lead with questions, not answers
- ▶ Engage in dialogue and debate and not coercion
- ▶ Conduct autopsies without blame
- ▶ Build red flag mechanisms that turn information into information that cannot be ignored

One of the primary ways to de-motivate people is to ignore the brutal facts of reality.

Historical overview

II

"If thinking is an intellectual response to a problem, then the absence of a problem leads to the absence of thinking".
(Theodore Levitt)

Intelligence in within business society started in the late 1960s and early 1970s, and sprang from the military and governmental spheres, where it remains deep-rooted today. The names of government intelligence agencies such as the KGB in Russia, CIA and Homeland Security in the USA and MI6 in the UK are familiar. Small countries like the Netherlands, too, have their intelligence agencies such as AIVD.

The book *The Art of War* by Sun Tzu, widely considered as the first work to describe the methods of military intelligence, teaches us that dealing with conflict is a matter of anticipating and adapting adequately to external change. How does this apply in business?

In a conflict, the wise general always seeks the most advantageous position. He uses his wisdom, alertness and awareness to benefit from the energy in any given situation, even an unfavourable one. He is aware that any battle, once engaged, will result in casualties, so he tries to settle a conflict without going to war. When war becomes inevitable, his aim is not to win at the expense of other competitors, but to try to gain strength through his competitors. His aim is to create improved access to resources, assets and means that are vital to the existence, integrity and development of his state.

1960-1970s

Sun Tzu explained to us long ago the importance of knowing one's enemy and knowing the terrain where a battle is likely to take place. In the 1960s-1970s, marketing entered our thinking of management and so did strategic management, both based on Igor Ansoff's theory of the "turbulence in our business environment". Companies began to collect competitor information, initially with a focus on operational and tactical sales and marketing. Information about competitors, usually brief, became part of the business plans. The key figures in this accumulation of information were librarians as information providers. Top management paid little attention.

1980-1990s

In this decade Michael Porter published his famous books *Competitive Strategy*,

Competitive Advantage, Porter on Competition and *The Competitive Advantage of Nations.* These taught the business community about all aspects of competition and the business environment. Porter's "five forces" model is still used in many companies as an important part of the strategy process. Many companies started with industry and competitor analysis. However, full senior management support was still lacking. In the US, benchmarking started; "introduced" by Xerox, this became an accepted management application to compare performance functions between companies and even between competing companies.

In 1986 SCIP, the Society of Competitor Intelligence Professionals, was founded. In the nineties, 'competitor' was changed to 'competitive'. Competitive intelligence became increasingly accepted as a management tool, principally, however, in the US.

In 1986 SCIP's mission was:

> *"To help professionals develop expertise in collecting and analysing information, disseminating competitive intelligence, and engaging decision-makers in a productive dialogue that creates organisational competitive advantage".*

In 2003 this mission changed to:

> *"The global organisation of choice for professionals engaged in competitive intelligence and related disciplines. SCIP will be the premier advocate for the skilled use of intelligence to enhance business decision-making and organisational performance".*

In 2005 again, the mission changed to:

> *"The mission of the Society of Competitive Intelligence Professionals is to enhance the success of our members through leadership, education, advocacy and networking".*

1990-2000s

In this decade two important books brought the awareness of competition into the spotlight. These were *Hyper Competition* by Richard D'Aveni and *Competing for the future* by C.K. Prahalad and Gary Hamel. New management topics such as core competences, core capabilities and strategic intents were introduced by Prahalad and Hamel, who have also regularly published in the Harvard Business Review on the need to establish competitive intelligence capabilities in companies at senior management level. In the US, competitive intelligence made a considerable initial impact and was soon accepted by all Fortune Top 500 companies. Competitive intelligence was recognised as essential for strategic decision-making and received much attention from top management. Companies began to allocate budgets and dedicated resources to the establishment of competitive intelligence activities. The subject also became a standard topic on the programme of business schools, and efforts were made to develop support tools for competitive intelligence activities with information technology solutions such as Outlook, Lotus Notes, Sharepoint, CI Portals, etc. Again, competitive intelligence mainly took off in the US. Europe only became aware of competitive intelligence in the late 1990s.

I was among those who pioneered competitive intelligence in Europe in the late eighties. At that time, most assignments came from major multinationals throughout Europe, mainly at divisional or business unit level. I will describe the European history of competitive intelligence below.

2000-
In the 21st century, competitive intelligence is fully accepted in the US as an important capability enabling the timely prediction of changes and disruptions in the business environment which could affect the company.

Europe and the rest of the world are becoming increasingly interested in the topic of competitive intelligence. Subjects such as "key intelligence topics", "early warnings", "strategic alerts" and "business blind spots", etc., have become familiar to management.

IT software-based solutions are entering the market, assisting and facilitating the flow of data and information in a better-structured and more accessible way. Also in Europe, competitive intelligence is becoming accepted to an increasing degree, especially by US-based companies and other forward-thinking enterprises.

Competitive intelligence in Europe
In Europe, competitive intelligence remains the most neglected management discipline in business. Very gradually, some businesses are beginning with competitive intelligence, usually with the allocation of employees within marketing, sales, R and D or business development. This approach can never hope to succeed, because competitive intelligence is a 'people' affair; appointing some individual, somewhere within the organisation to do something in intelligence of which most colleagues are not aware, is a strategy foredoomed to failure.

However, it is evident that some development is occurring within marketing. Some marketing departments, marketing services and market research departments have started marketing intelligence.

Limitations to intelligence within marketing are: Marketing intelligence focuses chiefly on market share, markets and customers, and lacks the overall view as well as the future overview of the competitive landscape; Marketing intelligence is still practised in too many cases as market research "plus"; Marketing intelligence in most organisations lacks senior management support; Marketing intelligence in most cases reports to the marketing manager or marketing director and consequently remains within a limited perspective; in the last 5-10 years marketing has lost ground in many organisations and thus credibility.

In my view, locating the competitive intelligence discipline within marketing is "the kiss of death". The definition of competitive intelligence I always use explains why it goes beyond the scope of marketing.

> *"The analytical and intellectual process that transforms disaggregated market, customer, competitor, supplier, technological and other key competitive data, information and knowledge into usable actionable intelligence to the key decision-makers. Focus is the key drivers of change. Aim is future oriented."*

I will explain in details what I mean by this definition and why it goes beyond the limits of marketing.

"Analytical": within competitive intelligence, analysis is the most important part.

"Intellectual": no system whatsoever can do this. We need our intellectual capabilities to create intelligence. We also call this the human factor or "human intelligence", which makes the difference between data-information-knowledge and intelligence.

"Disaggregated market, customer, supplier, technological and other key competitive data, information and knowledge": is about all the aspects in the dynamics of the external business environment which determine the long-term success of organisations. So management must have all the fragments of information readily accessible in a structured way. This is the lifeblood of every organisation. One of the first steps in the competitive intelligence process is to bring order and structure to the vast amounts of data and information. If this is not done as a first step, management will be submerged by a flood of data and information that makes no real contribution to timely intelligence. Most managers are managed by information; instead, they are able to manage information. Of course, they all have their control mechanisms and impressive cockpit displays but these don't explain WHY. The word "why" is one of the most frequently-used words in competitive intelligence.

"Competitive": competitive means strengthening the future competitive position of the organisation. How can the company stay ahead of the competition and how can it see changes in the competitive landscape in time?

"Actionable intelligence": the objective of competitive intelligence is to take actions for decision-making. This is the key. So competitive intelligence is not information-gathering and intelligence professionals should not be seen as information-providers. Unfortunately, in many organisations this is still the case. Neither is the comparison with knowledge management correct. Knowledge management has a finite scope and is applicable in many R and D and technology-driven organisations. Intelligence, on the other hand, has an infinite scope and should always direct towards the "window of opportunities". Competitive intelligence is never finished for the simple reason that the outside world is constantly changing.

"Key decision-makers": decision-making is the most difficult aspect of management. There are hardly any courses that teach management about decision-making. Once I was fortunate enough to attend an international course on decision-making, given by the management consulting and training firm Kepner Tregoe. So management is desperately seeking supportive management tools in decision-making. One might compare it this to the military, where the highest level of support for the most important decisions to be made is provided by intelligence. Why should the business world not learn about the use of intelligence from the military, as it has learned about strategy, also military in origin? In chapter X of Part I in this book, I will describe in greater detail the lessons we can learn from military intelligence. This pinpoints the need for competitive intelligence for senior management within many organisations as a "must have capability".

"Key drivers of change": famous is the statement that it is not the big companies per definition that will be successful, but those companies which are able to adapt in time to changes in the external environment. A perfect management tool still highly recommended is Michael Porter's 'five forces' model. If management are able to monitor those key five drivers of change consistently, they will hardly be surprised by changes in the external business environment. Could you imagine a modern pilot flying an aircraft without radar? Or generals entering a military campaign without intelligence? Of course not! Yet the vast majority of companies do not have in place any kind of monitoring or tracking capability; they lack any kind of company radar or a kind of watchtower that would enable them to anticipate changes in the dynamics of the external business world. I always ask management how they expect to be able to compete successfully, if they are unable to see the daily dramatic changes in the competitive landscape.

"Aim is future oriented": the primary focus of competitive intelligence is the immediate and mid-term future. Based on the lessons learned from the past and on an in-depth situation appraisal analysis of the present, management can create business foresights with competitive intelligence. By doing this in a structured and consistent manner, companies are in a position to anticipate future developments. Peter Drucker stated already many years ago that the future cannot be predicted, but future events can. The prediction time scale of competitive intelligence is on average 3-18 months based on decisions made now. Could competitive intelligence with such a range not guarantee the long-term success of the organisation? Beyond the space of 18 months, other management tools have a role to play, such as "the strategy under uncertainty model", described in Part II chapter 13, and scenario planning, also described in Part II chapter 12.

Finally, I should like to clarify the comparison between competitor analysis and competitor intelligence. Competitor analysis is generally carried out on an ad hoc basis at the time when strategy plans are being made, or as input for annual budget planning. In a majority of cases the result is a random picture which is updated once a year. In too many cases it merely offers a snapshot. Competitor intelligence is a complete in-depth intelligence analysis, focused on just one competitor, and is updated at least four times per year.

Creating a competitive intelligence regime inside organisations functioning 24/7 constitutes a "pre-condition for future existence".

Introduction to the competitiveness of nations

The aim of competitive intelligence is to strengthen the competitive position of companies, organisations or countries. Having a competitive intelligence competence in place means that management will possess better business insights today and improved in-depth foresights in the immediate future. The future cannot be predicted, however, as mentioned, future events can. Companies nowadays face rapid change and new dynamics in a world that has become truly global and international. The key driver has been the increasing widespread acceptance of the Internet, which started back in the mid-1990s. The World Wide Web is also described as ' a world without walls'. This has happened in the last decade, resulting in a world of increasing globalisation, internationalisation, deregulation and privatisation. Markets converge and customers can shop all over the world. The competitiveness of nations and companies is no longer limited by borders and frontiers. Competition has become fierce and competitive pressure will continue to increase.

In 2006, the G8 countries are represented by the US, Japan, Germany, France, United Kingdom, Italy, Canada and Russia. In 2020, it is expected that the G8 will comprise China, US, Canada, India, Russia, Brazil, Japan and hopefully the EU. Currently we face such up-and-coming nations as the BRIC countries: Brazil, Russia, India and China. This will change the international trading blocs in the world. Placing Europe at the centre, Europe will face from the left the US and Brazil, and from the right Russia, India, Japan and China. In the year 2000 at the Lisbon Summit, the EU agreed on the aim of becoming the world's leading knowledge economy by 2010. Will the EU succeed in realising this ambition? Unfortunately, it will not, and it is facing increasingly strong competitive pressure from the other trading blocs. The biggest problems confronting the EU are rigid labour markets, protectionism, and bureaucratic regulations which make it difficult to create the single European market without barriers, and thus diminish its ability to compete in the immediate future.

1   The competitiveness of Europe

"As the glory of Europe decays".

This depressing assessment of the EU's hopes of bringing about a revitalization of its economy so as to become the world's most competitive business environment comes at a time when Europe is struggling with unemployment, low economic growth, and public resistance to further integration and towards the elimination of internal barriers. European companies are making adjustments in investing in innovation and productivity improvements in the face of competition from Asian rivals with lower wage costs and less rigid employment laws. Examples of this are outsourcing and off shoring of business activities to India and both off- and near-shoring to the former Eastern European countries.

The challenges for Europe are to revitalize the labour markets, to increase the investments in research and development and innovation, education and to ensure fair competition. However, ambition is not the same as vision. For many years now Europe has lacked a coherent vision and a sequenced plan for its implementation. Europe should not seek to compete with China in manufacturing commodities but should instead invest heavily in research facilities, working in close collaboration with the business world with the ultimate drive to innovation.

Some examples of vision have been listed below: "a market-oriented confederation with European as well as national consciousness speaking with one voice", "take full advantage of outstanding potential present in people and culture", "Improve international economic competitiveness to such a degree that Europe can afford a high level of environmental protection and social cohesion", "become a leading knowledge-based and service-oriented society", "become the United States of Europe with shared budgets for defence, education, research, health and foreign affairs".

An international survey undertaken by the Italian consulting firm Ambrosetti among 35 executives of major companies in Europe, published in the Wall Street Journal in December 2005, lists five key priorities:
1. Improve the labour market flexibility
2. Introduce a tax exemption for R and D investments
3. Attract and retain the best students and researchers
4. Curtail unfair competition and illegal product imitations
5. Improve the link between private and public research.

In the same survey another key question was how to evaluate the current / future competitiveness level in 2015 of the EU, US, Japan and China. (1=low 10=high):

	Current	Future
US	8,09	7,76
China	7,82	8,38
Japan	6,59	6,79
EU	5,38	6,06

Unfortunately these recommended actions do not coincide with the agreement on the EU budget reached during the mid-December Summit 2005 in Brussels. I have listed the key estimated budget spending projections for the period 2007-

2013. The European Commission asked for 1.025 billion Euros, the European Parliament wanted 975 billion Euros; the final figure decided at the Brussels Summit was 866 billion Euros.

1.	Funds for restructuring and cohesion for poorer regions	308,0
2.	Subsidies for the agricultural sector	293,0
3.	Strengthening of competitiveness and research	72,0
4.	Foreign policy and support of underdeveloped countries	50,0
5.	Justice, security and migration	6,6
6.	Funds for globalisation	3,5
7.	Cost of administration	51,0

As will be seen from this, the EU will invest around 300 billion in subsidies for the agricultural sector. This is not in keeping with the aim of becoming the leading knowledge based region in 2010.

We must expect fierce competition in agriculture from China, the world's leading producer of fruit and vegetables. For example, of the total world production of apples (80 million tons), 50 million tons are produced in China. The production of soft fruits such as citrus fruits, grapes, cherries and prunes will increase in importance. In an attempt to stop the migration from rural areas to cities, the Chinese government initiated the Chongqing Ganges Citrus project near the Yangtze river, a project involving 25,000 hectares – more than the total production of Australia. With new infrastructure, warehousing and packaging processes in place, China will become the leading agricultural producer in the world. No doubt the EU will protect its farmers with subsidies, impose quotas on imports from China and seek as far as possible to protect its agriculture. But how long will these measures be necessary? Can the trend be arrested? Is the protection of the agricultural sector by in excess of 300 billion in subsidies commensurate with the aim of becoming the world's most competitive region?

We may conclude that there is still a huge mismatch between the ambitions of the business community, the ambitions of politicians and the actual projected budget which allocates 72 billion Euros for the strengthening Europe's competitiveness and research, representing 8.4 percent of the total EU budget for 2007-2013. It is difficult to believe, based on these figures, that Europe will ever realise the Lisbon Summit 2000 objective of "becoming the world's most competitive region in 2010". The target of the EU in 2000 at this summit was to spend 3 percent of GNP on R and D in 2010. It is estimated that in fact that percentage will be maximum 2,2 percent in 2010.

In early January 2007 the European Commission announced another ambitious long-term plan with regard to climate change. The greenhouse effect must be reduced by 20 percent compared to 1990 and the percentage of environmentally-friendly energy should increase to 20 percent of total energy consumption by 2020 compared to 7 percent in 2006: another very ambitious plan, while the earlier plans of Lisbon and of R and D will not be achieved at all. So what of this new plan for energy?

Another important aspect of the competitiveness of Europe is the position of education. Every year, Europe produces fewer graduates than the Far East. Education in Europe is less accessible for people from lower social backgrounds. But if Europe really hopes to compete in the future as a knowledge economy, it desperately needs massive investments in improving the education and skills of the working population. Life-long learning should be one of the key future indicators of success. In April 2006, the Lisbon Council, an independent think tank of scientists and entrepreneurs in Brussels, published its research study on the competitiveness of Europe. "If all our political leaders had been students, we would have given every one of them an F". The F stands for Fail. Europe has the highest tax burden in the world, governments have for years had budget deficits and in spite of this there is gross under-investment in education. The study calls it immoral to send children out into a world of increased competitiveness without giving them the best tools to survive. The situation in countries like the UK, France, Italy and Germany is even more dramatic, because they deliver the same number of graduates per capita as in the 1960s. Countries like Portugal, Ireland, Finland and Spain perform much better. Germany and France, which account for 35 percent of the European economy, are no longer among the world leaders in education and skills.

Countries and continents that invest heavily in education and skills will become strong economies. The better educated the population, the higher productivity will be. Ireland and Korea lead the field in productivity. But Europe still spends around 300 billion in subsidies on agriculture and 50 percent less per student compared to the US. Knowledge and skills are the key success factors for Europe's economic survival.

Furthermore, Europe lacks leadership. Schröder, Chirac and Berlusconi did not succeed in restructuring their countries' economies; Blair's position is under pressure. We must wait and see what new European leaders, Angela Merkel in Germany and the newly-elected leaders in the UK and France will bring to the table.

I am based in the Netherlands, one of the founding members of the EU. There is much discussion about what the strategy of the Netherlands should be as one of the small countries in Europe, especially after the no-vote for the new European Constitution in June 2005. Some speak of the European Dream where money should help people to develop themselves. This should not be seen as an objective per se and should be transferred to investments in leisure, entertainment and life-style enhancement. The European Dream is the opposite of the American Dream. The Platform of Innovation in the Netherlands has the following areas selected for future sustainable growth: food and flowers, water, high-tech systems and materials, creative industry, chemicals and personal services. These are the areas where the Dutch economy should develop in order to increase the country's competitiveness in Europe and across the world.

A good example is the case where the merger of three small European players in semiconductors would result in a strong European semiconductor industry. Intel has the global leadership with a total share of 15 percent of the world market. French STMicroelectronics, German Infineon Technologies and Dutch Philips Semiconductors have market shares of 3.7 – 3.5 – 2.4 percent. A merger would lead to 9.6 percent share of the world market, the second position after Intel and before number three, Samsung Electronics with 7.3 percent. However, Philips sold the semiconductors division to three investment companies in summer 2006. The company is now called NXP.

Dominique Moïsi, founder of the French Institute for International Affairs (IFRI), gave Europe a dramatic wake-up call: during a meeting in April 2006 in Paris a highly-respected Chinese business man, combining his time in Hong Kong and London, stated: "Europe is becoming a third-world country. Europeans spend their time on the wrong issues – constitution, welfare state and the pension crisis – and to the questions you raise you systematically give the wrong answers".

Europe is facing a bi-partite crisis: an identity crisis and a crisis of trust. European political leaders change their view of the world slowly; compare the dramatic speed of change in the Far East. They lack vision for the longer term and cling obsessively to their short-term interests. European political leaders have not won the respect of their Asian counterparts; contrast the achievements of the European business community in Asia. Asia regards Europe as a model of reconciliation, peace and prosperity. However, if the economic performance continues to fall, the key question is whether this view of Europe can be saved. Asians may come to regard Europe as a political version of Venice: a place where you can walk around full of melancholy for past glories, admiring its museum-like character.

"Strategy is like trying to ride a bicycle while you are inventing it".
(Igor Ansoff)

The American National Science Foundation stated in March 2006 that the foreign research and development activities of US companies tripled over the period the development of 1985-2005 compared to domestic activities, producing a domestic/foreign ratio of 1:3. In Europe the situation as regards the growth of investment in research and development is similar. The ratios for other countries are: Germany 1:2, France 1:3, United Kingdom 1:4, Netherlands 1:6.

Nyenrode University has published interesting research results on the background of this development within R and D; this research was based on 375 interviews with senior management from medium and large international companies. Three key reasons for this migration were established:

The first is the need to be close to markets and customers. Another important aspect is to ensure R and D in highly competitive markets. The second is cost. Countries low wages but a high educational profile are of interest for R and D; such countries include India, the Czech Republic, Ukraine, Poland, Russia and to a lesser extent China. The third factor involves programmes established by governments to stimulate the development of R and D facilities in their countries.

The migration of R and D will be even more pronounced in the years up to 2015. It is expected that 35 to 40 percent of all R and D activities will be re-allocated outside the Netherlands towards the US and the Far East, with the EU generally being excluded from this migration, chiefly because the EU lacks the necessary dynamics, is over-regulated, fragmented, and therefore globally less interested.

Another challenge is to establish alliances between R and D- driven companies. It is estimated that in 2020 the cost price of electronics, microelectronics and nano electronics will comprise 40 percent of R and D efforts. Add to this the cost of marketing, sales and logistics, and it becomes clear that future margins will be under huge pressure, which more or less rules out Europe.

One might conclude that Europe desperately needs new entrepreneurship. There is sea of knowledge available but new entrepreneurship is required to transform and translate knowledge to render it of value to society. However, in Europe we are dealing with a culture within society which has a structure of risk-avoidance. In such a culture, entrepreneurship will never flourish.

One cause of a lack of entrepreneurship might be the 'passive wage slave attitude' that prevails in Europe. In his book *Dutch Overconfidence*, Mathijs Bouman may have identified the reason.

The highly-skilled and well-educated Dutch (and this applies to the rest of Europe too), have been pampered far too much. The welfare state has built in all manner of security for a pleasant and easy life. These white-collar workers with salaries in excess of 40,000 Euros are not challenged to display entrepreneurial qualities. They enjoy job security; it is only the less-educated blue-collar workers who need protection.

In the Netherlands alone there are one million white-collar workers with salaries of 40,000 and above with no ambitions to become entrepreneurs. Much more effort should be made to push these workers towards greater flexibility, with incentives to encourage them to start their own businesses.

Another important aspect is the R and D competition with the USA. In Europe we lack the basis for research and science: consider the winners of the Nobel prize: for many years now the Nobel prizes have gone to Americans. In 2006, the

Nobel prizes for science, chemistry, physics, medicines and economics all went to American scientists.

How has France supported intelligence for the private sector? In France competitive intelligence is called "Intelligence Economique"

> *"The French government has seen the high value of Intelligence Economique for the private sector with the aim to strengthen the country's competitiveness".*

> *"The French government appointed a Minister of Economic Development for Intelligence Economique on par with the Prime Minister".*

The French are known for their pride in their country; they are even regarded as "Chauvinistic". France has always protected herself from the outside world by focusing strongly on French interests both at home and abroad. Intelligence is widely practised at both governmental level and within the military. It has been remarkable to see that the French government has also developed programmes for raising awareness within the private sector of how intelligence can be of great interest to large multinational companies as well as to small and medium-sized companies. In 1993, the French Government published the first report on "Intelligence Economique", the so-called "The Martre Report".

Definition: "Intelligence économique is the combined, coordinated research actions of information treatment and the diffusion of economic actions for strategic and operational exploitation". Intelligence économique should have four pillars:

1. Encourage the practice of intelligence économique at company level;
2. Optimise the transfer of information between the private and public sectors;
3. Construct data banks in the light of user needs;
4. Mobilize the training and education world.

Jakobiak, Member of the Martre Committee, identified five levels of intelligence: International level: strategy of State influence; Transnational level: Large multinational groups; National level: concerted strategy amongst decision centres; International level: inter-professional branches of activity; Base level: companies.

In 2003 the Martre Report was followed by "The Carayon Report: intelligence économique and social cohesion". The differences between this and the Martre Report were:

▶ The report was commissioned by Prime Minister Raffarin;
▶ It contained 38 proposals to enhance intelligence économique in France;
▶ It was more ambitious, more transparent and showed a higher level of government engagement.

The Carayon Report mentioned negative and positive outcomes as well as recommendations.

Negative outcomes:
1. Involvement of the "Secretatiat Générale de la Défence" SGDN. The SGDN has a strong focus on terrorism and the mafia. It has been admitted that involving the SGDN was a mistake;
2. Absence of value-creating strategies;
3. Hierarchical and secretive nature;
4. The role of the Prime Minister clashing with the inter-governmental representatives;
5. Limited sharing of information between the private and public sectors;
6. Ministry of the Interior: ongoing regional projects;
7. Ministry of Economics: insufficient resources and inappropriate hierarchical structures;
8. Ministry of Foreign Affairs: the entities of the diplomatic corps had unequal capabilities;
9. Education and research at the ministries: singled out for a lack of reflection towards intelligence économique.

Positive outcomes:
1. Higher education in intelligence économique has grown substantially;
2. Intelligence économique professionals forming a recognizable and focused group;
3. Intelligence économique awareness is well diffused throughout public and private sectors;
4. Small and medium-sized companies receiving assistance in training and implementation in regional projects.

Recommendations:
1. More engagement at the presidential level to overcome administrative inertia;
2. Creation of an "Economic Competitiveness and Security Advisory Board";
3. Appointment of a "Minister of Economic Development", working in the Cabinet of the Prime Minister since September 2006;
4. Embracing a "Eurocentric" approach to intelligence économique efforts;
5. More implementation at regional level.

In addition, in 2003 ATELIS was founded as a result of the Carayon Report. ATELIS is an institute combining the various organisations active in intelligence économique, including the Chambers of Commerce, which by nature operate close to the private sector across the country. The objectives of ATELIS are consultation with the regional SMEs, local government and institutes on competitive intelligence, training and applied research.

What lessons are to be learned from the French? Firstly, the French have recognized that intelligence is not solely the preserve of the government and the military, but is also of great potential interest to the private sector, which can benefit from intelligence économique to increase its competitiveness at both national and international levels. Secondly, the French have recognized that, in order to secure future French business interests both nationally and internationally, the French Government needed to take the initiative and lead to create awareness and acceptance of intelligence économique. Thirdly, the French government showed they were serious about intelligence économique by placing it at the highest level within the government: the Cabinet of the Prime Minister.

What is my recommendation for Europe and the EU? Please, just get on and do it! Most European countries could take France as their model for improving the competitiveness of their private sectors and the creation of a shared platform for increasing the competitiveness in matching the private with the public sector as well. By so doing, Europe will be in a position to catch up with the US and the Far East and become, maybe not by 2010, but certainly a few years later, the world's leading "competitive region". Perhaps the Lisbon target of 2010 can be realised in 2012-2015.

2   The competitiveness of China

> *"Everything you can do they can do too".*
> (Dr. Werner Hell of the Hell Yang Group in China)

Virtually everyone has been impressed by the Chinese and their fast-growing production rate, the most famous areas of which are textiles and shoes. Below you will see an overview of the explosion of Chinese and Indian textile exports to Europe and the US. In shoe-manufacturing the situation is similar, where China succeeded in increasing its world market share in the course of just five years to 62 percent of the total world production.

Case Textile Sector

" The deadline will come shortly and how will the reaction be?"

Facts & Figures:

- 1995 : Liberalisation of Global Textile Market by WTO
- 1997 – 2003: Not foreseen how China and India would develop.

- 2005:

	USA			Europe	
	2002	2005		2002	2005
China	16	>50		18	29
India	4	>15		6	9
	20	65		24	38

@ 2006, Rodenberg Tillman Associates

Source: FD 11.10.2004

Will the growth of China as production location for the rest of the world last for the next decennia? China, in common with every other country, is facing several problems such as oil consumption, pollution, population migration from rural to urban areas, prosperity interests in Western luxury goods, fashion, cars, living standards and much more.

However, one of the key problems China faces is the structure of its economy. China has a state-controlled economy. Many economic activities are heavily subsidized, for example textile and shoe-manufacturing. Surpluses in real estate speculation and over-investment are the pillars of the Chinese economy which lead to overcapacity. Examples are the real estate, steel, aluminium and automotive sectors. Such over-supply results in debts that are difficult to collect. The government is very powerful and civil servants are in control; not only do the 15 million households of civil servants control the economy, they cause the increasing imbalance between rich and poor as well as corruption. Of a working population counting 800 million people, 50 percent are employed in agriculture. Of the remaining 400 million, some 160 million have a fixed income, 200 million have no labour contract, and between 40-50 million are individually employed in such activities as shoe-shining, cigarette-selling, etc. China should consider restructuring from a state-owned economy towards a market economy; however, the power wielded by civil servants makes her reluctant to do so. Around 20 percent of the GDP in China is realised by foreign companies. Young Chinese preferably to seek employment with foreign companies, unlike young people in other Asian regions as Japan and Korea. The conclusion might be that there is a question mark over China's future competitiveness, which will influence the rest of the world.

Many executives have their heads turned towards China because of the country's cheap labour costs, manufacturing stability and lack of labour unrest. However, this also means massive dependence on China. According to an article about Sun Microsystems in CFO Global Outlook of 2007, every single computer in the world currently has at least one critical component that is made in China. Sun states: "Your suppliers have supply chains and their suppliers have supply chains, so people don't know what's from China". To obtain a better insight into the dependence on China, Sun Microsystems started with enterprise risk management.

> *"We need to be asking ourselves why is one region growing faster than the rest, or one country making more operating income than any other? Is there something that the rest of the of the world can learn from?"*
> (CFO of Dell in 2006)

Another example of how China has been subsidising its industry concerns the Dutch paperclips manufacturer Pinclip from Emmen. The company manufactures 400 million paperclips annually with two employees and 95 per cent automated production. Cost of materials and packaging make up 70 percent of the cost price. Paperclips are produced in all types, sizes and colours, also under brand names such as Perfecta, Zilvesta and Selecta. In 2004, they lost a major customer who decided to purchase their office supplies in China, where they could purchase paperclips at half the price. During the period 2004-2005 total sales decreased by 65 percent. It appears that China offers paperclips at half-price, which could be a case of unfair competition. Pinclip does have evidence that the Chinese subsidize this sector. The company has reduced its prices by 25-30 percent; however, the same thing happened in 2005 with an even bigger customer, who orders the paperclips now per container in China. The management has been very disappointed that customers travel to China, but don't make the effort to travel to the Pinclip company which is based close at hand in the Netherlands. In this case there is little the management of Pinclip can do; outsourcing is not an option because the production is almost fully automated and run by just two people. The company complained in early 2006 about the "Crash Team of Unfair Competition" to the Dutch Ministry of Economic Affairs.

In contrast, China is happy to open up and show the world that they can do more than merely produce commodities; consider for example Chinese Lenovo, which acquired the PC division of IBM, including the brand name Thinkpad, for a price of US$ 1.750 million. This acquisition made Lenovo the third-largest player in personal computers after Dell and Hewlett Packard. Lenovo also produces other consumer electronics such as mobile phones. To show the world what they can do, Lenovo was the first Chinese sponsor of the Olympic Winter Games in Turin in Italy, and they will be key sponsor of the Olympic Summer Games in Peking in 2008.

> *"Cash-rich Chinese acquirers have been painted as pillagers and plunderers, out to strip assets and rob jobs. The truth is very different".*
> (CFO of Lenovo in 2006)

The acquisition of the PC division of IBM by Lenovo was no easy affair. CFIUS, the US Institute of Control of Foreign Investments, did research on the consequences of the potential Lenovo acquisition. One of the key intelligence topics was what would happen about IBM's Research Triangle Park in North Carolina. They were asking themselves if the centre might also be used to start espionage activities. What were the conditions for the Lenovo staff who might also have access to the other companies in this Park? The Pentagon doesn't trust the Chinese and has stated that whatever the Chinese get from us might be used against us.

Other example is that the Pentagon forced Washington not to sell Global Crossing to Chinese Hutchison Whampoa in 2005.

In March 2005, the American Government Institute, which controls US mergers and acquisitions, finally approved the sale of the PC Division of IBM to Lenovo.

It is also interesting to observe how the US intelligence services as well as the Pentagon are closely linked to some US companies with a high level of strategic impact for the society. NSA, the National Security Agency, supported Microsoft with the security of the new software Windows Vista.

How quickly will China succeed in establishing its business in Europe? Consider, for example, the Chinese Hisense company which has started a business in the Benelux countries. Hisense is the market leader in consumer electronics in China. Its first product in 1969 was a transistor radio. In November 2005 Hisense established a business in the Benelux countries starting with flat-screen television sets priced at 20 percent below the well-known brands. In France and Spain Hisense is already on the market with an average market share of 3 percent.

This is a useful example, and demonstrates that Chinese companies are entering the EU, the US and the rest of the world. In 2005, Chinese Haier attempted to acquire US Maytag with the objective of introducing their consumer electronics business in the US. However, what we need to know is how quickly Chinese companies will succeed in gaining positions in Europe and the US. It took Japan some 30 years to gain a foothold in Europe. It took Korea 15 years to gain a foothold in Europe. We might expect it to take China 5-8 years to gain a foothold in Europe.

Are you familiar with the names of international Chinese companies? Here is an overview of some of them; all have over US$ 2 billion in sales:

- ▶ Eastern Communications
- ▶ China Putian
- ▶ Huawei
- ▶ Midea
- ▶ SVA
- ▶ BOE Technology
- ▶ TCL
- ▶ Changhong
- ▶ Galanz
- ▶ Desay
- ▶ Shanghai Electrical Group

In addition, many multinational companies from Japan, Korea and Taiwan have established their businesses in mainland China and the big US and European multinationals all have their partnerships with the CMs, Contract Manufacturers, the OEMs, Original Equipment Manufacturers, the OBMs, the Original Brand Manufacturers, the ODMs, the Original Design Manufacturers and the EMSs, the Electronics Manufacturing Service providers.

> *"China is now more than just a factory of the world. It is a market that is too big to ignore, so every multinational company needs a "China strategy". Unfortunately, China is probably the most difficult market in which to plan. There are many ways a strategy can go wrong, from branding issues to not attracting the right employees to letting the cost of building scale spiral out of control. CFOs need to manage these risks carefully, taking advantage of risk transfer and insurance where appropriate".*
> (Peter Wong, Regional Director AIG, Hong Kong, in CFO Global Outlook 2007)

China's CNPC has given Russia a loan of US$ 6 billion for the nationalisation of Yukos. In return, Russia will supply China with oil for the next 6 years. In China, there is a desperate need for commodities. In October 2004, China's Sinopec signed contracts with Iran for gas and oil worth US$ 70 billion. In November 2004, China will invest US$ 100 billion in Brazil, Argentina and Chile for the next 10 years to secure supplies of steel and copper. In August, president Chavez of Venezuela travelled to China to negotiate a deal for oil supplies over the next 10 years.

3   The competitiveness of the USA

For many years the US has been, and is still, the engine of the world economy
as well as the world's leading economy. Other economies, China, of course, Latin
America, Russia, India and since 2006 Europe too, have shown growth. The trade
deficit in the US is 6,5 percent of the national trade balance. But every nation has
from time to time a trade deficit or surplus aware that there are few countries
where the balance is even. However, the 6,5 percent trade deficit counts almost 70
percent of total deficits in the world, and this is alarming: some 3 billion flows to
the US every day to close the deficit gap, around 800 billion a year, equivalent to
the total US annual defence budget. This unstable global situation is discussed
at every meeting of the G8 and the IMF. How long is this going to go on? Is the
rest of the world prepared to finance the US economy much longer? The cause
of this huge problem is the imbalance between savings and investments. In the
US savings are lagging behind and the money for keeping up investments has
to come from abroad. Another way to look at it is that as a nation the US spends
more than it earns. In the 1980s and early 1990s the Americans saved about 10
percent of their income. Now this percentage is minus 1,5 percent. But it's not
only the American people who overspend: so does the US government. Two other
indicators confirm the dramatic development of the US economy. In the past,
1980s/1990s, the US shares have made up 60 percent of GDP. In 2006, this
percentage increased to 120 percent despite the downturn on the Stock Exchange
since the Internet bubble of 2000-2001. The same comparison can be made with
the other key indicator, house prices. In the past, the share of houses was 100
percent of GDP. This percentage has now increased to around 165 percent. So, if
income stabilizes and assets increase over time, people feel themselves "rich on
paper". To spend more in this way means that people have to borrow money with
collateral. This borrowing takes place at the cost of the rest of the world.

These indicators make the US vulnerable, and a downturn in the US economy
will have a powerful negative impact on the rest of the world. Pimco, the largest
investor in bonds in the US, has developed a very interesting scenario. If China
would genuinely open up for "friendly" investment, float the currency and create
a better legal system, most of the world's capital investment would flow to China,
along with a vast "brain drain".

The US will lose its leading position as the world's strongest economy and
will change its role from that of an economic shaper into that of an economic fol-
lower.

It's obvious that China is set on a clear path; this was evident from the Chi-
nese President Hu Jintao's visit to the US in April 2006. During this visit, the
President spent more time in Seattle with Bill Gates of Microsoft and with Boeing
Aircraft Industries than with President George W. Bush.

The expected downturn in the US economy, be it sudden or gradual, will probably lead to greater sustainability in the future and a more balanced competitiveness in the next few years up to 2010.

A very strong factor in the competitiveness of the US is the drive to win. Comparisons can be made with the world of sport: in Europe most of us are happy to achieve a draw in a game; it means we didn't lose. But in the US people are very disappointed with a draw; second is nowhere. This is a crucial difference between Americans and the rest of us: the will to win.

4   The other new competitors of BRIC: India, Russia and Brazil

China will become the manufacturing centre of the world. India will become the back room of the world. India has a fast growing sector of the population which is highly-educated and able to provide services at 10-20 percent of the labour cost in the EU, Japan and the US. This applies especially to information technology services; many Western companies have already discovered this and have adopted a policy of off shoring, transferring their IT activities to India.

Around 50 percent of the Fortune Top 500 companies purchase software solutions from Indian companies. At first off shoring concentrated on software development, application development, system integration, hosting, technical control of applications and data and external networks. Recently, business processes such as administration, call centres, data control and research have been added.

In the press many announcements have been made in the last couple of years about companies that have transferred their back-room offices to India. Examples of off shoring include the following financial institutions; the figures show the number of Indian employees.

Number of estimated employees in 2006:

HSBC	7,000
JP Morgan Chase	5,000
Deutsche Bank	2,000
Lehman Brothers	1,000
Goldman Sachs	750
UBS	500

Other financial institutions have outsourced their IT activities to leading IT companies such as EDS, IBM, LogicaCMG, all with back-room offices in India. New names of companies with India-based back-room offices are Office Tiger, GenPact and InfoSys Technologies with Bangalore as the new "Silicon Valley" of India. India is fully aware of its potential ability to conquer the world in the 21st Century by combining intelligence with business.

"Due to Russia's size, capex has been much higher than in the West, resulting in nega-
tive cash flow for many firms. But we are nearing a turning point where relative capex
will begin to fall and cash flow worth billions of dollars will be generated. Then, Russian
firms will look to make significant investments beyond their own borders".
(Roger de Bazelaire, Senior VP Strategy and Financing, Moscow, in CFO Global
Outlook 2007)

The competitive power predicted for to Russia and Brazil in the near future is
based on the countries' immense resources. Both countries have enough resources
of commodities to be competitive for their own sectors and the additional ability
to export their resources. One example is oil. Countries whose oil consumption
exceeds their ability to produce it will face huge problems. The US, Japan and
China are already facing this situation; in the foreseeable future the problem will
increase. Russia will become a major supplier of oil and gas to the EU, Japan and
China, and in consequence these countries will become increasingly dependent
upon Russia. The question is whether China, which already is active in securing
commodities supplies from Africa and Latin America, will take the initiative to
protect them by means of military force.

Examples of how China has already secured their supplies of commodities:

1. In 2005 China's CNPC gave Russia a loan of US$ 6 billion for the nationalisa-
   tion of Yukos Oil in 2005. In return, Russia will supply China with oil until
   2011.
2. In 2005 China's Sinopec signed with Iran for the delivery of gas and oil worth
   US$ 70 billion.
3. In 2005 China intended to invest US$ 100 billion in Brazil, Argentina and
   Chile to secure supplies of steel and copper until 2015.

The future economic growth of Brazil will come from rapid agricultural exports.
After the US and the EU, Brazil is the 3rd largest exporter of agricultural products.
Exports to Russia, China and the Middle East grow by over 20 percent per year.
It seems that Brazil has around 100 million hectares potential farmland available
for further growth. By comparison, the Netherlands has 1,9 million hectares of
agricultural land. At the Doha discussion of the WTO, the will to open up world
trade in agricultural products stood at the head of the Brazilian Government's
agenda. Together with India, Brazil leads the G20 countries in the ambition to
eliminate import barriers in the US and EU. If the EU, for instance, should decide
to open the door to poultry from Brazil, it may be expected that poultry farming
in Europe will disappear. Together with other sectors in agriculture, this implies
a major threat for the EU.

Moreover, Brazil is a member of the Mercosur, the Free Trade Zone in Latin
America, whose members are Argentina, Brazil, Paraguay, Uruguay and Ven-
ezuela. Mercosur can be seen as an important accelerator for Brazil and with no

doubt will strengthen its competitiveness as one of the key competitive nations in the immediate future.

5   How to increase the competitiveness of nations?

In 1957 Nobel Prize winner Robert M. Solow explained productivity growth of 20 percent by the production factors labour and capital. In general, we know that the remaining 80 percent of growth of productivity is determined by the development and application of knowledge. This is the reason that knowledge is seen as the only differentiating factor for sustainable competitive advantage. More people employed or additional capital only goes part way to accounting for an increase in productivity. Neither the size of the company nor the sector in which it operates makes a difference. Many research studies confirm a positive relation between knowledge productivity and the growth of net profits and the positive development of cash flow.

Knowledge productivity is the result of the variety of knowledge sources, the interchange of knowledge sources as well the level of usage of knowledge, the development, exploration, exploitation and infrastructure of knowledge. It's all about the productivity of knowledge and not about the ownership of knowledge. The productivity of knowledge needs to be managed in three ways. Firstly, knowledge can lead to advantages for the company such as new products, economies of scale, new business development and innovation. Secondly, the storage of knowledge must be effected so that knowledge becomes a genuine asset for the company. The situation has changed from one where companies are flooded with information to one where they are starved for knowledge. Thirdly, knowledge shows us the way to new competences, such as developing new markets and new channels of distribution. Knowledge will drive innovation, which strengthens the competitive position based on knowledge as a new asset and knowledge as competence. Companies are able to develop increased knowledge productivity both independently and in close cooperation with suppliers, customers or alliance partners.

However, it is rather disappointing that there are so few companies and organisations that have a well-developed knowledge capability in place. In most cases, large companies and organisations do have knowledge capabilities in place, but the majority of companies have no structured process of knowledge management. Knowledge management and innovation involve inspiration. The main reason is that organisational knowledge is as much about the people in an organisation as the organisation itself. Those companies that have understood that knowledge management can do as much for them as research and development and marketing have taken the first important step in the right direction. Knowledge management is a management tool that provides a multitude of tangible benefits at strategic and operational levels.

The crucial first step is to generate commitment at top management level. Only if the organisation has the buy-in of top executives it will be able to proceed to the next step: working out the right conceptual mix. In this phase organisations must accept that there is no one-stop-shop solution for knowledge management for their organisation. Rather, they need to work out a solution that is tailored to the individual needs. Only a tailor-made concept for the organisation will win the buy-in of employees, and this is vital, since it is they who will turn the concept into reality. But the task is still not finished. Such ventures take time and for organisations to be really successful it is necessary that they remain constantly involved in the concepts they have initiated.

6   The key to the competitiveness of nations and companies: beyond knowledge towards competitive intelligence

One of the important drivers of success in business is competitive intelligence. Competitive intelligence goes beyond knowledge management. Knowledge management looks down the hall, while competitive intelligence looks out of the window of opportunity. Competitive intelligence drives the five key drivers of change crucial to every company: markets, customers, competitors, technologies and legislation; it is future-oriented and, above all, "actionable". It is actionable because the emphasis in competitive intelligence is on equipping senior management to take better decisions and to understand the strategic impact of decisions before and after the supposed actions: The before-action-reviews and the after-action-reviews, BARs and AARs.

Competitive intelligence triggers inspiration by cross-fertilizing ideas within research communities in-house, innovation centres and via trend-scouting, monitoring and exchange of ideas in external markets. In fact, external ideas acquired through purchase or lease account for much of the inspiration of the world's most innovative companies. More fundamentally, competitive intelligence reduces perspiration along the entire value chain of innovation management. A comprehensive competitive intelligence capability or regime targeting innovation enhances responsiveness to market opportunities. It improves research and development investment decisions and lowers the related research and development project cost and attrition rate, all through the efficient and effective enrichment of information and knowledge towards intelligence. Competitive intelligence accelerates product development and prototyping through rapid collective intelligence exchange. The transfer of experiences in patenting and licensing reduces the risks of delays for legal product approval, plant start-up and market entry. Many companies say that the turnaround phase is over and that they are entering a new phase of growth. In turnarounds the focus is on cost-cutting skills. However, a phase of growth is uncertain and less predictable. What is needed is creativity; the current skills, capabilities and competences must be redirected. One of the new skills that can open many new windows of opportunity is competitive intelligence.

Besides the operational benefits within marketing intelligence departments, competitive intelligence may yield major strategic advantages for an organisation. It may help to sustain or expand a company's knowledge portfolio and to reduce related business risks. Like tangible resources, a company's know-how is a marketable commodity. Intelligence-based knowledge can be bought and sold on the market or exchanged with other companies. However, the largest proportion of a company's know-how and competence is never documented as it resides in people's minds. This implicit knowledge is traded on the job market together with its human owners. So there is a great need to retain knowledge and intelligence before it walks out of the door of the organisation.

What does the organisation need in competitive intelligence and when? Can we plan ahead and purchase or hire accordingly? September 11, S.A.R.S, the bird flu, pandemic or terrorist attacks (London, Madrid), natural disasters (tsunami, New Orleans) radiation leaks, hurricanes (Florida), earthquakes (Japan, California), firestorms (France, Spain, Portugal), chemical attacks (Japan), have all demonstrated yet again the limitations of planning and forecasting.

The company needs to be sufficiently flexible and agile to react and adapt quickly to unexpected situations. The strategic value of competitive intelligence is not the knowledge about the future, but rather the ability to respond to future events through the availability of the appropriate competitive intelligence. Competitive intelligence about alternative distribution channels, about the capabilities of local subsidiaries or about product substitutes, helps companies survive times of crisis. In-depth competitive intelligence provides both options and scenarios for senior management which will reduce business risks.

The implementation of a competitive intelligence capability enables the management of organisations, whether they be small, medium-sized or large, to strengthen its competitive position.

The ten important objectives of competitive intelligence are:

1. To forewarn management of sudden developments in the fast changing dynamics of the external business environment;
2. To create timely business insights about threats and opportunities;
3. To establish a consistent input into strategy processes;
4. To prevent management from dwelling on the past, demolish arrogance and stop complacency;
5. To continuously identify the company's own strategic blind spots as well gaps in the strategies of competitors;
6. To monitor pro-actively emerging events in the converging sectors of industry;

7. To create early-warning signals in order to increase own performance in markets and with customers, with the objective of remaining one step ahead of competition;
8. To create a consistent and good performance because intelligence concentrates on the five key drivers of change: markets, customers, competition, technologies and legislation;
9. To improve the objectivity of decision-making processes as competitive intelligence acts as the critical watchdog;
10. To act in a pro-active, more intelligent way, being more alert to opportunities in the market place.

Senior management as well middle management will agree that these ten objectives of competitive intelligence are vital to every organisation and company in the world. They all perceive the need and urgency. However, the general acceptance of competitive intelligence as a management discipline faces a number of difficulties.

Let us first consider senior and top management. A list of the support tools senior management have at their disposal would be as follows:

Management information systems, balance score cards, customer relation ship management, performance management driving by key performance indicators, accountants, lawyers, supervisory boards, other stakeholders, and last but not least the management team or executive management team representing core activities as well as such functions as strategy, marketing, sales, business development and R and D. Listed companies have, in addition, audit committees. All the above-mentioned are mainly concerned with the internal aspects relating to how organisations are steered, and all focus on management and control, and to a much lesser degree the outside world.

> *"But the most important decisions are not taken inside the company but outside the company".*
> (Per Erik Kihlstedt)

What tools does senior management have which concern the outside world? They have their teams active in strategy, marketing, sales, R and D, information and knowledge management. All of these deal to some extent with the outside world. However, the key problem of dealing with the outside world by means of these various functions is the lack of a shared information platform, despite the numerous information technology tools available, and the fact that no monitoring system, radar or watch tower is in place.

The second factor concerns the many people employed at middle management level. All of these people are fully convinced of the need to have a competitive intelligence capability in place. But they are all under tremendous pressure of time and work, a pressure chiefly caused by ponderous internal management and control systems: performance management, balance score cards, information technology, quality management and control, project management and so on.

The result of these management and control systems is that people are hired to just do their jobs and have less time available for new initiatives and innovation. They are evaluated through systems that set colleague against colleague; in the resultant pressure, creativity vanishes. Tempering such rigid performance assessments enables individuals and organisations to become more comfortable with risk-taking and with failure. Over time, rigid systems cause employees to focus on competing with each other, rather than collaborating. With so much emphasis placed on the tools and tricks of performance management, it's easy to lose sight of what is genuinely important: conversation and dialogue. This is the crux of the matter. This is also the main reason why "people-driven activities", such as information and knowledge management, new business development and innovation, are squeezed in most organisations.

So on the one hand we have senior management who have a variety of management and control systems at their disposal and on the other hand middle management oppressed by rigid performance assessment measures. However, "competitive intelligence starts with the guy at the top". Not all senior managers and top managers welcome strong dynamic colleagues and support teams. If they are considering having a competitive intelligence competence in place, they should not expect these competitive intelligence professionals to be yes-men.

After all the objectives and strategies of companies and what's best for these companies are often incompatible with managerial ego-trips. Take, for example, the mania for mergers and acquisitions.

7   Competitiveness by protectionism

One of the objectives behind the creation of the EU in 1958 was the free movement of people and trade between the member states. Almost 50 years later we are seeing a new phenomenon of globalisation and internationalisation in Europe which is in conflict with the fundamental principles of the EU. In 2006 we saw increasing efforts to protect "strategic" sectors of industry. This started with the bid by Mittal Steel India to acquire the European Steel Group Arcelor in January-February 2006, a great "shock" to the European Steel Society. Arcelor itself came into being as the result of the merger of several steel companies active in France, Belgium, Luxembourg and Spain. The French government were the first to protest against this acquisition because of Areclor's "strategic importance for France".

Italian-based Enel announced in February 2006 their aim of acquiring French Suez. Again the French government was not happy with this initiative on the part of the Italians. The French government immediately started a counterattack by

initiating a merger between Gaz de France with Suez. This met with strong pro-
tests from the Italian government. In Belgium the merger of Gaz de France with
Suez resulted in an almost 100 percent monopoly in the energy market for the
Alliance of Gaz de France.

In February 2006 the German company Eon announced a hostile bid on Spanish Endesa. The Spanish government reacted with the statement that "Endesa
should stay Spanish". However, Gas Natural, based in Catalunya in Spain,
announced that it would keep to an earlier bid on Endesa. Volkswagen in Germany agreed with Porsche Germany for a 18,5 percent stake in the Volkswagen
Group.

The reaction of the French government is truly astounding. France has a very
open economy with one-in-seven employed French people working for foreign-
based companies in France. France is more open than the economies of the Netherlands, Germany or the UK. But France is not recognized as one of the leading
open economies in Europe. Mergers and acquisitions in Europe are fine, just so
long s they take place outside France. The problem is that France is one of the
countries with the greatest number of civil servants, partly because France Post
and EDF are still state-owned companies and because in public organisations
which have been privatised, employees retain the status of civil servants including full pension arrangements.

In September 2003, the merger was announced between the national and
state-owned Air France with Dutch KLM. Did the Dutch Government react? Did
we hear from the French Government? Of course we didn't hear from the French.
On the contrary, the French were extremely happy that Air France had acquired a
successfully-performing international airline like KLM. In the Netherlands, KLM
was regarded as a national treasure on a par with other Dutch-owned companies
like Hoogovens, now Corus, DAF, now Paccard and Fokker Aircraft Industries,
part of DaimlerChrysler, which two years after the acquisition went bankrupt.

Despite the influence of the French government, the following companies
are on the "list rouge" as potential acquisition targets according to the French
newspaper La Tribune: Arcelor Steel, Carrefour Supermarkets, Casino Supermarkets, Danone Dairy, Saint Gobain Glass, Societe General Banking, Suez Energy,
Thomson Electronics, Vivendi Universal Media.

As a result of this protectionism of energy interests in France and Spain, the
Dutch energy market reacted to renew the consideration of splitting the supply/
delivery/logistics of energy with the other energy activities of the Dutch players
Nuon, Eneco, Essent and Delta. In addition, the European Commission reacted
in April 2006 to 17 of the 25 countries of the EU to force them to really open up
the energy market for liberalisation. At the same time the Commission Chair
Mr. Barroso warned the French to take steps to prevent France from protecting
another 11 listed sectors, which the French Government sees as possessing "strategic importance" and as vital for the national economy.

But how much longer may sectors of nations' industries be regarded as of strategic importance or vital, and how much longer are national governments going to protect these sectors? To answer this I have listed three key questions:

1. Do companies generate most of their revenues from their country of origin?
2. Is the management of these companies mainly comprised of citizens from the country of origin?
3. Are most of the staff in these companies citizens of the country where it is based?

Research published in the Dutch financial paper the Financieele Dagblad of February 18 2006 showed that the answer to the three key questions is "No". The research was conducted among the largest Dutch companies listed on the AEX of the Amsterdam Stock Exchange.

Decreasing influence of Dutch management in AEX listed companies (in%)

	1995	2000	2005
In the Boardroom	83	68	57
In the Supervisory Board	80	72	61
In Staff	72	53	47
In revenues	29	18	12
From the shareholders (Dutch origin)	33	15	14

This example confirms that the basic or national inheritance of Dutch companies such as Fokker, DAF, Hoogovens, KLM, VNU (The Nielsen Company) perceived by the people in the country no longer coincides with the perceived national inheritance of the management of the AEX-listed major international companies in the Netherlands. The expected growth in mergers and acquisitions as well as the growing influence of Private Equity Firms in coming years will probably further decrease the influence of Dutch management in Dutch-owned companies.

8   Mergers and Acquisitions

"When growth is scare, doing deals in order to add revenue quickly may be appealing, but you never want to make an acquisition for the sake of it. We stick to specific objectives when buying. Our objectives are all about deepening domain competence, filling out service lines, obtaining access to new markets or enhancing our technological footprint".
(Suresh Senapaty, CFO Wipro, Bangalore, in CFO Global Outlook 2007)

In the last 10-15 years many studies have confirmed that around 70-80 percent of all mergers and acquisitions have failed, begging the question as to why so many

Executive Boards, CEOs or Supervisory Boards persist in this mania for mergers and acquisitions. Is the aim of mergers and acquisitions to achieve synergy, to achieve efficiency, increased shareholder value, strategy gaming like "stratego", better strategic fits or is it all about management ego? Early in 2006 KPMG published the results of research into all mergers and acquisitions above US$ 100 million that took place in 2002-2003. Key findings were:

- ▶ 43 percent of all mergers and acquisitions did not result in added value for shareholders;
- ▶ in 31 percent of cases shareholders benefited;
- ▶ in 26 percent of cases shareholder value decreased;
- ▶ but 90 percent of the companies imagined shareholder value to have increased;
- ▶ 66 percent of the companies did not find the projected synergy advantages;
- ▶ Only 20 percent of the buyers had a plan to explain the advantages;
- ▶ It takes a period of 9 months to obtain the sense of control, because of differences in culture, IT-systems, measurements and rules and financial reporting;
- ▶ Only 60 percent had a plan how to proceed after the official agreement to merge.

The merger and acquisition mania started again in 2002-2003, after a downturn in 2001.The year 2000 was a top year, according to KPMG's research US$ 1.397 billion. In 2005, it was US$ 517 billion. It is expected that the activities will strongly increase in 2007-2010 mainly because of low interest rates. In 2006, over US$ 3100 billion was spent on mergers and acquisitions.

An overview of merger and acquisitions announcements in the first quarter of 2006:

- ▶ Eon and Endesa followed by Gas Natural   22.0
- ▶ Linde and BOC   12.0
- ▶ Nasdaq and London Stock Exchange   3.5
- ▶ Eurosnext and Deutsche Börse   19.0
- ▶ L'Oreal and Body Shop   1.0
- ▶ Mittal and Arcelor   25.8
- ▶ Suez and Gaz de France   70.0
- ▶ Ferrovial and BAA   12.6
- ▶ CVC/KKR and AVR   1.4
- ▶ Consortium on VNU   7.5
- ▶ Dubai Ports and P and O   5.9
- ▶ Sonae and Portugal Telecom   10.7
- ▶ BNP Paribas and BNL   10.8
- ▶ Adecco and DIS   0.6
- ▶ Prudential and Aviva   25.0

▶ Merck / Bayer and Schering   16.3
▶ Alcatel and Lucent   19.0
▶ Johnson & Johnson or Boston Scientific and Guidant   22.0
▶ AT&T and BellSouth   75.0

All together we are talking about 310 billion Euros for these 19 mergers and acquisitions, and this is only 10 percent of the total number of US$ 3,100 billion in 2006. Based on the study made by KPMG, the drop in shareholder value may be estimated at around 80 billion. There is no doubt that this will be reflected by a corresponding number of lay-offs. We also should bear in mind that 60-80 percent of all mergers fail, according to numerous studies carried out over the past ten years.

The most frequent reason for the failure of why mergers and acquisitions has been the differences in culture between the merging organisations. However, a new study by KPMG, published in January 2007, showed that this argument of differences in culture is over-simplification. They define culture as a so-called "catch-all word" which makes it meaningless. John Kelly, head of the integration consultancy at KPMG states: "you can also blame the weather for why mergers fail". Of course cultural aspects are of relevance; but management should take responsibility for the failure of mergers and acquisitions; it is human nature to blame everything but oneself when things go wrong. It is easy to put the blame of 'culture'. To generate the money for mergers and acquisitions is not the hardest thing in the world, and too little time is spent on the integration of the organisations. The results of KPMG's research show that 80 percent of respondents admitted that they were not well prepared for the integration. In 2001, the thesis of Frits Grotenhuis already proved that it is not differences of culture that are the main reason for the failure of mergers and acquisitions, but leadership and vision. Frits Grotenhuis also stated in 2001: "the influence of culture on the success of a merger can be managed".

> *"Organic growth is difficult to achieve and acquisitions are back in fashion since early 2006. Will companies learn from the missteps they made in the past? I have my doubts. At corporate level, survival rates are very low, so we have a new generation of managers about to make the same mistakes as their predecessors. The implications for the markets are serious. People are buying shares based on promises of growth levels that will not be achieved".*

There is no doubt that competitive intelligence can fundamentally contribute to the success of mergers and acquisitions. What is vision? Simply stated: vision is what I see and you don't yet see. It all has to do with the near future related to the future competitive landscape. One of the key objectives of competitive intelligence is to identify the current and future competitive landscape and to act accordingly.

Static versus dynamic. Using the metaphor of farmers versus hunters. Competitive intelligence is per definition dynamic; by identifying the business opportunities before your counterparts, you are always dealing with moving targets.

The key players for loans, in billions, for mergers and acquisitions in 2005 in Europe were Royal Bank of Scotland (26.1), Barclays (11.6), Morgan Stanley (11.4), BNP Paribas (11.2), JPMorgan Chase (10.4), Citigroup (9.8), Deutsche Bank (9.3), Merrill Lynch (8.0), Credit Suisse (7.2) and GE (7.0).

Globalisation in food retail with mergers and acquisitions

In the 1990s the big food retail chains held the belief that the local food retail business could become global. Dutch Ahold opened shops in China and Thailand and acquired food retail chains in Spain, Argentina, Sweden and the US. Similar initiatives were taken by French Casino and Carrefour, US Wal Mart and British Tesco. Because of the scandals within Ahold the new management had to discard most acquisitions, Carrefour sold its acquired food retail chains in Chile, Japan and Portugal, Casino wants to generate 2 billion Euros from divestments. Professor Brakman of the University of Groningen, the Netherlands, and Maikel Batelaan do not agree with the ideal picture of the global player who wants to obtain a global presence by means of numerous global strategic acquisitions. The most sold cars in the economic regions EU, US and the Far East are regional brands, except for Toyota. This is the same picture as in many other sectors of industry. Globalisation is not global but regional and only strong brands do not adapt to regional conditions. Examples are Coco Cola, Nike, Apple, Toyota.

Too many managerial boards have embarked unsuccessfully on the road to internationalisation and globalisation. Dutch companies such as KPN, Ahold, Buhrmann, Aegon, VNU have tried to achieve success by means of acquisitions. The result has been a dramatic drop of 60 percent in shareholder value.

9   Private Equity Firms

The failure of many mergers and acquisitions has created new opportunities for venture capitalists and Private Equity Firms. Private Equity Firms in particular are very active with a focus on companies that have not been successful in mergers and acquisitions and others which have shown hardly any growth in some years. They claim that these companies are ready for dismantling. The Private Equity Firms are cash-rich and have the backing of pension funds, which in the past five years have turned their backs on stock exchanges. The overriding aim of Private Equity Firms is to make profit. The lack of the economic drivers of mergers and acquisitions on the part of Boards and CEOs lays the field open to Private Equity Firms. The great advantages possessed by Private Equity Firms are freedom of action, less interference with corporate governance, less need for transparency.

Companies which they withdraw from the stock exchange are no longer obliged to report on a quarterly basis to please the financial world, and banking analysts are no longer looking over their shoulders.

> *"The combination of high levels of liquidity at private equity firms and trade buyers, increasing acceptance of secondary sales among private equity firms, volatility of the markets and the need for certainty on the terms of sales are all making IPOs less attractive".*
> (James Stewart, ECI Partners, London, in CFO Global Outlook 2007)

Prime targets of Private Equity Firms are those companies that have been active in mergers and acquisitions or have not produced the necessary growth. Most of those failed, in addition, to develop to create value. You might well conclude that the strategy and tactics of many Boards of Directors have been unsuccessful. We know that mergers result in redundancies. There are hundreds of examples in many sectors of industry where many people have lost their jobs. The announcement in April 2006 of the merger between French Alcatel and US Lucent indicated at an early stage that around 9,000 of the total number of 80,000 employees would be made redundant.

The key activity of Private Equity Firms is to fragment companies so as to improve competitiveness. I had the impression that in these cases, too, many people will lose their jobs. However, the opposite is the case. In December 2005, the Centre for Entrepreneurial and Financial Studies of the Technical University of Munich, Germany, conducted an in-depth study for the European Private Equity and Venture Capital Association. The research showed that Private Equity Firms and Venture Capitalists created about one million jobs during the period 2000-2004. Private Equity Firms created over 600,000 new jobs and the Venture Capitalists over 400,000 jobs.

This contrasts with the numerous redundancies in well-known major companies such as ABNAmro Bank, ING Group, Rabobank, KPN, AT&T, MCI, Bellsouth, Unilever, Wolters Kluwer, Michelin and the automotive companies General Motors, Ford, Daimler Chrysler, Volkswagen Group and Nedcar. The list is far from complete.

However, the management of a company can also take its own initiatives to clean up its portfolio of business activities. A good example is General Motors (GM), which made a loss of US$ 10.6 billion in 2005. GM sold its stakes in Isuzu of Japan (1971), Suzuki (1981) and Fuji Heavy Industries, the holding company of Subaru, in the US Delphi Automotive and its healthy finance division General Motors Acceptance Corporation (since 1919 contracts worth US$ 1,300 billion for sales totalling 158 million cars. Value of assets in 2005 was 310 billion). Together with the decision to lay off another 30,000 people and offering early retirement to another 105,000 employees, one might conclude that GM is in big trouble. Big trouble, because when companies start to sell their silverware, it's the beginning of the decline. It's amazing that GM, with a US market share of 42 percent in the 1980s, dropping to 25 percent in 2005, should have got into such a state. The current market capitalisation of GM is estimated at US$ 12.5 billion compared to over US$ 200 billion for Toyota, which has a share of 13.5 percent in the US market.

However, it is not only GM that has faced problems on the US automotive market. Also Ford Corporation and to a lesser extent DaimlerChrysler have not performed according to expectations. We should not conclude from this that the automotive sector in Detroit, home base of GM, Ford and DaimlerChrysler, has not been able to recover from the successful market incursions by Japanese and Korean auto manufacturers in the early 1980s. The cause of the decline in the American automotive industry has been the combination of vehicles that didn't meet customers' needs, bad management, corporate dyslexia, market blind spots, complacency and arrogance.

The big three have attempted to find hierarchical solutions to their problems. If problems occur in production, staff try to solve the problems. Toyota, for instance, gave all employees the skills, the tools and the leeway to solve problems as they arose and to prevent new problems before they occurred.

> *"I see no scenario whatsoever where Toyota will pass us in market share".*
> (Dieter Zetsche in February 2002, CEO DaimlerChrysler US)

A prime example of the huge ego and arrogance of a CEO. Toyota surpassed both DaimlerChrysler and Ford on the US market and will become the world's leading automotive company in 2007.

Case: DaimlerChrysler

Another result of a bad merger or acquisition was Daimler and Chrysler in 1998, followed by the acquisition of a 30 percent stake in the Mitsubishi Motor Corporation of Japan.

Case DaimlerChrysler

---

1. Facts in 1998:

- – Daimler Benz merged with Chrysler in 1998
- – Timing: Top of the market
- – Aim to become Global Player with 30 percent share in Mitsubishi ("If you can't beat them, merge")
- – Aim of synergies/year round Euro 1.5 billion
- – Share price of Euro 100 in 1998
- – Analysts were very positive

Case DaimlerChrysler

---

2. Previous achievements of Juergen Schrempp:
   - Ten years Daimler Benz South Africa
   - Restructuring of the Mercedes Benz Truck division in the US
   - Restructuring of DASA Aerospace Germany
   - CEO of Daimler Benz in 1995
   - Acquisition of Chrysler in 1998
   - CEO of DC in 1998

Case DaimlerChrysler

---

3. Conclusions in 2005:
   - Announcement of DC to withdraw as CEO on July 29th
   - Loss of Smart since 1998
   - Loss on Mitsubishi stake
   - Quality problems at Mercedes Benz Brand
   - Increasing sales of Chrysler because of new launches
   - Share price of Euro 36
   - Increase of share price on 29.07.2005 of 10%
   - Schrempp has been at DC for 44 years

I gave an overview in the diagrams of what has happened since both companies merged "as equals"; however, the end result was the acquisition of Chrysler by Daimler. This was a typical acquisition by a CEO on an ego-trip, in this case Jürgen Schrempp, who acquired the nickname "Der Macher". By the way, in 1998 the entire finance sector was positive about this merger. However, we might conclude that it was a failure. Only a few years ago Chrysler in the US improved its performance, synergies have not been realised, the withdrawal from Mitsubishi, huge losses for many years with Smart, and finally quality problems with the core brand Mercedes Benz. To this could be added marketing problems as a cause of the problems in branding. Firstly, the SmartforTwo, which is a very strong and different concept of mobility which was destroyed by the introduction of the SmartforFour. Secondly, Mercedes Benz which markets cars varying in price from 18,000 Euros to over 150,000 Euros and violates the basics of marketing in terms of brand equity, brand values and brand image. In addition, the company has been facing huge quality problems with Mercedes Benz, including several "call backs". In the 1970s-1990s Mercedes Benz was the leading brand in the luxury sector of the car market. But the brand has been passed by brands such as Lexus, BMW, Audi and Maserati. The aim of the merger in 1998 was synergy and better shareholder value. But doesn't the share price tell you something about shareholder value? At the time the merger was announced, the share price was 100 Euros, in 2005 the share price dropped to 36 Euros. On July 29th 2005, the day Jürgen Schrempp announced his resignation as CEO of DaimlerChrysler, the share price increased by 10 percent.

Case: Automotive sector

What do Volkswagen, PSA/Peugeot/Citroen, BMW, Fiat, Ford, Porsche, Toyota and Suzuki have in common? The answer is quite simple: "family". Apart from Toyota and Suzuki, the various families control around 55 percent of the automotive sector in Western Europe. Although they are not always fully in control, they own strategic stakes are well connected with other stake owners. The Peugeot family has still influence in France, the Agnelli family still invests in Fiat, the Quandt family in Germany is a major shareholder in BMW, Mini and Rolls Royce, Bill Ford is on the Board of the Ford Motor Company and Ferdinand Piëch of Porsche has a strategic stake in Volkswagen. The success of an automotive company is dependent upon the success of new car models. What explains the success of these family-based automotive companies compared to less entrepreneurial automotive companies? These families believe in defensive strategies for the long term. They do not believe in mergers and acquisitions (BMW admitted that acquiring the Rover Group was a mistake). The Quandt family took the tough decision to shed the Rover Group, based on an emotional analysis rather than an economic analysis.

The family-connected automotive companies rely heavily upon real innovation and new technologies. Mercedes Benz preferred to go down the road of acquisitions such as Chrysler and Mitsubishi Motor Corporation, and has been struggling ever since 1998 with image and quality problems, a rigid focus on short-term shareholder value and a product portfolio which is inconsistent in terms of brand equity and brand values.

What can we expect from the Private Equity Firms, which have listed as potential targets many other companies that have not performed in respect of growth, profitability and innovation? Just in one country, such as the Netherlands, potential targets of Private Equity Firms could include ASMI, Ahold, Unilever and Philips, while the battle of VNU in April 2006 remains after the failed merger between IMS Health and VNU at the end of 2005. The aim of the Private Equity Firms is to increase economic value and economic growth rather than shareholder value.

The financial basis upon which Private Equity Firms finance their acquisitions is relatively simple. If they want to acquire a company with a market value of 8 billion Euros, they invest around 1 billion themselves, and borrow the remaining 7 billion from banks and pension funds. This is favourable, if interest rates are relatively low. After the acquisition they split up the acquired company, because the individual parts generally have a higher market value than the initial total market value of the company as a whole. Example: KKR (US) bought the Dutch retail group VendexKBB for 2.4 billion and changed the name to Maxeda. After one year they sold the real estate of Maxeda for 1.4 billion market value with a book value on the balance sheet of 0.8 billion. Within one year KKR realised a profit of 600 million on a total investment of 2.4 billion.

> *"I am a great supporter of private equity. They wake up sleeping managers and give companies new objectives. These kinds of financers make companies better".*
> (Jack Welch, former CEO of GE in FD January 9 2007)

The economic value of companies acquired by Private Equity Firms will increase in the medium term combined with an increased shareholder value in the short to medium term. Operational processes will be improved, unnecessary costs will be cut and revenues should be increased in order to pay the interest on debts. Because the average time a Private Equity Firm owns the company is five years, they will have no interest in costly long-term innovation programmes. In the long run, this will damage the competitiveness of the acquired companies. Another disadvantage of the strategy game played by Private Equity Firms is the new situation of rising interest rates and high level of debt which will be impossible to pay in the future; this will be of great detriment to the acquired company. On the other hand, there are advantages: a fast, efficient and effective managerial approach, growth of employment after the first year, the creation of a vision of where the company should be going, and the ability to implement changes at an early stage.

One of the key objectives of competitive intelligence is to prevent companies being taken by surprise by sudden developments in the business environment. Within the world of private equity, many Boards of Directors are still overtaken by surprise. An FD article lists ten recommendations to help avoid surprise attacks on Boards of Directors by private equity firms:

1. Don't be surprised. Be prepared and don't wait too long before adapting the company's strategy. Don't close your ears to the outside world: change your strategies. Waiting too long, weak results and poor performance will lead to high interest on the part of private equity firms. Three Dutch companies faced this situation in 2006: Royal Ahold, CSM and VNU. Ahold even started merger negotiations with Belgian Delhaize to protect itself.

2. Open up a dialogue with activists from private equity firms. Both the Chairman of the Supervisory Board and the CEO of VNU have been fighting against the corporate raiders Templeton, Fidelity and Eric Knight.

3. Look for allies. Corporate raiders cleverly manipulate the press and the media with the aim of increasing the shareholder value of the target companies. Boards of Directors should act even more cleverly. Open up to the press,

find new allies among financial institutes, involve the trade unions and the employees' council. One good example of a company which did this is Dutch Stork.

4. Demolish protectionism. Loyal shareholders will lose shareholder value through protection regulations, making them vulnerable to corporate raiders to avoid the "Dutch discount of 10%". Protection regulations have a negative impact on the development of the stock price. So it is recommended that the share warrants be done away with, both A versus B shares as well preferential shares.

5. Speak with the corporate raiders. Start an open debate; impress upon them the strategy and the "personality" of the company. Seek support from the media and from shareholders. Create your scenarios with the potential outcomes and be prepared to adapt the company strategy. Don't allow a wedge to be driven between the Board of Directors and the Members of the Supervisory Board.

6. Pay back surplus cash. A good strategy to keep the company out of the hands of raiders in private equity firms is to pay back the any surplus to the shareholders, either to buy own shares or in the form of an extra dividend. Good examples of companies which did this are Nutreco, Euronext, TNT and KPN Telecom.

7. Keep the company structure transparent. Companies with a non-transparent structure are prime targets for private equity firms, even such huge companies as Royal Dutch Shell or Unilever. Eliminate poorly-performing sections or activities within the company which are being supported by the successfully-performing sections. One good example is the planned buy-out of Organon, the pharmaceutical division of AkzoNobel.

8. Do the work yourself and don't give private equity firms the opportunity to do it. Restructure, sell off poorly-performing activities and improve operational margins. Royal Philips has long been targeted by private equity firms. It has sold off the so-called 'bleeders' as well as the semiconductor division and has redefined its strategy for consumer electronics, domestic appliances and medical devices. Unilever has sold off its frozen food division, and TNT its logistics division.

9. Fulfil your promises. A good example is Numico, where the new CEO restructured the company completely in 2003, defined new objectives and strategies and asked the shareholders for the time to implement them. In 2006 Numico had the highest price-gains ratio in the AEX-listing on the Amsterdam Stock Exchange.

10. Keep out of the courts. The outcome of legal battles is always an imponderable. Furthermore, this is not the best way to ensure shareholders keep their faith in the company. It may be better for the Unions or the employees' council to go to court.

The added value of competitive intelligence

What is the added value of competitive intelligence in relation to these ten recommendations, and what are the benefits if companies have a competitive intelligence capability in place?

▶ Not to be taken by surprise. One of the most important objectives of competitive intelligence is to avoid surprises. Think of Frederick the Great's statement: "To be defeated is forgivable to be surprised not";

▶ The aim of competitive intelligence is to create an intelligent and alert organisation;

▶ To be cleverer than your rivals. Remember the words of Sun Tzu: "Know your enemies and know yourself and in a hundred battles you will never be in danger".

▶ Clear strategies. Strategy is what the company wants to do in the outside world. Intelligence is what the outside world wants to do with the company. It is a precondition for the development of successful strategies that those strategies are consequently and consistently fed with competitive intelligence.

▶ Shed weak company activities and/or bleeders. The aim of competitive intelligence is to keep ahead of the competition. CI professionals supply decision-makers with the appropriate "actionable intelligence" with the aim of avoiding persisting with poorly-performing activities.

▶ Competitive intelligence is key in monitoring the execution of the current & future strategies in the dynamics of the external business environment.

▶ Competitive intelligence is per definition future-oriented. It helps senior management to identify new market opportunities in time.

The big advantage which has resulted from the market entry of corporate raiders or activists in the private equity firms in the business world is a tremendous increase in alertness within the managerial boards of companies. Clear and transparent strategies appear to be a pre-condition for survival, and this is something senior management does not necessarily possess. With interest rates low since 2001 and their targets of 20 percent ROI, I assume there will be an increase in the area of private equity firms. Another important advantage is that the acquired target companies receive greater freedom to seek expansion.

Case: Competition in the backyard of The Greenery

The Greenery is a Dutch cooperation of vegetable and fruit producers. Total revenues in 2005 was 1.6 billion Euros. The Greenery has developed in recent years from an auction organisation into more of a trade organisation, with an estimated share of 4 percent of the European market. In 2006 the Belgium-based United Vegetables and Fruit Masters, Uni-Veg, acquired the Italian Bocchi Group which has 75 percent of sales in Germany, with Dutch products as well to the rest of Europe, Brazil and Mexico.

Uni-Veg was established in 1983 and controls the total value chain from grower, harvesting, warehousing and distribution. Customers of Uni-Veg are located in Benelux, Spain, Portugal and Poland. With the acquisition of the Bocchi Group they have now covered the white spot of Germany. Both companies complete their portfolio of products with estimated revenues in 2006 of 1.8 billion Euros. The success of Uni-Veg is the different business model where customer intimacy is central meeting new consumer needs. The business model of the Greenery is still based on the supplies of the producers offered via the auction. Uni-Veg, the relatively new kid on the block, has a different, more successful business model, and has just surpassed the Dutch Greenery as one of the former key players in Europe. The big question is whether the Greenery had insights and especially foresights into the future dynamics of the competitive landscape. So far as I am aware, this was not the case.

Case: Telfort and the eye of the storm in mobile phones towards a bumpy ride

We know that the mobile phone market is a very dynamic, ever-changing market. Mobile phone operators do not have strategies to last beyond one year on average. Customers are creatures of whim, and their behaviour capricious. Mobile phone operators need to adapt quickly to the fast-changing market circumstances. For management, too, it has been a question of dynamic decision-making, with little notion of the clear road ahead. In the mid 1990s, large companies showed great interest in benefiting from the opportunities offered by the mobile phone markets. ING Group was one of the founders of Libertel Mobile Phoning, which later became Vodafone. There has been hardly a clear consistent vision of the best way of adapting to the fast changes, resulting in a tremendous strategy game of investing and de-vesting. Strategic choices have faced fast changes, needing to act with decision in "the eye of the storm". Dutch Telfort is a good example of this.

- ▶ 1995: the founding of Telecom 2, the joint venture between Dutch National Railways NS and British Telecom BT as new entrant and new competitor to KPN, the national Telecom player in the Netherlands
- ▶ 1996: change of the name Telecom 2 starting with business-to-business and later the acquisition of the GSM licence
- ▶ 1998: start of mobile phone activities
- ▶ 1999: start of replacing of KPN phone booths at railway stations
- ▶ 2000: NS sells its stake of 50 percent to BT, which acquires 100 percent ownership
- ▶ 2001: split of Telfort into two companies, one for mobiles – Telfort Mobile, one for fixed lines, BT Ignite
- ▶ 2001: BT Wireless, the holding company of Telfort, listed on stock exchange under the name MMO2
- ▶ 2002: change of the name Telfort Mobile to O2

▶ 2003: MMO2 sells O2 Netherlands to venture capitalist Greenfield Capital Partners

▶ 2003: the previous name Telfort is brought back, and Telfort starts price competition, with excellent market success, growing faster than its direct competitors

▶ 2004: a private investor buys a stake of 52% in Telfort for 200 million Euros

▶ 2005: KPN buys all shares of Telfort at the price of one billion Euros

The key question is why KPN made no move in 2004. They already had a serious interest in Telfort. Did the action of the private investor who in 2004 paid 200 million for a 52% stake take them by surprise? If they had acted already in 2004 it would have saved KPN around 600 million Euros. Did KPN have a competitive intelligence capability in place? The answer is no, although throughout the company there was some intelligence-gathering operation. The problem was that these intelligence activities were unstructured and did not represent a collective effort. An additional problem was that competitive intelligence was not organised close to the executive committee. The management of KPN must have been happy when they finally acquired Telfort in the summer of 2005. The price they paid was 600 million too much, chiefly because of the lack of any proper competitive intelligence capability. How are companies ever going to be able to compete if they do not maintain a constant watch on their competitors, 24 hours a day and 7 days a week?

In such a case KPN should have had 100 percent insights into Telfort, and full answers to the following 12 key intelligence questions:

1. What are Telfort's objectives?
2. How does Telfort intend to realise these objectives? What are their strategies at the strategic, tactical and operational levels?
3. How does Telfort plan to compete, how does Telfort compete?
4. What is Telfort's strategic intent?
5. Who is the management of Telfort? What are their achievements, how do they think, what are their business and personal networks like, what are their personal interests?
6. How does Telfort define success?
7. What does Telfort believe about the market, themselves and their competitors including KPN? What assumptions do they make?
8. What are Telfort's capabilities, what are their potential weak spots, what could they do?
9. What will Telfort do next?
10. How will Telfort respond?
11. How effective will Telfort's response be?
12. What will be our Before-Action-Reviews of our action-based assumptions?

Case: Numico

Numico is the Netherlands-based European leader in baby food. Since the 1999s, the company has been in transition and in 2003 returned to their core activities in baby food and clinical foods for hospitals and the elderly. It has cost Numico around 4 billion Euros because of inappropriate acquisitions in 1999-2002. Now the company is back on track again, although the company's equity is relatively low. In my previous books I have already described how wrong the decisions of the executive committee and the Supervisory Board have been.

Now I will briefly describe some instances in which arrogance on the part of management resulted in failure to take competition seriously.

In mid-November, 2005, the retail chain Kruidvat, active in Health and Beauty and a subsidiary of Chinese Hutchison Wampoa, introduced a new range of baby food under private a label. Numico is the market leader in baby food for the 0-2 age range. Numico's reaction was: "We don't see the attack of Kruidvat as a threat. No doubt Kruidvat will take a small part. The competitive landscape will not change that much. Brand loyalty with baby food is high: 85 percent at the first birth and 65 percent at the second birth". Numico feel confident because of previous experience, when UK-based Boots also made an attempt to sell baby food, but were unsuccessful. In late 2005, Numico increased the price of baby food by 25 percent; the price of Kruidvat's baby food is 40 percent below the Numico price level.

In March/April 2006 Numico engaged in a lawsuit, claiming that Kruidvat had violated their baby food patents. Why did Numico only respond to the competition from Kruidvat 4 months after the latter penetrated the market? In December 2005 Numico stated that it would not be a threat to them. In early April 2006 the courts decided that Kruidvat had not violated Numico's patents. We might conclude that this is a typical example of managerial arrogance in refusing to take competition seriously. Numico should have taken Kruidvat very seriously indeed, because this retail chain has almost 800 shops in the Netherlands and another 6,500 in Western Europe!

Another factor difficult to understand was the decision to appoint Rob Zwartendijk, for a fourth term of four years as chairman of the Supervisory Board of Numico. In the first place, Numico violated the corporate governance Code-Tabaksblat, which allows members of Supervisory Boards to act for a maximum of three terms. Secondly, and even more critically, Rob Zwartendijk was Chairman of the Supervisory Board at the time of the unfortunate acquisitions made by Numico during the period 1998-2000, which in 2001-2002 cost the company some 4.5 billion Euros in investments and divestments; these included the acquisition of Rexall Sundown and GNC, both based in the USA. Mr.Zwartendijk approved the acquisitions! Mr.Zwartendijk approved the divestments! Mr.Zwartendijk accepted as Chairman of the Supervisory Board a loss of 4.5 billion Euros. How delighted must the employees of a company like Numico be, a firm that makes such disastrous appointments? The headline in a Dutch financial newspaper commented on the appointment of Mr. Zwartendijk for another 4-year term " The local playground club does it better".

Will Numico get back on track? At the start of his term the new CEO Jan Bennink communicated the new company message: "high growth, high margin". In 2004, Numico acquired EAC Nutricion with the brand Dumex for 1.2 billion Euros. Numico's total debt has increased from 1.1 billion to 1.8 billion, which is the same as total annual sales in 2004 of 1.8 billion. EAC is active in China, Malaysia, Thailand and Southeast Asia. The total revenues of EAC are 350 million Euros and profits of 50 million Euros. The size of the middle market in China was estimated at 595 million in 2015. So this acquisition promises to be of great value long term.

For many years Numico enjoyed a very comfortable market position in Europe in health care nutrition. However, the company will face a formidable competitor in Nestle, which has acquired the medical-nutrition division of Novartis pharmaceuticals at a cost of US\$ 2.5 billion. This means that Numico may expect fierce competition from Nestle, the world's leading food company. Should Nestle also succeed in acquiring Novartis's Gerber baby food division, then the competitive battle of Numico with Nestle will be engaged on all fronts.

Case: Mobile Phones

The mobile phone market is an extremely competitive market with an ever-changing competitive landscape. Key success factors in this sector are economy of scale, cost leadership, fast adaptation to unmet consumer needs, combined with new technology, design of the product combining the right mix of features and the immense power of marketing.

The market shares of the global players in 2005:

1.	Nokia	33.0
2.	Motorola	19.0
3.	Samsung	12.5
4.	Sony Ericsson	6.5
5.	LG	6.5
6.	Siemens	4.5
7.	Others	17.0

Others are NEC, Matsushita known for the brand name Panasonic, Toshiba, Mitsubishi Electric and, in the past, brands like Philips and Alcatel. Annual sales of mobile phones have increased from around 100 million in 1997, 420 million in 2000, 800 million in 2005 to an estimated projection of 1,200 million in 2010. Recently companies like Matsushita, Toshiba and Mitsubishi Electric announced their intention to withdraw from the market, because they were unable to compete with the powerhouses Nokia, Motorola and Samsung. Early in 2005 Siemens already left the field, selling its mobile phone operation to Benq in Taiwan. In 1997 Nokia started to establish a competitive intelligence capability, which has now been up and running for many years.

Case: STMicroelectronics Complacency?

From an average annual rate of 17 percent between 1960s-1980s, the semiconductor industry slowed down to around 6 percent growth between 1995-2005. Over the period 2006-2015, the sector's growth expectations are estimated at 8-10 percent. However, STMicroelectronics did not perform all that well in the last couple of years. CFO Carlo Ferro stated: "It's a case of corporate complacency". What went wrong? The spectacular highs of the tech boom left "ST middle management feeling that they had delivered, and so they relaxed their focus". The challenge in 2006 was to shake up the company again. Carlo Ferro saw that he could play a pivotal role in helping "our management understand how their actions are perceived externally by our shareholders".

What lessons can we learn from STMicroelectronics? One of the objectives of competitive intelligence is to eliminate corporate complacency.

Case: Boeing and Airbus

Boeing and Airbus have been locked in fierce competition for years. Both have an excellent portfolio of aircraft. Airbus relied on the assumption that planes should be bigger; in 1999 they undertook the development of the huge A380 with a capacity of around 800 passengers. Boeing first misled Airbus, announcing their response with a larger Boeing 747; however, they started to develop a completely new aeroplane for 250-300 passengers, the Dreamliner 787, with a longer range combined with an average of 20 percent less fuel consumption.

Another perfect example of Boeing's competitive strategy has been the completely redesigned Boeing 747-8. Because of the huge problems with the A380, Boeing reacted very quickly to the changing competitive landscape. Lufthansa have already ordered 20 new planes of the 747-8 type.

Both companies will benefit from the growth market that is China. According to an interview with the management in the Herald Tribune end of November/early December 2006, Boeing has identified that China currently has around 800 planes with 11,000 pilots. Estimates by Boeing and Airbus indicate that in 2010-2025 another 2000-2400 new planes will be needed with 55,000 pilots.

Case: ABNAmro Bouwfonds

ABNAmro Bank is one of the leading top-4 banks in the Netherlands, together with ING Bank, Rabobank and Fortis. In 1999 it acquired Dutch-based Bouwfonds, active in real estate development and real estate financing with total assets of 1.2 billion Euros. The current CEO of ABNAmro, Rijkman Groenink, who at the time of the acquisition was fully involved, acquired Bouwfonds from the Dutch

Council Group. At this time Rijkman Groenink made a statement: "A beautiful additional activity fitting perfectly in the European ambitions of ABNAmro bank". Real estate was been seen as a sector with strong growth potential which could give the bank access to other markets. At the end of 2005, only five years later, management explained that much had changed and that management now had other priorities. The new focus would be on the mid section. The business and private markets and customers should increase ease of access to other products and services. In this new strategy real estate development and financing was less appropriate. Bouwfonds' mortgages, with a market value of 27 billion Euros, would be excluded from this divestment, and would be transferred to ABNAmro, under the brand name of Bouwfonds for the time being.

The rationale for the divestment was also efficiency and cost-cutting at ABNAmro, to a total of 600 million Euros in 2007 and beyond. The estimated market value of Bouwfonds has been estimated at 1.2 – 1.3 billion Euros.

The question that needs to be asked is why an acquisition like this no longer fits company strategy after just five years. Is it down to incorrect wrong strategic choices, lack of vision, inappropriate assumptions and estimates at the time the decision was taken to make the acquisition?

Case: Fierce competition in food retail in Europe

Between 2001-2006 the European economies were flat; consumers adapted to this situation by spending less money in retail and seeking out cheaper options, such as less expensive products and private labels.

Germany. Metro faced quite a number of problems with its supermarket formulas Real and Extra. German consumers decreased their spending on eating and drinking because of the downturn in the economy. Metro decided to close 150 of its 750 retail outlets.

France. In France the situation more or less mirrored the situation in Germany. Price competition forced the biggest retail group, Carrefour, to lower its prices in 2004-2005 (in total a value of 700 million Euros). Carrefour recovered with its supermarkets because of these price cuts and survived in the price war with its discount competitors.

Belgium. Carrefour entered the Belgian market but it faced two formidable competitors, Delhaize and Colruyt. Colruyt especially is a keen and highly successful veteran of price wars.

United Kingdom. The price war is conducted between the big retail chains Tesco, Sainsbury, Asda (acquired by Wal Mart), and WM Morrison. Since Wal Mart acquired Asda, Tesco has lowered its prices time after time. Sainsbury reacted too late and is struggling to recover.

The Netherlands. Since the economic downturn in 2001 the discounters Aldi and Lidl have benefited from the price war in the Netherlands. The year 2005 was the first to see pressure, with stable shares of the market for Lidl at 3.8 percent and Aldi at 9.5 percent.

Case: Apple Computers

It was a very smart decision of Apple to open up its software for Microsoft Windows. This decision was taken in early April 2006. Most people are used to Windows; now they can change to Apple Computers. Windows can be used on a MAC but not at the same time. Around 90 percent of computers worldwide have Windows. Apple has only a 2 percent share globally. When Apple decided to open-up its iPod, sales of the iPod exploded to capture a market share of 82 percent of all music carriers in 2005. The unexpected strategic move by Apple is extraordinary. In January 2007, Apple announced the successor of the iPod, the iPhone, which combines the functions of a mobile phone with those of a photo camera and an iPod.

Case: C&A-H&M-Zara

The Dutch clothing company C&A regains its position in fashion after fierce competition in the late 1990s. C&A, founded in the Netherlands in 1841 by Clemens and August Brenninkmeijer, is Europe's biggest fashion retail chain. In 2005, its total sales amounted to 5.2 billion Euros. But it took C&A years to recover from the competitive battlefield in which it was challenged by newcomers like H&M, Zara, WE and Mexx. In the 1990s C&A changed its fashion collection on average 2-3 times a year, while its new rivals offered new fashion on an almost weekly basis. Cost-cutting was the first action towards regaining profitability by implementing a central purchasing system, with the result that the same fashions, in the same styles, colours and sizes should be offered in every shop in Europe. In addition, shops were closed down in the UK and US to secure the rest of the business. The action was to rethink the basic concept adopted by C&A in the past: high quality at affordable prices with flexible fashion collections developed over 6-9 weeks, and a less rigid purchasing system. Because of this, C&A is back in business again, meeting the challenge of the fast fashion brands H&M and Zara with the right response. So C&A no longer lag behind, and management now have plans to extend business activities to the former Eastern European countries, Turkey and Russia.

The lesson the company learned is that you neglect new rivals at your peril; competition must always be taken seriously. C&A showed itself capable of adapting to new market conditions mainly because of its financial reserves; but few companies get so much time to recover. In the end, C&A's recovery took 5-6 years.

What has been the key to the success of Zara and Hennes and Mauritz (H&M)? Zara has around 800 shops and H&M around 1200 shops worldwide. Zara passed H&M in 2005, their sales increasing by 21 percent to 6.7 billion Euros. What factors have governed the success of these fashion chains? A perfect balance of the internal and external focus on fashion. The first factor is that both companies fully control production. The second factor is the fast development from concept to point of sale. On average, this takes 6 weeks. The third factor is that they hardly ever have "special sales" dictated by poor sales figures. The fourth factor is the excellent internal information systems from cash registration, indicating precisely which lines are the fast runners. The fifth factor is the surprise factor of presenting new fashion. Women are aware of this, so it produces dynamic trade. The sixth, and perhaps most important, factor is the contribution of the creative teams which constantly monitor external developments – consumers on catwalks, at airports, shopping areas, sport events, movies and other events. It seems that Zara, for example, has some 200 of such teams travelling the world with the aim of discovering new fashion behaviour and trends.

"Intuition is one of the X factors separating the men from the boys".

Innovation as the key to success

In April 2006, Business Week published its annual report on the world's top 25 leading innovative companies. The list included Apple, Google, Toyota, Microsoft, GE, P&G, Nokia, Starbucks, BMW, Wal Mart, Intel, Samsung, etc. Together with the BCG, Business Week conducted a global study among 1100 executives. The CEO of IBM, Samuel Palmisano, stated: "The way you will thrive in this environment is by innovating – innovating in technologies, innovating in strategies, innovating in business models". Innovation is much more than new products and is also about reinventing business processes and creating new markets that meet unmet customer needs. Globalisation and the Internet widen the potential of new ideas. The challenge is to select and execute the right ideas and bring these on to the market fast. In the 1990s, innovation focused on technology, quality and cost. Today, innovation reaches beyond technology. The research in this global study identified three key areas of innovation: process innovators (GE, Toyota), product and services innovators (Sony, Samsung) and business model innovators (Southwest Airlines, Dell, Virgin). Companies that represent all three categories of innovation are P&G, Nokia, IBM and IKEA.

A useful example of innovation currently taking place is P&G, who have exchanged their traditional in-house research and development process for an open-source innovation strategy called "connect and develop". They have made a collective effort of their innovation, connecting networks of consumers, scientists, suppliers and universities.

Five important areas for innovation have been identified: Open the company labs, expand the opportunities and initiate collaboration with suppliers, customers, sharing software codes with programmers and tap networks of scientists and entrepreneurs to benefit from the world's best ideas.

1. Become innovators in chief. More than 50 percent of the respondents of the survey said that responsibility for driving innovation lay with the CEO or Chairman. Without solid support from the top, innovation efforts will get lost in the morass of short-term demands.

2. Measure what matters. It is difficult to track the results of innovation. Innovation cannot be reduced into a single number; balancing risk is always part of equation.

3. Innovation needs co-ordination and collaboration; it cannot simply be 'switched on' at will. Building creative companies take synchronization from the centre, cross-boundary collaboration and structural change to the organisational chart.

4. Mining customer insights. Getting inside the minds of customers is essential
    for insights that lead to innovation.

The same article in Business Week also gives an overview of the constraints of
innovation, the methods by which to measure successful innovation and where
the investments occur (percentage of respondents)

First, the overview of the constraints listed by the respondents:
1.	Length of development times	32%
2.	Lack of coordination	28%
3.	Risk avoiding culture	26%
4.	Limited customer insights	25%
5.	Poor selection of ideas	21%
6.	Inadequate tools to measure	21%
7.	Lack of ideas	18%
8.	Marketing or culture failure	18%

Second, the overview of the methods to measure innovation success:
1.	Overall growth of revenues	56%
2.	Percentage of sales from new products and/or services	50%
3.	Customer satisfaction	47%
4.	Return on investment in innovation	30%
5.	Number of new products and/or services	30%
6.	New product success ratio	20%
7.	Higher prices	11%

Third, where the investments in innovation take place:
1.	Improving existing products and/or services	32%
2.	Creating new products or services for new customers	29%
3.	New products or services for new customers	21%
4.	Reducing products or service cost	21%

This survey of Business Week and the BCG shows that there still is a long way
to go towards successful innovation. Is it worthwhile? Does innovation pay off?
Does it improve long-term shareholder value? Is it not the only way to survive in
the long run?

I can answer these four questions in the affirmative. Let us consider the results
of the 25 leading innovative companies listed in the Business Week article.

More than half the top 25 companies generated better profit margins and
higher stock prices in the period 1995 – 2005. The innovative companies achieved
median profit margin growth of 3.4 percent a year since 1995, compared with 0.4
percent median of the Standard and Poor's Global 1200 companies. The median

of the annual stock price was 14.3 percent, which is 3.0 percent better than the Standard and Poor's 1200 Global companies over the period 1995 – 2005. "Innovation is allowing companies to grow faster and have a richer product mix", according to the head of BCG's innovation practice. Almost 50 percent of respondents in the global survey stated that they were dissatisfied with their returns on investment from innovation.

Case: Nedap

Ton Scharenborg and Eric Venema of the Dutch electronics and automation company Nedap attended our international Master Class Competitive Intelligence in March 2006. They were very enthusiastic about the two days of teaching, sharing and practising of competitive intelligence, and invited me to visit them at their headquarters at Groenlo, Netherlands, which I duly did in May 2006; this proved an extremely interesting visit for me. First we toured the facilities for over an hour; this was followed by discussions and pooling of information. Nedap is a medium-sized Dutch company operating in Belgium, UK, France, Germany and Spain. The company is labour and knowledge-intensive with a bias towards technology and engineering. What, in my view, makes Nedap so special, so different and so successful? These are some of the extraordinary drivers of Nedap's success:

1. Nedap is a medium-sized Dutch company driven by innovation and strong entrepreneurship.
2. Company vision: "challenges enrich life".
3. Philosophy: limitations and problems live between the ears of humans. This also means that possibilities and solutions live between the ears of humans.
4. "Customers are our employer", not the company itself.
5. At Nedap they don't talk about employees, but colleagues.
6. This is a strongly innovative company represented visually by a tree: the left side of the tree shows the existing operating markets and the right side of the tree shows the "young" markets. So they don't speak about their company products and services, but about markets and customer target groups.
7. Since 2000 company growth has been sustainable and organic with the same number of people. So there was no cost-cutting by redundancies, unlike almost every other company in the difficult years 2000-2005.
8. Sustainable growth in added value per individual over the period 2000-2005.
9. If numbers in a business section approach 100, the work force is divided into small teams to generate maximum involvement, entrepreneurship and customer success.
10. The co-workers are constantly challenged to improve every aspect of their operation.

These are just some of the reasons behind Nedap's success. This company should serve as an example to many companies in Europe. Nedap is highly skilled and labour-intensive, knowledge-intensive and innovative, creating long-term share-holder value. The overall motto is: "in order to survive in a turbulent business environment it is necessary to be ahead of change, to develop new markets, to control the rules of competition and never to become satisfied with the current situation". In other words " it's you who govern the future".

Revolutionary new solution making safe water affordable for millions of people: Naïade

The Naïade product is a stand-alone, solar powered water purification unit which can be set up and operational within 30 minutes. No special infrastructure is required and the single unit can meet the clean water requirements of 350-400 people at an estimated cost of around one Euro per person per year. This revolutionary new solution has also been developed by Nedap. This innovative water purification system combines well-established solar energy and UV-water treatment technologies and offers cheap and safe water to millions in the developing world. Nedap has won many prizes for this unique solution. One of the statements made by an international jury was as follows: "Massive potential in the battle against water-borne diseases, particularly in remote areas in the developing world".

In December 2006, I had the opportunity to speak with the management of Nedap about this revolutionary solution. The Naïade product has been available on the world market since 2004, and because it can help so many people with safe water in the developing countries in South America, Africa and the Far East, I was deeply impressed. I am convinced that this solution should be broadly accepted by all International Institutions and National Governments in their support for developing countries. The management of Nedap has presented their revolutionary solution at numerous trade fairs around the world; at these events, people at the top level of international institutions such as the UN, WHO, the International Red Cross, IMF, World Bank, heads of state, ministers of national governments and leaders of NGOs all met and spoke with representatives from Nedap, and they were all very impressed. The overall reaction was: "You should contact the relevant departments of the people involved". The management of Nedap is currently working on a new additional business model, trying to reach directly the responsible people in distant NGOs who are working in the field in the crisis areas of South America, Africa and the Far East. Another target group will be the business world. In many companies, management is increasingly interested in taking more responsibility for those who are suffering hardship in developing countries. Just one Naïade solution at a price of around Euros 3,500- will give 400 people in Africa safe, healthy water for a whole year and more.

Enterprise Intelligence, creating the intelligent and alert organisation

In 2004, I published my second book in Dutch under the title "Enterprise Intelligence, creating the intelligent and alert organisation". In it I describe how we can integrate business intelligence, organisational intelligence and competitive intelligence. In this chapter, I shall explain how important it is to continuously monitor the external business environment. I have not seen many solutions that can do this, nor do I know of many companies that have implemented such a monitoring solution.

Such insights don't pop up overnight. For many years I have been recommending to a number of management teams the implementation of a monitoring system, radar or watch tower, in the interests of perceiving changes in the dynamics of the business environment in time. Early in 2004, in Sweden, I met Per Erik Kihlstedt, the author of the book "The Baseline Revolution". He got me interested in his new ideas for improving the management of organisations, especially as regards issues concerning my expertise in competitive intelligence. One of his key messages was that the success of companies relies heavily upon the business relationships a company has established. These business relations have a direct influence on the company and its freedom of action within the marketplace. Per Erik invited me to a week-long workshop, where I learned a great deal about a different way of looking at the outside world. We agreed to introduce his way of looking at companies in the Benelux countries, based on his "freedom of action" philosophy. This philosophy fitted in perfectly with our competitive intelligence best practices. In May 2004, we agreed that I should transform his book into some white papers based on and related to our competitive intelligence best practices.

So I have adapted and fine-tuned Per Erik's philosophy and basic management concept of freedom of action for companies. In this chapter and the next (chapter VI, entitled the Fourth Economy), I will describe his ideas, which I have adapted in keeping up with our expertise in competitive intelligence.

Just as war and diplomacy will never be the same again, neither will business or our national and global economy. There are many who seek to lull the business community into denial of the dramatic changes that have occurred. They try to make us see events as just "business as usual". Others, while acknowledging that we are in a period of rapid and dramatic change, still believe we can muddle through somehow with the same old traditional management tools. One of the important new management tools, which may be seen as "a pre-condition for existence" is enterprise intelligence. The aim of enterprise intelligence is to create an intelligent and alert organisation.

Organisations achieve intelligence and alertness if they have been successful in transforming the vast streams of data, information and knowledge into intelligence. In too many cases, organisations are drowning in data and information, and are unable to reach the next level of knowledge and intelligence. Enterprise intelligence combines the three intelligence areas of business intelligence, competitive intelligence and organisational intelligence.

Business intelligence

The first intelligence area is business intelligence. The aim of the information technology industry is to order, structure and render accessible the vast stream of internal data and information supported by management information systems, data warehousing, data mining tools, balance score cards, company performance dashboards, etc. However, the stage of knowledge and intelligence has not yet been reached. The IT sector markets these applications as business intelligence solutions, but unfortunately doesn't bring an ounce of intelligence to the table.

"Enterprise Intelligence, creating the intelligent and alert organisation"

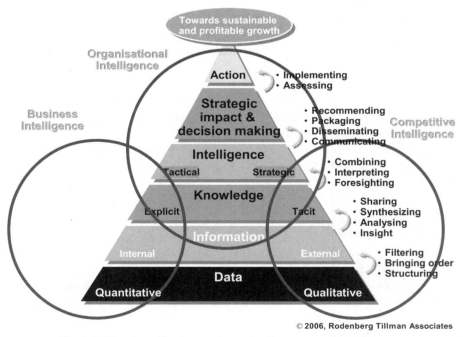

© 2006, Rodenberg Tillman Associates

"In intelligence the issue is not what to read but how to read"

Business intelligence has become a buzzword. "Business intelligence is concerned with the discovery of information, and its use to reduce the cost and increase the value of operational activities," according to the Butler Group. So it's all about dealing with the discovery of information with the aim of reducing costs and increasing the value of day-to-day operations. The diagram shows where business intelligence is placed within the intelligence pyramid.

Competitive intelligence

The second intelligence area is competitive intelligence. Competitive intelligence is the organisational means and analytical and intellectual process that transforms disaggregated market, customer, technological, competitive and other data, information and knowledge into relevant and usable intelligence for users who can act on it. Competitive intelligence aims to be future-oriented and actionable. Within the intelligence pyramid shown, competitive intelligence deals with qualitative data, external information, tacit knowledge resulting in strategic intelligence for improved decision-making and the assessment of the strategic impact on the organisation. Competitive intelligence is a comparatively new management discipline; not many companies have professionally implemented a competitive intelligence competency to date. Most companies with a competitive intelligence capability are major international companies. A very important dimension of competitive intelligence is the gathering of data, information and knowledge of the outside dynamics and fast changes in the external business environment in a structured and consistent way and bringing this in from the outside. The focus of competitive intelligence is always on the "drivers of change" faced by every company: markets, customers, competition, technology, legislation, etc. Having implemented a competitive intelligence capability with a focus on these drivers of change means that management will never be surprised by any change in the dynamics of the external business environment. But most companies do not have it and will therefore always be surprised by changes of market conditions, changes in the competitive arena, new disruptive technologies and new customer needs.

"No IT system in any company can generate intelligence".

Organisational intelligence

The third intelligence area is organisational intelligence. Organisational intelligence deals with people. No IT system in a company can generate intelligence. People alone can create intelligence. Huge amounts of money are invested in IT systems. But, if we want to become smart as an organisation, we'll need to emphasize the I of IT, not the T: the I of IT is all about information management. We must help and support our employees within the organisation to improve their skills in dealing with the vast streams of information, analysing, sharing and disseminating information within the organisation. We will never solve these problems by continuing to invest in more T of IT. 60-70 percent of all investments in IT still do not come up to expectations. All companies measure the cost of IT investments, only a few assess the effectiveness of IT. The volume of information doubles every 18 months, while the availability of people capable of analysing the information decreases dramatically.

Organisational intelligence is positioned in the middle of the intelligence pyramid, and is closely related to the areas of business intelligence and competitive intelligence. As already mentioned, people in organisations are the only valuable resource capable of transforming data, information, knowledge into relevant and useful intelligence. People alone create intelligence.

Top management requirements
The requirements, if management are to successfully lead a business, are the same as the objectives of enterprise intelligence.
1. To prevent surprises from the external business environment
2. To have timely foresight of the threats and opportunities faced by the organisation, and strategies to transform these threats into opportunities
3. To make informed strategic choices
4. To continuously identify the gaps in the company's own strategies as well the gaps in the strategies of competitors
5. To monitor developments within the sector and beyond
6. To anticipate unforeseen developments
7. To monitor early warnings from the internal and external dynamics of the industry
8. To keep in view the key drivers of change in the competitive arena: markets, customers, competition, technology, legislation and beyond.

The conclusion is that enterprise intelligence is a strategic management responsibility of top management. All the above top management requirements deal with the outside world. It is of growing importance for management to introduce new measures that will enable them to manage the business environment more effectively.

> "Not even the US despite its position as the only remaining superpower can handle war on its own. They need more than ever to develop support, alliances, networks and relationships". And so also companies have to.

Management must learn to handle the challenges of fast and unpredictable change. Traditional management solutions such as forecasting, trend analysis, extrapolation, planning based on past performance, discounted cash flow analysis, net present value, real options, SWOTI analysis, traditional strategic management processes, and, last but not least, "business as usual", are no longer effective. Instead, flexibility, agility and freedom of action will be the new important conditions for success. Diagnoses of threats and opportunities in the present situation will be more important than prognoses. Turbulence is nothing new in our business community; speed and the fast pace of change are not the only dimensions to be considered.

Freedom of Action: The Business Position

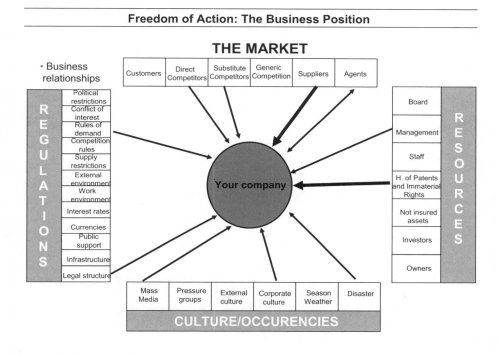

Source: The Baseline Revolution

So how does management handle one of the big dilemmas, the great paradox for top executives, the need to make decisions about a future that is not only uncertain, but in reality unpredictable? How can one establish a platform for making decisions that will shape a company's future, one way or the other? Small wonder that business executives, just like all other human beings over the years, have desperately sought ways to deal with this paradox, ways to predict the future, using anything from crystal-gazing to discounted cash flow, striving to escape from the futility of forecasting. The fact that it is not only difficult but downright impossible has not prevented many people in various roles and with widely different tools and techniques from offering their forecasting services to frustrated executives.

It's obvious that past performance is no indication of future results; neither is looking forward through the rear view mirror.

In management, to have any chance at all of coping with the future, we need to carefully examine the present, especially the quality and strengths of the company's business position and its relationships. All one can do is to analyse the present, especially those parts that do not coincide with what everybody knows and takes for granted, beyond traditional accounting. Strategic decision models that rely on accounting-based data, on trend extrapolation and forecasting-back casting have never been reliable. Today, they are increasingly unreliable and irrelevant.

The need to understand and manage the company in its living environment, in an inter-connected economy, will call for a new focus on what is good for a company. First, moving from a balance sheet focus to a relationship focus. Second, distinguishing between good and bad relationships. Basically, we need to redefine the company as a network of relationships. Treating the company as an isolated unit, as accounting does, is revealed as a major factor in management and other applications.

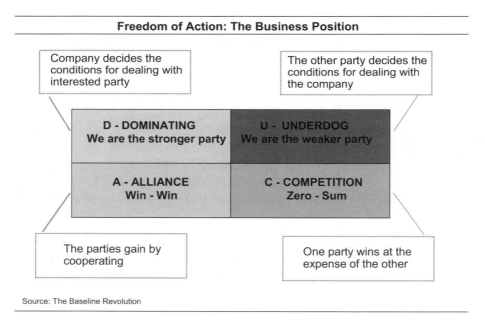

Freedom of Action: The Business Position

Company decides the conditions for dealing with interested party

The other party decides the conditions for dealing with the company

D - DOMINATING	U - UNDERDOG
We are the stronger party	We are the weaker party
A - ALLIANCE	C - COMPETITION
Win - Win	Zero - Sum

The parties gain by cooperating

One party wins at the expense of the other

Source: The Baseline Revolution

A company with a heavy balance sheet including big investments in fixed assets, real estate, factories, machinery and so on, loses its freedom of action. It tends to be locked into the business it has chosen. In a world of no change, such a position may have its benefits. But few companies, if any, today live in a world without change. The demands of change and flexibility head the list for most companies.

Only companies that prioritise relationships over fixed assets have a chance of adapting to new situations. But how is one to measure the dependencies the company has in its relations with other stakeholders and parties? A "managing your business environment" scheme will have to provide us with methods and measures designed to report and assess dependencies. It is all about the ultimate strategic asset "Freedom of Action".

Case: Gazprom

"Despite all the huffing and puffing about terrorists and hackers, mother nature remains business's biggest saboteur".

"A victory for the new Russia" was the heading of an article in the FD in December 2006. The basic reason given was the reduction of Shell's stake in the Sakhalin 2 project from 55 to 27.5 percent: a perfect example of loss of position and the freedom of action as a company, based on vital changes in business relationships in the external environment. Gazprom obtained the majority stake in the Sakhalin 2 project and will be one of the new energy powerhouses over the next 30-40 years. What is the situation?

Russia is no longer dependent on the world, especially Europe. Europe is now fully dependent on Russia's energy policy, and both European governments as well as fuel companies face a new challenge in how to manage these relationships successfully. Take for example the cutting off of gas supplies to the Ukraine by the Kremlin in January 2006. This had a knock-on effect on gas supplies to Italy and Austria. Europe suddenly woke up to the fact that it is highly dependent on current and future gas supplies from Russia. Another wake-up call for Europe came in January 2007 with Belarus. Russia decided to cut off the oil supplies to Belarus, with the direct effect of cutting off oil supplies to Poland and Germany. Some key facts:

1. The Board of Gazprom is very close to the Kremlin. CEO Alexei Miller was Minister of Energy until 2001; he is the confidant of Mr. Putin. Dmitri Medvedev is chairman of the Supervisory Board of Gazprom and Vice President of Russia. Victor Khristenko, Minister of Energy, and German Gref, Minister of Economic Affairs, are both in the Board of Directors at Gazprom.
2. Energy has become the focus of Russian politics. The key question is the future role of Mr. Putin after the 2008 Russian presidential election.
3. The strategic intention of CEO Alexei Miller is that Gazprom should become the world's leading energy company, with future growth focus areas in Europe, Asia and the US.
4. Perspectives of the market capitalisation:
   ▶ The value of Gazprom in December 2006 was calculated at US$ 273 billion;

▶ The value of Shell is US$ 228 billion, BP US$ 218 billion and ExxonMobil US$ 443 billion;

▶ Strategy of Gazprom: firstly the exploration and production of oil and gas and secondly the integration of the value chain by obtaining footholds in Europe in distribution and marketing. Gazprom has already established alliances with German-based EON Ruhrgas and Wintershall. In the UK they have made a bid for Centrica.

5. The big challenge for Gazprom is to explore new oil and gas fields in remote and inaccessible areas such as the Yamal peninsula and the Barents Sea. For both these fields Gazprom will need alliance partners for future exploration, because the growth in the production of gas is expected to slow down from 550 billion to 560 billion cubic metres.

The challenge for governments and energy companies in Europe is now to identify both the business and personal management relationships within the overall landscape of Russian energy. The next step is to monitor this Russian competitive energy landscape daily; in so doing, the requisite clarity will be ensured which will enable decision-makers to act and counteract. An example of such a competitive landscape might resemble the competitive landscape we developed earlier for UK-based British Petroleum.

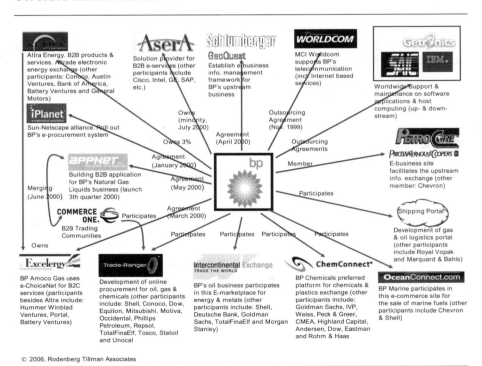

The Strategic Road to "Freedom of Action" follows a step-by-step process which starts with relationships.

1. A company that has good relations with its stakeholders tends to receive in return at the very least acceptance, and very often more than that: active support from forces in its environment;
2. A company that receives acceptance and support from its environment encounters fewer restrictions and obstacles;
3. Fewer restrictions and obstacles mean a stronger negotiating position;
4. A strong negotiating position leads to higher value-added and a bigger share of retained value-added;
5. Increased value-added and a larger retained share of the value-added means better earnings, better chances of survival and opportunities for growth.

I strongly believe in the victory of common sense over theories and bureaucracy, so I think it is worth the effort to get the heavy stone rolling. This is why any new system should aim to be:

▶ Relevant: establishing a platform for strategic management and board of management decisions;
▶ informative: providing meaningful information about the company for investors, analysts and all other stakeholders;
▶ objective: the norms and priorities of the person making the report should not influence the outcome;
▶ measurable, to allow for comparisons with other businesses, irrespective of company size, type of business or geographic location as well as for comparisons over time;
▶ consistent, so as to minimize any possibility of manipulating the results.

The solution I propose provides a coherent model. It meets the need to have a radar in place that will monitor important indicators of company progress, success or failure, a solution that helps management and other stakeholders to make better choices. It suggests appropriate measures, but is not constructed solely on the basis of financial data. Instead, it helps companies to create internal and external reports that will provide relevant and meaningful information.

> "We must begin to organise information from the outside, where the true profit centres exist. We will have to build a system that gives information to those who make the decisions".
> (Peter Drucker)

Our aim is to encourage companies to experiment with this monitoring solution and to show traditionalists that an outside-the-box solution is feasible also in this traditions-laden field. I hope that this experimentation process will create awareness that there are better viable alternatives. This may help ease the feelings of uncertainty and fear that many will experience as it becomes increasingly obvious that the old models are inevitably breaking down.

It looks at the company within the living context of its environment, not in isolation, as traditional accounting does. The most important feature is that it offers several ways for management, as well as other stakeholders, to monitor company progress towards the achievement of this objective.

> *"My message to the business world is clear. We are moving fast away from managing what we know to the management of uncertainty. To deal with this uncertainty, senior management must understand the management discipline of competitive intelligence to avoid being surprised by changes in the external business environment".*

Top management requirements

Diagnoses of threats, opportunities and business risks in the present situation will be more important than prognoses. So how does management handle one of the major dilemmas, the paradox facing top executives, the need to make decisions about a future that is not only uncertain, but in reality unpredictable? The requirements of management in order to successfully lead a business are the same as the objectives of competitive intelligence.

1. To prevent surprises from the external business environment
2. To obtain timely foresights about threats and opportunities faced by the organisation, and strategies to transform these threats into opportunities
3. To make correct strategic choices
4. To continuously identify gaps in the company's own strategies as well the gaps in the strategies of competitors
5. To monitor developments within the sector and beyond
6. To anticipate unforeseen developments
7. To monitor early warnings from internal and external dynamics of the industry
8. To keep in view the key drivers of change in the competitive arena: markets, customers, competition, technology, legislation and beyond.

This means that competitive intelligence is the strategic management responsibility of top management. All the above top management requirements deal with the outside world.

The result of the process is a unique evaluation of the company's current business position. The key to the process is a clear structuring of all important relationships. To establish this, all relevant relationships are defined and classified in respect of kind and strength, and then combined with the result graphically presented.

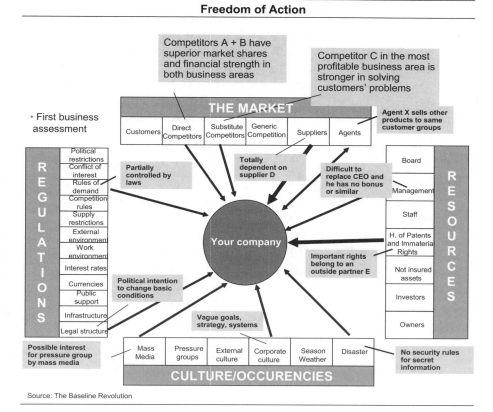

Freedom of Action

Competitors A + B have superior market shares and financial strength in both business areas

Competitor C in the most profitable business area is stronger in solving customers' problems

• First business assessment

THE MARKET

| Customers | Direct Competitors | Substitute Competitors | Generic Competition | Suppliers | Agents |

Agent X sells other products to same customer groups

REGULATIONS

- Political restrictions
- Conflict of interest
- Rules of demand
- Competition rules
- Supply restrictions
- External environment
- Work environment
- Interest rates
- Currencies
- Public support
- Infrastructure
- Legal structure

Partially controlled by laws

Totally dependent on supplier D

Difficult to replace CEO and he has no bonus or similar

RESOURCES

- Board
- Management
- Staff
- H. of Patents and Immaterial Rights
- Not insured assets
- Investors
- Owners

Your company

Important rights belong to an outside partner E

Political intention to change basic conditions

Vague goals, strategy, systems

Possible interest for pressure group by mass media

| Mass Media | Pressure groups | External culture | Corporate culture | Season Weather | Disaster |

No security rules for secret information

CULTURE/OCCURENCIES

Source: The Baseline Revolution

"Most managers don't have the balls to make decisions. Instead of going to war to kill, they go to war to evade bullets".
(Leopoldo Pujals of TelePizza in *Forbes*)

This new intelligence-based monitoring diagnostic tool does not rely upon any traditional numbers analysis. It does not compress all the information into an income statement or balance sheet. Rather, the intelligence-based monitoring solution identifies what is essential in and around the company, presents it and allows conclusions to be drawn from it. The focus is on relevance and perspective rather than on precision.

It is entirely based on the statement that "the most important decisions are not taken inside your company, but outside your company". Will management have the courage to work with this new intelligence-based monitoring solution? That's the question, isn't it?

Case: Shell and Gazprom

Freedom of action was the key issue for Royal Dutch Shell in the Sakhalin 2 project. What happened and how did Shell lose its freedom of action? In the early 1990s, the US company Marathon Oil started developing the vast oil and gas fields around the island of Sakhalin. After a couple of years it became clear that this project was too big and too complex for Marathon Oil. In 1995, Shell took over and signed the Production Sharing Agreement. Shell received a stake of 55 percent in Sakhalin. The initial investment was US$ 10 billion and the Russian state was to be able to share in the profits after Shell's return on their total investment. At the time oil prices were low and Boris Jeltsin was President of Russia. In 2002-2003 Shell's production came under pressure, and, in 2004, the scandal of the reserves became public. Shell had underestimated the complexity of Sakhalin and in the same year the management was replaced. However, by then Russia had a new president, Vladimir Putin.

Mr. Putin sees the energy sector in Russia as the absolute top priority for the nation's future growth and wealth. He fought to retrieve the majority stake in Gazprom and succeeded in regaining full control of Yukos Oil. In 2005, Russia became interested in Sakhalin.

In July 2005, the Kremlin announced that Gazprom had acquired a 25 percent stake in Sakhalin and in exchange Shell had received a 50 percent stake in the gas field of Zapolyarnoye. Early in August 2005, Shell announced an increase in their investment in Sakhalin from 10 to 20 US$, and that production would begin in 2008 rather than in 2007. This was too much for the Kremlin, and was the beginning of extremely difficult negotiations, the outcome of which was a drop of Shell's stake in Sakhalin from 55 to 27.5 percent in 2006.

This example shows that we should never second-guess how relationships will develop over time, and how a company's share can change from a "dominant" to an "underdog" position without warning. One of the key focus areas of competitive intelligence is identifying, managing and monitoring changes in business relationships. I do not claim that Shell neglected this management area; but the freedom of action model shows us how we might prevent similar situations from arising in future.

> *"We didn't foresee the enormous pressure on us from the side of the ecology".*
> (Jeroen van der Veer, CEO Shell, *Telegraaf*, January 8 2007)

The Fourth Economy[1]

We have just started on the 21st Economy, which is seen as a period of sweeping and profound change, in some respects more dramatic than many of us might wish. Just as war and diplomacy will never be the same again, neither will business and our national and global economy.

The changes originate in the simultaneous arrival of a wide range of technological, economic and social sources and forces with far-reaching consequences. They affect almost all aspects of human life, in almost every part of the planet, including our business and our economy. Many of the most engrained patterns from earlier times will have to be reviewed. Including many of the most sacred shibboleths of the business and economic community.

> *"To be able to exploit these changes as opportunities for our companies, executives will have to understand the realities of the Next Society and will have to base their policies and strategies on them".*
> (Peter Drucker)

There are many who seek to lull the business community into a sense of false security and a denial of the dramatic changes that have taken place.

They try to make us regard what is happening as just another phase of " business as usual ". Others, who recognize that we are in a period of fast and dramatic change, still believe that we can muddle along with the same old management tools.

The "new economy" was seen as a temporary phenomenon, a craze. The years 1999-2001 were known as the 'Internet bubble'. This quickly turned into a cliché. For these two reasons I shall not use the term again. Another important reason to avoid the term 'new economy' is that it implies a conflict between a new and an old economy.

We are at the beginning of an era that will change much of what we have taken for granted in society, in the economy and in the way we run countries and companies. Peter Drucker calls it "The Next Society". We respectfully submit that this different society is already well on the way. In a wider context, it might be called "the fourth world order". Since we will limit our focus to the new aspects for

---

1   This chapter is based on a white paper written after my workshop with Per Erik Kihlstedt in Stockholm in 2004. The white paper was based on my new business insights from this workshop as well as on Kihlstedt and Johnsson's book *The Baseline Revolution*.

business and the economy, Kihlstedt will modestly call this new era "The Fourth Economy".

Despite its significantly different character, the fourth economy does not conflict with previous economies. It builds on the industrial third economy, just as the industrial economy developed from the earth-based second economy, which in turn was preceded by the first economy of hunters and gatherers. Each new economy has made significant contributions to mankind.

The first economy still exists in some areas of the world, not to mention all those in the developed countries who enjoy hunting and fishing as serious leisure activities. In some economic pursuits we are still in a hunter-gatherer economy. Fishing has been, and remains, one such activity, although fish farming is now a fast-growing business, moving fishing from the first economy into the second. The second economy was an improvement on the first economy in that it provided a certain degree of stability and reliability in basic supplies such as food, clothing and materials. Wealth in the second economy was created by earth-based processes. To be rich was to own land.

The third economy added machinery, mainly for manufacturing and transportation. It gave man new physical strength and power and added speed and productivity to physical processes, including second economy processes, such as new equipment and processes for mining and agriculture. Wealth in the third economy was created largely through manufacturing processes. To be rich was to own factories, machinery and capital.

The fourth economy takes mind-based processes to previously unimagined levels of strength, power and speed. This adds up to a tremendous potential for productivity increases in mind-based processes, increasingly significant in pure fourth economy companies, but also in companies rooted in the second and third economies. Wealth in the fourth economy is created through mind-based processes, exchange of ideas and above all information and knowledge. However, the fourth economy is more than an IT-based "new economy".

A perfect example of the coexistence between the four economies is India with a world-leading software development practice in a country where people still plough with oxen.

Management in the Fourth Economy

> *"For companies being a step ahead of competition is more important than it ever has been".*

The fourth economy presents great threats and opportunities, immediate and indirect risks and benefits, and new and far-reaching challenges for management, business and the economy. Let us list the most important drivers of the fourth economy:

1. New sciences and technologies; the fourth economy is a high-tech economy with a very broad technology base including, but certainly not limited to, information technology. Biotechnology, astronomy, nanophysics, new energy sources (wind, hydrogen, fuel cells), new materials, composites, new thinking including complexity and chaos theories and new priorities of time are only a few examples of science and technology forces that impact on society in large, broad segments of the economy and ultimately on individual companies.

2. Trans-national awareness; the fourth economy builds on a previously unknown combination of advances in transportation and communications, which in some cases have all but eliminated distance as a decision factor. Apart from the business sphere, but certainly affecting it, this has encouraged intense ideological, political and religious contacts. One result is a broad and strong trans-national awareness, working in a WWW environment, a world without walls.

3. A new base for wealth creation; in the fourth economy, economic growth is fuelled primarily by minds in interaction, not, as traditionally, by physical resources or capital. One significant feature of the new wealth creation processes is that, unlike physical assets, the human mind is not a fixed, limited resource. The fourth economy has the potential for unlimited growth, provided the mind-based resources are supported and developed through education and free exchange, and given the preference they deserve. This affects many old political and business priorities, practices and measures.

4. Multiculturalism; the fourth economy favours variety, diversity, multiculturalism since interaction between different minds is a stronger force in generating new solutions than interaction between identical or similar minds. Diversity, linked to the concept of minds in interaction, is a distinctive potential source of wealth creation and productivity enhancement, a kind of mental entropy function.

5. A search for common protocols; the fourth economy calls for common protocols, along with a high level of tolerance for trial-and-error development. A good example of this is the international development of wireless communications in the 1990s. Clinging to an analogue system, rather than moving to digital, in a technology standard not embraced by the rest of the world, the 1990s were for the US largely a lost decade for wireless communications, whereas the rest of the world, especially Europe and Asia, has made extremely rapid progress.

6. New concepts of time; new concepts of time have influenced thinking and practice since Einstein. In the fourth economy the time factor has been eliminated from many processes, undertaken in "real time". Paradoxically, time is often a more critical resource than capital, resulting in management approaches like time to market and the need to stay ahead of the competition.

For companies, being a step ahead of the competition is more important than ever.

7. New waves of creativity; the fourth economy, through new and rapid forms of interaction, has the potential to develop into a global win-win economy of practically unlimited human creativity.
8. New forces of conservatism; in the fourth economy conservative forces, sometimes with religious fundamentalism as a strong element, will oppose the dynamic power of minds in interaction, ideas exchange, transparency and openness. In the long run, however, the world without walls is strongly positioned to win over isolationism.
9. New roles in government; the role of governments does not disappear in the fourth economy, but many priorities will be refocused toward investment in human development, education, health care and mind-based infrastructure.
10. New powerful countries: the BRIC countries, Brazil, Russia, India and China, are increasing in strength. Over the next two decades these new powerful countries will dramatically change the existing world order.

> *"The fourth economy has consequences on the macro level and at company level. The success or failure of countries, systems and companies will be decided to a larger extent by their ability to encourage, adapt to and benefit from the new conditions."*

A clear focus on threats and opportunities inherent in the new situation will be required of executives and managers at all levels. This will call for bold approaches in business, including new diagnostic systems and new measures to support success and protect against unnecessary failure.

From the Broad View to a New Management Focus business life is all about making choices. It is also about taking responsibility. We need the broader view for a full perspective, but then, for a sharper focus, we must reduce the confusion of trends and influences to a few major factors or characteristics. The sources and forces that drive the fourth economy are largely found outside the economy in a narrow sense, while some of their impact is visible in economic terms. Business executives and managers must widen their scope to include social and political changes, since these affect business in a multitude of different ways, including the usefulness of accounting.

"Action without thinking is dangerous. Thinking without action is useless". In business practices we see the two, thinking and action, as complementary. One is impossible without the other. We need new thinking to grasp what is going on in the dramatic paradigmatic shift to the fourth economy. Then, to put thinking into practice, we need well-considered action. Finally, appropriate action will call for new management tools.

Management will face three specific challenges:

1. The Age of discontinuity. Unprecedented speed of fast, unpredictable change, replacing the step-by-step or "business as usual" patterns of earlier economies. Rapid and unpredictable change and the impact it has on society, the economy, business and human minds, was dramatically called to the world's attention in 1970 by Alvin Toffler, with the publication of his book "Future Shock". Peter Drucker, in the same vein, called our time "The Age of Discontinuity".

2. The Age of Mind-Based Wealth Creation. In previous economies natural resources and physical assets were the driving forces in wealth creation. Today, wealth is created primarily through the interaction of mind-based factors. Management writers like Peter Drucker first signalled the changing emphasis from earth-based and capital-based assets to non-financial, mind-based value drivers as the main agents of wealth creation. In the early 1990s this led to many new initiatives.

3. The Network Economy. Strong and intricate networks of relationships, interdependence between people, companies and countries, and their environment are the keys to company survival, growth and earnings. The traditional "autistic" view of the company as an independent legal unit is increasingly replaced by the view of the company as a living organism. The crucial dimension is the constant exchange between the company and its environment. The practical consequence is that every company has to be seen and evaluated in its context, not in isolation.

> *"Recent management trends such as just-in-time, daily deliveries, outsourcing, offshore, time-to-market, alliances, mergers and acquisitions, etc., tend to reduce or eliminate balance sheet assets as the carriers of company value. Traditional balance sheet assets are replaced by relationships with suppliers, customers and business partners. Rapid and unpredictable change, one of the three features, is in itself fed by the other two, mind-based factors accelerated by communications and relationships".*

Three features are suggested as more significant in the fourth economy than ever before. Society as a whole, the economy and most businesses today:
▶ are exposed to fast and often unpredictable change;
▶ depend on mind-based, non-financial performance factors as opposed to physical assets as drivers of wealth creation;
▶ are closely interrelated and interdependent.

The three characteristics interact to reinforce each other. The new conditions are powerful enough to dramatically challenge old concepts in business management and analysis. Beyond the limits of the economy, they are also the strong driving forces in international politics, diplomacy and warfare of the 21st century. The attacks of September 11 2001 and the ensuing war were totally unforeseen and unpredictable. The conflict is about ideas, not about territory or resources, and alliances and relationships play an outstanding role.

Beyond Accounting to New Real Time Solutions for Valuation of Companies

I cannot claim authorship of the headline "The Failure of Accounting", no matter how much I should like to. It is a quotation from a source which can claim much greater authority in these matters than I can. It was first used as the headline of an editorial in no less a publication than CFO Magazine, as early as December 1994. The consequences of the failing accounting system have been dramatic. Decisions based on or influenced by accounting data have led to financial losses of hundreds of billions of Euros, if it is possible to count them even. Disastrous mergers and acquisitions that should never have taken place, mistakes in bank lending that forced enormous write-offs, venture capitalists who destroyed shareholder value, analysts' advice that led to huge investor and pension fund losses and auditing processes and risk assessments that looked in entirely the wrong direction, lured by the "good old accounting system". As an example, I may name the accounting scandals at Adecco, Global Crossing, Xerox, Parmalat, WorldCom, Enron and Ahold. Hundreds of thousands of people lost their investments through inaccurate audits, amongst them the top five in the world. Arthur Andersen became the victim of the Enron drama and was forced to close down the company. Despite the most reputable advisors on the US market, Enron went under. According to the book "The Rise of the Rogue Executive" Arthur Andersen received an annual fee of US$ 50 million from Enron. In addition, in 1999 Merrill Lynch earned fees of US$ 40 million and McKinsey earned annual fees of US$ 10 million from Enron.

Accounting started out as a specialised tool. It had one main function: to register business transactions. This was Luca di Pacioli's sole intention when he laid down the guidelines for accounting in 1494. This role of keeping the ongoing records of the transactions of a business is also one that accounting continues to perform reasonably well.

> "Accounting has been over-stretched into serving as guidelines in strategic management, decision-making and valuation of companies. It has been forced to serve as a misleading basis for valuation in due diligence processes. It has been deformed into meaningless ratios and twisted to fake support for decision-making at the stock markets, in investments, in financing and in bank lending processes. Accounting data have been misused as platforms for prognoses, predictions, trend extrapolation, unsustainable forecasting models and other oracle methods. It has been transformed from a specialized precision instrument to an all-purpose tool".

After more than 500 years, accounting should be returned to its own sphere, its only legitimate function, the direct registration of business transactions. Our economic needs deserve alternative systems for other applications such as business reporting, decision-making and valuation.

We need systems that focus on relevance above apparent precision and that give us useful and reliable information about "the fundamentals that move companies today".

However, it seems to be the general experience in virtually all fields that radical new approaches are seldom, if ever, introduced without an established profession. When they advocate change, they tend to come up with small steps of evolutionary change. If there is a need for revolutionary change, outside input appears an essential part of the process. Accounting has clearly failed to come up with the goods when it comes to meeting many of the needs of the present day.

In this chapter my aim is not to explain everything that is questionable in the current accounting system. I should just like to point out inadequacies, with one of the current business buzzwords: shareholder value. Creating or increasing shareholder value has been widely trumpeted as the ultimate strategic objective for boards and management. It has been presented as a reason for hundreds of thousands of mergers and acquisitions, although the objective has rarely been achieved.

Rather than measuring the wrong factors, down to decimals, I will address the issue of measuring the significant factors. This cannot be done with price tags based on an old purchase price or on a possible resale price, but on the impact on the fundamentals of survival, earnings and growth. Will this lead us to precise numbers to the last decimal point? No, it will not. "It's better to do something approximately right than to do it 100 percent wrong".

What is the Perspective of the New Management Solution?

> "Not even the US despite their position as the only remaining superpower can handle war on their own. They need more than ever to develop support, alliances, networks and relationships". This applies to companies too.

In the 21st century companies must learn to handle the challenge of rapid and unpredictable change. Traditional management solutions such as forecasting, trends analysis, extrapolation, planning based on past performance, discounted cash flow analysis, net present value, real options, SWOTI analysis and traditional strategic management processes, and, last but not least, "business as usual" are no longer helpful as they used to be. Instead, flexibility, agility and freedom of action will be the new important conditions for success. Diagnoses of threats and opportunities in the present situation will be more important than prognoses.

Turbulence is nothing new in our business community and the fast pace of change is not the only dimension to be considered. It adds to the drama of our time that change comes in so many shapes and from so many unforeseeable angles; technological change, change in marketing methods and approaches, new competitors entering the market from unexpected places, new constellations of stakeholders and companies, and government action in the form of deregulation and changing public opinions, trends and fashions.

> *"Earlier we could use the metaphor of sailing when we discussed management. Today, management is more like white water kayak rafting in class E rivers".*
> (Percy Barnevik)

So how does management handle one of the major dilemmas, the paradox facing top executives, the need to make decisions about a future that is not only uncertain, but in reality unpredictable? How can one establish a platform for decisions that will shape a company's future, one way or the other? Small wonder that business executives, just like all other human beings over the years, have desperately tried to find ways to deal with the paradox, ways to look into the future, using anything from crystal-gazing to discounted cash flow, trying to escape from the futility of forecasting. The fact that it is not only difficult but also downright impossible has not deterred numerous people in various roles and with widely differing tools and techniques from offering their forecasting services to frustrated executives. It's obvious that past performance is no indication of future results; neither is looking forward through the rear view mirror.

In management we have to carefully examine the present, especially the quality and strengths of the company's business position and its relationships, to have any chance at all of dealing effectively with the future. All one can do is to analyse the present, especially those parts that do not fit what is generally known and taken for granted, and usually go beyond traditional accounting. Strategic decision models that rely on accounting-based data, on trend extrapolation and forecasting-back casting have never been reliable. Today they are increasingly unreliable and irrelevant.

The need to understand and manage the company in its living environment, in a connected economy, will call for a new focus on what is good for a company. Firstly, moving from a balance sheet focus to a relationship focus. Secondly, distinguishing between good and bad relationships. Basically, we need to redefine the company as a network of relationships. Treating the company as an isolated unit, as accounting does, is a major factor in management and other applications. I should like to demonstrate this by the following case study.

Case: Truefresh, The Virtual Salmon Company

Truefresh is based in New England, USA. It has delivery contracts, but not employment contracts, with salmon fishermen along the coasts of Maine and Massachusetts. The fishermen deliver their catch to a freezing facility. Truefresh doesn't own this facility, but has a contract with it, including a licence for a flash-freeze process that creates high-quality frozen salmon. Each fish is individually packaged at the freezing facility, wrapped in Truefresh-labelled plastic emballage. The fish are then delivered across the US by a network of freeze trucks, none of them owned by Truefresh, but working for Truefresh on a contract basis. At the end of the network are resellers. Again, these resellers are not owned or employed by Truefresh but work for them on a commission basis. Truefresh itself has a very limited number of employees. What of its balance sheet? Maybe a couple of desks and laptops. Not much to show a traditional banker. The whole "value" of Truefresh is in its network, its relationships.

This example illustrates the role played by interaction in value creation and growth in the Fourth Economy:

▶ Company survival, earnings and growth are built by minds in interaction, inside and between companies.
▶ Intellectual "brain-based" exchange is not enough. Motivation and other emotional drivers are needed to create action. We call this "passion".
▶ Homogeneity is not the best driver of value. Diversity, well managed, is more productive between individuals as well as between co-operating companies.

A company with a heavy balance sheet including big investments in fixed assets, real estate, factories, machinery, etc., loses its freedom of action. It tends to be locked into the business it has chosen. In a world without change, this position can have its benefits. But few companies, if any, today operate in a world without change. The demands of change and flexibility are at the top of the list for most companies. Only companies that prioritise relationships over fixed assets have a chance of adapting to new situations. But is one to measure the dependencies the company has in its relations with other stakeholders and parties? A new reporting system will have to provide us with means and methods of reporting on and measuring dependencies.

This new reporting system exists, but not in our traditional accounting system. It is all about the ultimate strategic asset "Freedom of Action".

The Strategic Road to "Freedom of Action" follows a step-by-step process, which starts with relationships.

Four new fundamentals

Four new fundamentals and statements form the competitive intelligence solution. It has been designed to show the company's performance, its strengths and weaknesses in terms that are relevant to our time. This management solution has the potential to considerably improve fair disclosure, transparency and accountability in management, reporting, analysis, auditing, investing and financing. Each of the statements reflects factors that are crucial to a company's success or failure in the fourth economy. In combination, they are more reliable and considerably more relevant for decision-making processes than traditional accounting data.

New four Fundamentals

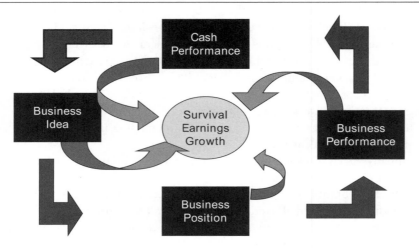

Source: The Baseline Revolution

The Business Idea aims to answer the classical question "What business are we in?". This should ensure that the company has and retains a clear focus: if you don't know where you are going, you are likely to end up somewhere else. It is also the most explicit way to express the management's vision of where it hopes to take the company. It is a carefully and structured way of identifying and presenting the company's business concept, mission and vision.

The Business Position aims to answer the crucial question "Who pulls the strings?". Surprisingly often, unexpected outside relationships exercise a high degree of influence and even control over a company. Competitive intelligence makes it possible to scrutinise and access the company's relationships, to monitor and measure the dependencies and threats that limit or affect the company's most important strategic asset, its freedom of action.

The Business Performance aims to answer the questions "What's on their minds?". In any free market economy, perceptions among stakeholders play a deciding role in helping or allowing a company to grow and develop. It identifies and monitors a number of the most significant drivers influencing wealth-creation decisions in five relevant areas outside the company, indicators of company performance and success.

The Cash Performance starts with the traditional cash flow question "Where does the money come from and where does it go?". This management solution selects cash flow rather than other financial tools, partly because it is more relevant than profit but also because it is less subject to manipulation and consequently more reliable than income statements and balance sheets. The world's most important and respected management consultant expresses this preference in no uncertain terms: "Profit is secondary, cash flow matters most".

The four factors are strongly indicative of a company's success or failure, and are consequently important when seeking to define, measure, monitor and report. The four factors are leading indicators which should be considered and evaluated in most of the decision-making situations faced by boards and management groups today. These factors are also what analysts, investors, lenders, bankers, venture capitalists, risk managers, auditors and other stakeholders should monitor in a consistent and systematic manner, for the simple reason that they will offer more transparency, a more relevant and timely picture of the company than the inadequate indicators of traditional reporting. They go beyond the catchwords of full or even fair disclosure to build a platform for relevant disclosure.

The four factors together represent a new overall perspective on what drives a company today. They meet a balanced all-inclusiveness test, are highly indicative of a company's chances of survival, earnings and growth. Practically all functions in a company today can be outsourced; however, these factors are so essential and so close to the core of the company that they can never be outsourced. They can be monitored regularly and measured with the desired degree of precision. Unlike accounting, which reflects past performance, competitive intelligence systems solutions point to crucial pro-active features. They offer to assess present threats and possibilities and find ways to strengthen the company's strategic and operational position.

The Four Fundamentals – a more detailed view

The Business Idea

The starting point of the Business Idea process is the identification of a perceived need in a defined group of customers, a group that is big enough to provide a satisfactory base for the company's business. The company can survive and prosper if it satisfies this need, usually in competition with others. Conversely, the Business Idea expresses the willpower of the original entrepreneur in a new company and of the owners and executives in more established companies. The official story is that businesses exist to satisfy consumer need. However, in reality it is equally true that they exist to provide an outlet for the ambitions, priorities and drive of those in charge, the owners, board members or top executives. The two sides of the coin, customer needs and owner ambitions, come together in the Business Idea.

The only value that any asset, hard, soft or liquid, creates in an ongoing business is based on how it is perceived by customers, investors and others to work towards the company's express and declared mission, its Business Idea. This is why the company's Business Idea, or the business ideas of each separate subsidiary, division, segment or business unit, are such essential benchmarks against which to check every resource the company applies and every step the company takes.

"Defining the business idea is often the most difficult part of an analysis. The difficulties emphasize the importance of the process. Very often in this process the management finds that the company holds more separate business ideas than they were aware of, or that the organisation of the company is not well aligned with the structure of the business ideas as it could be".

"When we talk about the business idea in this context we are not talking about a "fluffy" general statement that is just hype or a nice buzzword. We are talking about a truly well worked-out platform for the company, division or the business unit".

For a formalized approach to the definition of a company's business idea, it is possible to obtain additional support by answering a number of questions and checkpoints. Based on the answers, a management group can develop a specific and detailed description of what constitutes the "heart of the business" and what criteria should be identified as the essentials to monitor and prioritise. I have found that a process that considers the following 21 questions is well worth the time it takes.

It will be helpful for structuring your company's business idea and making it relevant to all stakeholders involved.

1. List all products/services the company sells, regardless of whom they are sold to.
2. List all types of customers/clients to whom the company sells, by business group, size or otherwise.
3. Make appropriate combinations between products/services and types of customers/clients.
4. Check for each combination the crucial question "Why does the customer/client buy this product/service?" Give the answer preferably in the format "in order to be able to......"
5. Proceed by asking "Why does this customer group want to be able to.......?" If the answer is still specific to the products/services sold, repeat the question until the answer is no longer specific to the products/services sold.
6. Take the second last answer (the last answer specific to the products/services sold) and use it as a definition of "customer need".
7. Verify that the definition does not contain comparatives such as "better, stronger, wider" or similar. If it does, change to plain positives, "good, strong, wide" etc.
8. Group the combinations above in the order a) customer need, b) customer, c) product. You now have a skeleton of business areas.
9. Check whether the products/services are exposed to direct competition (the customer can buy the same or a very similar product/service from someone else).

10. Check whether the need can be satisfied by alternative competition (the customer can satisfy the need by a different method/product/service).
11. Check whether the need is exposed to competition for the discretionary buying power of the customers (the customer can refrain from satisfying the need in question).
12. Are all customers end customers or not end customers? They should be in the same situation.
13. Is there a geographical limitation for which customers we focus on?
14. What is the customer's typical situation when making the purchasing decision? (acute/ need-planned/ need-routine/ need-unplanned/ need-spontaneous/ buying-need based on feelings).
15. Who makes the final decision to buy or not to buy and to choose one supplier over another?
16. In case of direct competition: "What are the most important factors that the customer assesses when he/she decides from whom to buy?"
17. In case of substitute competition: "What method constitutes the most severe competition in satisfying the need of the customers?"
18. In case of substitute competition: What are the most important factors that the customer assesses when he/she decides how to satisfy the need?"
19. In case of competition for the discretionary buying power of the customers: "What are the best answers to customer questions like "why should I spend my money to satisfy this need?"
20. Check that the answers to the last three questions do not overlap (two answers with the same meaning).
21. What are the most important competencies and resources we need to develop to respond to what is important to customers?
From *The Baseline Revolution*

Working from the answers to the 21 questions it should be easier to arrive at a clear definition of business ideas. In the process it is likely that several issues will arise which demand difficult decisions and choices. Making these choices now will help avoid confusion later and support intelligent decisions about organisation, structure and other policy issues.

This starting point is a thorough penetration of the business idea(s) of the company. The business idea is the benchmark and the most important checkpoint for all subsequent decisions and evaluations. It is also an expression of the central willpower without no business can exist. The result serves as a platform for the management and the board as well as for the outside analysts and investors.

The Business Position
The business position is the second of the four fundamental factors.

The purpose is to clearly show any strategically significant limitations to the company's "freedom of action". Here the crucial question is "Who pulls the strings?"

Companies do not exist in a vacuum, as traditional accounting appears to assume. The network economy is a reality. Companies like all other living organisms exist and thrive in a constant exchange with their environment. The deeper we get into the fourth economy, the more we realise that the old concept of fixed boundaries between a company and its environment is becoming outdated. The links between the company and its environment are the relationships.

Today, many important management issues, including outsourcing, off-shoring, contract manufacturing, R and D contracts, supplier contracts, franchising and other forms of dealer and reseller relationships, partnerships and other alliances tend to make the border less and less distinct.

The variety and multitude of relationships and the impact they can have on company survival, growth and earnings, make it increasingly important to identify, monitor and measure them.

To successfully manage a company and to evaluate its strategic potential and the threats it faces, no instrument is more important than a diagnosis of its relationships, alliances, current and future competitors and network counterparts. Companies who have thoroughly diagnosed their position in relation to other players in their market, who know the strength of their most important relationships and how they support or counteract company priorities, have the upper hand compared with companies who don't.

Evaluating a company's crucial relationships is an important part of strategic management, especially in today's network economy. This is why a competitive intelligence-based systematic diagnosis of such factors is indispensable as a fundament element of a relevant reporting system. It is a necessary step in getting and keeping a company focused on its "freedom of action".

A company's "freedom of action", its number one strategy priority, is largely controlled by conditions in the company's environment. A business position diagnosis shows the strategic links between the company and its environment and the strengths and weaknesses that those links provide to the company. Positive links between the company and its stakeholders are strong indicators of business success. Negative links show potential threats to the company's future.

> *"The Business Position is defined through a systematic review of the relationships that the company depends on for its survival, earnings and growth. This is the single most decisive group of factors in assessing a company's strategic potential and risks, yet is nonexistent in traditional accounting, which does not recognize any assets or reliabilities outside the closed company box".*

The clue to such a diagnosis is a clear structure of all important relationships. To establish this, all relevant relationships are defined and classified by kind and strength. The relationships will be defined and classified; they will be measured and finally combined with the following results.

As an additional instrument the diagnosis provides a list of emerging events that clearly shows the potential threats that the company is exposed to. The threats shown in the list of emerging events are crucial in assessing the strategic situation of the company under analysis and are consequently highly relevant.

▶ to the board and management of the company in choosing strategies and evaluating alternative courses that the company can take;

▶ to a consultant firm considering a merger or acquisition in a due diligence process;

▶ to an auditing firm or risk manager during a risk assessment process;

▶ to any stakeholder in assessing his/her ongoing involvement with the company;

▶ to investors or venture capitalists planning to invest in the company;

▶ to a bank or other lender considering a loan to the company.

The Business Performance

Business performance, the third factor of the four fundamentals in our definition, does not meant the numbers that come out of the accounting process. Business performance is a range of factors that influence company survival, earnings and growth. To find these conditions, one must leave the company compound. Many of the decisions that influence company success or failure are made outside the closed circuit of board and management.

> *"When customers love you, they tend to buy from you, when employees like the company they work for, they do a good job, when investors trust you, they stay with you".*
> (Jack Welch)

> *"Sex appeal is 50 percent what you have and 50 percent what others think you have".*
> (Sophia Loren)

> *"The assets that really count are the ones accountants can't count yet".*
> (Thomas A. Stewart)

Jack Welch, Sophia Loren and Thomas Stewart seem to agree that success is intangible. Many of the conditions for company performance, success or failure, are ultimately set by an ongoing flow of individual decisions by customers, employees, investors, opinion-makers and other stakeholders. The fact is that, in any democratic market economy, most of the decisions affecting a company's survival, earnings and growth are not made in the boardroom on the top floor. The most important decisions are made:

- ▶ by customers deciding to buy or not to buy, or to buy from your company or from the competition;
- ▶ by employees, deciding to work for you or somebody else, and if they work for you, whether to put in that extra value-adding effort or not;
- ▶ by investors, banks and lenders, deciding whether or not to put money into your company, and on what conditions;
- ▶ by public opinion makers taking a stand on issues that affect your company's business or political environment;
- ▶ and many others.......

What they know, think or feel about your company affects what they do, their buying, work and investing behaviour. Close monitoring of those perceptions and preferences gives stronger clues to present and future company success and failure than immaculate detailed accounting data. A company that wants to be step ahead needs to monitor these data as part of its reporting system.

Competitive intelligence-monitoring is a practical way of addressing this issue. In business performance, as described before in the areas of business idea and business position, it helps to eliminate the fuzziness that some accountants and business people still seem to connect with the "soft" value drivers. A natural approach is to define the important influence centres and then find a way to monitor them.

I will suggest five broad areas that most companies are more or less concerned with. In each, a number of specific performance and perception factors can be identified, structured and assessed.

"Five Value Added Axioms": maintaining good and open relations with the investment and financial community gains confidence, a basic condition for investor appreciation; this is known to and respected by those who create and influence its public framework, it finds more support and encounters fewer obstacles; where management has defined and communicated clear and understandable visions and strategies, it will be found easier to gain cooperation and support from employees and other stakeholders.

How may we capture this process and integrate it? Let's look into this sector by sector. The four blades of the propeller below drive company performance. The shaft that holds them together and makes them turn is leadership.

Five driving forces of company performance

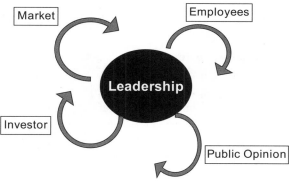

Source: The Baseline Revolution

1. The market

The market segment identifies, reports and measures crucial factors that affect success or failure in the market place, ultimately in terms of market share and price tolerance. The road to market share and price tolerance goes through awareness of the company amongst customers and potential customers, their perceptions, the brand position in their minds, their satisfaction with the company and its products/services, their loyalty expressed as repurchase and other factors. Building and measuring such factors is a crucial part of company survival, growth and earnings and should consequently be an integrated part of the competitive intelligence-monitoring company system.

2. The employees

Employees are a major cost and value-building factor in most companies. As companies move towards service rather than products, employees are an increasingly immediate source of sales, revenues and earnings. A company's ability to attract, keep and develop good talent makes employees a distinct success factor. The employee sector defines and measures non-financial factors that ultimately affect value added per employee, e.g. in terms of productivity and innovation.

Their competence and professional skills, their enthusiasm, motivation and loyalty, the spirit with which they interact between themselves and with clients and customers, their willingness to endorse and work by corporate mission and standards, the empowerment they get from management, the corporate culture, are all crucial to productivity, innovation and other company growth and earning factors.

Measuring non-financial performance and perception factors in the employee segment offers essential support to company management and provides important data to stakeholders.

3. The investors/financial world

The investors and financial world report critical factors that affect the cost of capital and ultimately the performance and share price of the company. It is the source of much of the working capital in the company.

Investor satisfaction with the company, obviously its overall return, but also such non-financial performance factors as long term growth, reputation, market position, the quality and reliability of information it provides, company leadership, are all factors that ultimately affect the share price and the cost of capital, whether borrowed or invested.

4. The public opinion-makers

The public opinion section recognizes that in all democracies companies operate with the formal or informal approval of public opinion. In this public opinion section, the company reports and measures factors that lead to an essential strategic objective of most companies: "licence to operate". The factors basically stake out a company's way to deserving its relative independence, in its turn critical to company survival, earnings and growth.

The public opinion section includes public policy-makers in the company's sphere of interest, local, national and international politicians and administrators, industry leaders, regulators, the media and opinion-maker groups.

Acceptance of the company as a good member of all communities where it operates, a good "corporate citizen", is a frequent phrase to cover what needs to be done and measured in the public opinion section. Successful work helps remove hurdles and paves the way for smooth and mutually beneficial relations between the company and its political and semi-political environment.

5. The leadership

The leadership of the company is perhaps the single most important section affecting success or failure. The visions and strategies of the leadership, the corporate culture and behaviour the leadership encourages, the broad acceptance and endorsement of basic concepts that the leadership generates, are all critical to company performance and results.

Successful work in the leadership section leads to supportive behaviour from the company's constituents. Monitoring the recognition and respect the company leaders enjoy provides a measurement of the support they are able to generate from all stakeholders, both within and outside the company. Such support is powerful and helps to create "freedom of action", the difference between the company's operating in a headwind or tailwind climate, which, in turn, affects the reactions the company can expect from the other four sections described above: the market, the employees, the investment community and the public sector. Together these make a great contribution towards company survival, earnings and growth.

Measuring the Business Performance

All the factors described above may have the potential to support or destroy company survival, earnings and growth. However, these factors are not called "assets" or "capital" nor are it the aim to simplistically assign to them a "value" in dollars or Euros. Strategy is seldom a matter of decimals. One practical approach, avoiding getting bogged down in interminable discussions about fine-tuning measurements into decimals or fractions, is to conflate all performance and perception measurements into a seven level scale like the following:

+3 (superior)	green light
+2 (much better than)	
+1 (somewhat better than)	
0 (approximately the same)	
-1 (not quite good as)	
-2 (worse than)	
-3 (significantly worse than)	red flag

This runs parallel to the levels in the business position monitoring and has three comparison options:
▶ The Benchmark option – better than/not as good as competition
▶ The Progress option – better than/not as good as last year, last quarter or last month
▶ The Target option – better than/does not meet management objectives

Measurements should be made in a consistent way, using accepted techniques and methods, preferably approved by the company's auditors. Ideally, the Business Performance Statement should include previous data for comparability over time.

Business Performance Summary Measurement (scale +3 +2 +1 0 -1 -2 -3)

	Against Competition	Over Time year/quarter	Against Company Objectives
Markets			
Awareness			
Brand Position			
Customer Satisfaction			
Customer Loyalty			
Zero Neglect			
Balanced Total			
Employees			
Awareness			
Expertise			
Motivation			
Empowerment			
Quality/Innovation/Productivity			
Balanced Total			
Investors/Finance			
Awareness			
Ranking/Ratings			
Investor Satisfaction			
Board Performance			
Balanced Total			
Public Opinion			
Awareness			
Knowledge			
Issue Management			
Support			
Confidence			
Balanced Total			
Leadership			
Awareness			
Support for Values/Ambitions/Objectives			
Support for Strategies			
Confidence			
Balanced Total			

The list suggested is not necessarily complete, but may serve as a starting point for a company that wants to include non-financial performance factors in its reporting process. On the other hand, each company should feel free to define the factors that are essential and relevant to its situation.

Cash Performance, a step beyond cash flow

The purpose of this fourth of the four fundamental factors is a bold but feasible way to show not only where the cash comes from and where it goes, but also how the cash flow supports company strategies. The crucial question here is "How does our money help us to achieve our strategic objectives?"

Even a traditional cash flow statement provides a better view of the company's strategic and operation situation than an income statement, especially if it provides sufficient details, comments from management and a sensitivity analysis for each important line. The main reason is that cash flow tends to be more reliable and have higher credibility. Is it totally reliable? No. No accounting statement is. But many experts agree that it is less subjected to "creative accounting" practices than income statements and balance sheets. Cash flow provides relatively fair disclosure in a more intelligent and reliable way than income statements.

In a traditional cash flow calculation, the purpose is usually to arrive at the free cash flow, the cash flow available to the owners. Operational costs are deducted to arrive at generated cash flow and investments are deducted to arrive at the final cash flow.

However, the Cash Performance Statement prioritises an advanced version of the cash flow statement. This advanced statement has a triple focus. Firstly, to show how the cash is generated, where it comes from and how it is used, and to relate it to the strategic and operational objectives of the company. Secondly, it is an improvement not only over traditional income statements and balance sheets but also over traditional cash flow statements. Thirdly, it is less susceptible to fraud or misrepresentation, whether intentional or otherwise, and provides unequalled clues both to the process of cash generation and, even more importantly, to management's strategic use of cash resources.

A Cash Performance Statement with accompanying "sensitivity analysis" links important items in the cash flow with key indicators in the Business Idea and in the Position Statement. The sensitivity analysis gives management an opportunity to add qualitative comments to the company and its stakeholders. Ideally, statements include last year's data for comparability. Companies with several business units make one Cash Performance Statement for each business unit and then consolidate them. Each relevant line is analysed and commented on by management.

Cash Flow	Amount last year/this year	Management Comments
Cash flow from operations		
– Revenues,		
– (broken down if relevant)		
– Changes in operational assets/liabilities		
– Other changes in receivables		
– (broken down if relevant)		
– Other changes in liabilities		
(broken down if relevant)		
– Taxes paid		
– Net cash from operations		
Cash flow from investing		
– Changes in financial receivables		
– Investment changes		
(broken down if relevant)		
Net Cash from investing		
Cash flows from financing		
– dividends paid		
– Options programme		
(broken down if relevant)		
– Changes in other liabilities		
Net Cash from financing		
Net Change in cash and equivalent		
– Starting Cash and equivalent		
End Cash and equivalent		

Further improvements to be made concern:

1. Estimate cash flow used to improve unfavourable conditions that limit the company's strategic goal: freedom of action
2. Estimate cash flow used to protect favourable conditions that support the company's strategic goal: freedom of action
3. Add these two cash flows and calculate them as a share of total cash flows generated by the company

4. Calculate the share of total cash flows, including financial transactions which have been spent but not used for the strategic purpose of improving "freedom of action".

This part of how cash is strategically used is the new part. The information we seek has nothing to do with whether a payment is seen as a cost or as an investment in traditional accounting.

Cash flow starts with payments to the company from customers who have bought products or services. The funds are used by the company to pay suppliers, employees, investors and other stakeholders. Already at this level, management can allocate resources or buy services to deal with strategic issues. These are then included in company operational cash use. Management can also use the cash flow for special efforts of an investment nature to protect the company's freedom of action. Paying off a loan to reduce an unfavourable dependence on a banker or lender can be a strategic act within the scope of the recommended programme.

For each payment the company has to define whether it aims at improving any of the relationships indicated, and if so to what extent. This question has to be explored further to avoid arbitrary comments as much as possible.

The guiding principle has to be that management, as a minimum, must keep cash flow, defined as inflow minus outflow, at a level required to keep business at its present level. We call the remaining cash flow "Cash Flow To be Managed" (TBM). Company auditors should be involved in establishing this level. Checking the way management handles TBM gives an indication of the direction management moves. Problem areas prioritised by management show the future focus. Information at this level can be described as "direction-oriented".

A term for the portion of TMB used for strategic action is "Cash Flow For Strategic Action" (FSA).

"Focus" and "Charge", two Cash Flow Ratios to Monitor Dividing FSA by TBM generates an interesting measure, showing how focused management is towards company strategic development. The resulting quotient is named the "focus" ratio.

A management team that uses TBM for other purposes than strategic purposes will get a low "focus" measure. A management team using the whole TBM for strategic purposes gets a "focus" measure of 100. Using more than 100 percent for strategic measures means either a reduction of liquidity or external financing. Measuring the increase of liquidity, including any externally provided means, during the selected period, gives a measure of how much cash management has saved for future needs. This is measured in Cash Available (CA) divided by TBM and the resulting ratio is called "charge".

Of all financial data that the board, the owners, lenders, bankers, investors and other stakeholders should monitor, cash flow can be seen as the most important.

With access to these measurements for a given period of time, you are able to compare these with real business development. Has the business idea developed over time? Has the strategic business position improved? How successful has management been from an operational perspective? Getting this information from conventional accounting is hard, not to say almost impossible.

The process and the key numbers apply irrespective of business, company size or geographic location. The process offers significant improvements in transparency.

Executing competitive intelligence on cash flow monitoring this way makes it possible to support not only strategic management and crossroads decisions, but also the key corporate governance issues. It identifies the four areas where serious threats and potential problems often originate. It helps the board and management to focus their attention on critical issues rather than on meaningless columns of more or less irrelevant numbers.

A first step toward a renaissance in corporate governance, in the sense of a higher sensitivity to strategic priorities, might be that most of all board meeting agendas, and at least one meeting per year, started with four recurring business priority items:

1. A review and updating of the company's Vision and Mission Statements, its Business Idea(s), the process by which the Business Ideas have been established, and the level of endorsement by various stakeholders.
2. A review and updating of the company's Business Position, changes since the previous meeting, and action taken by the management to eliminate or reduce serious strategic threats facing the company.
3. A review and updating of the company's Business Performance Statement, with a special focus on "red flag" items, the items where the company either has not made adequate measurements or has received low scores or where the scores have deteriorated since the previous measurement review.
4. A review of the detailed Cash Performance Statement, with management comments and feedback on strategic application of funds and where the "Charge" or "Focus" measures have revealed that insufficient funds have been allocated to strategic priority areas.

After a strategic process of this kind the Board knows that it has given attention and time to the important conditions for growth, earnings and survival, the factors and forces that are really the board's primary responsibility. They are, incidentally, also the primary responsibility of management and the cornerstones of relevant reporting and disclosure.

Then the board and management can always proceed with traditional items such as management reports on operations and finance.

Major strategic crossroads decisions would benefit from a review of the two or three major alternatives that are being considered, from the perspectives of these four fundamentals:

1. How are the Business Ideas affected by the choice of one or the other alternative?
2. How will the Business Positions come out, under one or the other of the alternatives?
3. How will our selected Business Performance factors be affected by various alternatives?
4. How will our Cash Performance be affected by either of the alternatives?

Chances are that a board discussion along these lines will help the board make a considerably more enlightened decision than if these aspects are not considered.

One more thing is obvious and proves the point that these issues are not selected arbitrarily. If none of these four factors are affected, then the choice is not really a strategic issue!

> *"Virtually every serious study done shows that it is very difficult to bring off a successful merger".*
> (*Business Week*, October 1997)

Many studies in the recent past have shown that about 70-80 percent of all mergers and acquisitions in the world fail. The most dramatic example is of course the merger already mentioned, the acquisition one year later, of Daimler Benz and Chrysler into DaimlerChrysler. Tens of thousands of people were laid off and the value of the new company fell by US$ 40-60 billion over the period 1998-2006. At the time of the merger, Chrysler had the highest profit per car of any automobile maker in the world. Its reported earnings were a considerable part, in fact half, of the combined company's profit. Chrysler's Grand Cherokee was the strongest brand in the fast-growing Sport Utility Vehicle segment. All of this has vanished under the management of DaimlerChrysler.

In general, the conclusion to be drawn from the doleful track record of acquisitions, even in the financial arena, is that mergers and acquisitions require more than financial skills. When things go wrong, it's for business reasons more often than financial reasons.

The whole attitude to mergers and acquisitions must change. Too much of the "due diligence" practiced in preparing mergers and acquisitions is steeped in the traditions of legal, financial and accounting practices and procedures. Methods of a different kind need to be developed and applied. M and A processes based on accounting have had their day. Their records speak for themselves. A "simple" improvement would be to treat M and A more as business transactions, not primarily as financial transactions. If they had been seen with a business focus before, during and after the event, there would have been much higher chances for success.

A business perspective with a focus on people and relationships, rather than a financial perspective focused on numbers, would reveal what accounting can never achieve. Some of the conditions and qualities, as well as risk and threats, of any two companies involved in a merger are simply not visible when seen through the eyes of traditional accounting-based practices.

Mergers and Acquisitions: basic facts:
1. are forward looking operations – accounting is not
2. are business transactions – not primarily financial
3. succeed or fail, just like most – accounting has no way to include such factors other business ventures, because of people and relationships

There are better ways to run an all-inclusive due diligence process than to rely on financial and legal procedures. But that requires a new approach, covering important business fundamentals, not accounting.

The four fundamentals in the new management report solution provide clues to a successful merger, or warn the Boards when conditions are precarious. The key is a check-up on the Business Idea of the two companies, their Business Position before and after the merger, the Business Performance situation and the Cash Performance. Competitive intelligence monitoring is able to do this.

It would not have been applicable to come up with a post-merger-analysis on the dramatic DaimlerChrysler case. What we know is that in cases where a competitive intelligence capability has been used in preparing and executing mergers and acquisitions, one of two things have happened:
1. Quite frequently, the analysis has resulted in a recommendation not to pursue the merger plans
2. When the analysis has ended in a "green light", it has not only provided a guide for the merger deal. It has also supported a due process for the execution and follow-up of the merger.

What is the differentiating factor for success?
The main reason for its success is that a competitive intelligence approach goes beyond accounting data and penetrates deep into the basics of company life, into the fundamentals of the business in the two companies in question.

Stage one in the process compares and analyses each of the companies concerned in respect of the four fundamentals, Business Idea, Business Position, Business Performance and Cash Performance. Stage two in the process is repeated for an estimated view of the potential in the combined company.

When this process is carried out it usually reveals clearly and in great detail important similarities and differences between the companies, risks and potential threats, as well as opportunities. In a positive case where a merger appears to be justified, the competitive intelligence process will show that the combination eliminates certain weaknesses which appear more strongly than in the two companies separately.

In other cases, the weak points of the two companies pull in the same direction, so that the combined company becomes more sensitive to some threats than the two individual companies one by one. The combined company should have a higher degree of "freedom of action" than the individual companies would have had. Competitive intelligence creates a very clear platform for the strategic pre-merger discussion and decision-making process of the two boards and management teams.

I will summarize the highlights of the different approach competitive intelligence achieves.

Compared to accounting-based reporting, this competitive intelligence approach provides a more reliable basis for fair and relevant disclosure. It meets the new management requirements of looking at the company from the outside. It offers a platform for decision-making in strategic choice situations, in mergers and acquisitions including due diligence, in investment and lending decisions, in auditing and in risk management.

It defines company success as survival, earnings and growth. The primary strategic goal is "freedom of action". Competitive intelligence provides methods to monitor and measure the company's freedom of action.

▶ It advocates a systematic and consistent review of the company's business idea, its visions and mission statements.

▶ It assesses the company in its networks, in business position terms showing its dependencies on relationships that can make or break it.

▶ It keeps track of selected performance and perception factors which the company does not own, or even control but upon which the company is dependent for its success.

▶ It tracks the cash flow, both its sources and its uses, and relates the cash flow to company strategies.

Competitive intelligence does not depend upon a traditional numbers analysis of financial details in company accounting. It does not reduce all information into an income statement or balance sheet. Rather, competitive intelligence identifies what is essential in and around the company, presents it and allows conclusions to be drawn from it. These conclusions are presented in data and information with a focus on relevance rather than precision.

This approach of competitive intelligence is a way of thinking and acting designed to show company performance in terms that are relevant to our time. It presents four fundamental statements: Business Idea, Business Position, Business Performance and Cash Performance.

Each statement reflects an important group of fundamentals, factors and forces that are crucial for company success or failure in the fourth economy.

A competitive intelligence capability has the potential to considerably improve transparency and accountability, to support management, reporting, valuation, auditing, investing and financing decisions. In this context we must never forget:

> *"The most important decisions are not taken inside your company, but outside your company".*

Competitive intelligence cases at public events

"Competitive intelligence is fundamental to how we drive our business".

In 2003 and 2005 SCIP Benelux, the Society of Competitive Intelligence Professionals, organised two events with the objective of getting together with the competitive intelligence professionals based in the Benelux countries. I myself chair the SCIP Benelux chapter and it's always a great challenge to track down professional who are willing to share their competitive intelligence best practices within their companies. I will give an overview of the highlights of some of the presenters at these SCIP Benelux events.

In order to become successful in competitive intelligence the three intelligence areas of business intelligence, organisational intelligence and competitive intelligence should be integrated. This new concept is called Enterprise Intelligence, on which topic I published my second book in 2004. Business Intelligence can be seen as the umbrella name of numerous IT-based software solutions devised to better order, structure and access the internal information flows, workflows, management information systems supported by tools such as data warehousing, data mining, business performance management tools as balance scorecards and dashboards.

The challenge for competitive intelligence professionals is to relate the results of these business intelligence solutions to external business environment dynamics, seen as the domain of the competitive intelligence management discipline. However, the key success factor in enterprise intelligence is people, who must be seen as the intellectual capital of the organisation as well as the most important assets on a company balance sheet. This area of human intelligence has been defined as intelligence of the people within the organisation. By carefully balancing the responsibilities, capabilities and tasks of people, organisational intelligence will become the bridge over the gaps between business intelligence and competitive intelligence. The aim of organisational intelligence is to develop the ability of people to transform the data, information and knowledge into policy-making, improved decision-making and business forecasting. (see the diagram at page 76).

Competitive Intelligence Services at Solvay Belgium
Francis Gallez of Belgian-based Solvay shared his vision with participants in the competitive intelligence activities at Solvay. CI at Solvay started in 1997 by

establishing a so-called "Watch Team". In the last couple of years Francis has succeeded in making the "CI-Master" the centre of external agents and provided services, resulting in a secured watching system and portal-based open-access system. The competitive intelligence-focused organisation at Solvay consists of a champion, a crew of observers, a team of experts, a network of internal information sources and a network of external information sources. Intelligence at Solvay means inquiries and cleverness, and is seen as ever-watchful and always strategic. In 2003 there were three key pillars to the Competitive Intelligence Service: firstly, a computerised and secured knowledge management system. Secondly a business and market focused watching organisation, and thirdly, the opportunity to take advantage of company networks and communities of business practices.

Intelligence at Pfizer, the Netherlands

Paul Boeren explained how in the pharmaceutical company Pfizer intelligence drives strategic decisions in order to build sales throughout the product lifecycle. The aim is to minimise risks and maximise opportunities. The growing intelligence gap between the growth of data and information and the decreasing availability of analytical personnel within Pfizer has been recognized. For Pfizer, improved management of the intelligence change process focuses on three areas. Firstly, the structures and processes – people, processes and partnerships. Secondly, training and development towards the strengthening of the general and technical competencies of the organisation. Thirdly, change management dealing with vision, strategy, short-term gains and business success. The mission of the intelligence capability at Pfizer has been redefined as follows: "business intelligence, as partner in business decision-making, will pro-actively guide the strategies and operations by objective presenting value added internal and external business insights and recommendations to business decision-makers". As a result the profile of intelligence officers at Pfizer has been changed from that of providers towards that of internal consultants. The provider function in the past was reactive, providing data and information, whilst the current internal consultant role is pro-active, selling insights and recommendations.

Competitive Intelligence at Royal Dutch Shell

Christiaan Luca of Shell presented an interesting view of intelligence-based Play Mapping. Three focus areas were explained. Firstly, know where you are as organisation. Secondly, know where you want to go as organisation. Thirdly, make a forward plan. To know where a company such as Shell is, Christiaan presented an industry analysis of the upstream oil business as well as the Exploration and Production trend analysis. To know where you want to go as a company, an analysis of the strategies of the key players in the upstream oil business was presented. The most interesting part of Christiaan Luca's presentation was the Forward Plan, where Play Mapping and Scenario Analysis were demonstrated:

the Technology Play Mapping. This offers a comprehensive overview of the technical and competitive landscape by describing the four dimensions: business needs, market dynamics, key players and competencies. The objective of the Forward Plan is "timely" insights and identifying priorities to enable the right strategic decisions. In the Technology Mapping exercise six steps were identified: issue framing (1), secondary research (2), visualisations (3), primary research (4), analysis (5), and action (6).

The conclusion drawn by Christiaan was that there are plenty of tools and enough information that is publicly available, however, you need stamina and hard work, and finally, that strategy development and execution need broad consultation, communication and cooperation.

Competitive Intelligence at La Poste

Koen DeVos, competitive intelligence manager at the Belgian postal company La Poste, presented the competitive intelligence activities in the postal market. Competition is increasing with the entry of new rivals British Royal Mail, German Deutsche Post and Dutch TPG on the Belgian postal market. Koen showed us three relevant dimensions currently faced by La Poste: firstly, a better understanding of the internal business processes and human-related issues. Secondly, an improved understanding of former, current and prospective customer characteristics, behaviour and attitudes with respect to postal matters. Thirdly, to obtain an in-depth understanding of the market environment and competitive landscape. The aim of the intelligence focus at La Poste is the "translation of data into added-value or decision support for the company". To get a better understanding and to be able to manage the intelligence process, three levels of intelligence activities have been identified: strategic, tactical and operational intelligence.

Competitive intelligence at La Poste has been positioned within Strategy and Business Development as a corporate support function. They work closely with the intelligence professionals of the marketing intelligence department. The corporate function is responsible for the management of the public data sources.

One of the first steps is the development of a knowledge database with the objective of providing a platform for easy storage and retrieval of all market intelligence-related knowledge available at La Poste. The objectives are to create a shift from individual to shared knowledge (1), to ensure the availability of the best data (2) and finally to avoid reinventing the wheel (3). Koen finally came up with following learning steps. The technical part is the easiest one, however it takes time. Data is a cost; only if it improves decision-making it is beneficial for the organisation. Finally, no users without content, no content without users.

Competitive Intelligence at AkzoNobel Resins

Nuplex Resins is the former AkzoNobel Resins company. The introductory message of Mario van Wingerde was "How you gather, manage and use information will determine whether you win or lose". At Nuplex Resins the mission of CI is the competence to analyse the company's external environment and convert hard and soft information into knowledge about the company's own position. Intelligence is actionable information about the external business environment that could affect Nuplex Resins' competitive position. Intelligence is focused on four key areas: customers, competition, markets and technologies. The intelligence function is linked with global marketing and is part of the global management team. Key success factors that made intelligence happen at Nuplex Resins are: executive sponsorship, strong focus, first organisation and than IT support, involving as many people as possible, strong project management and finally keeping it simple, building on current resources and infrastructure.

Competitive Intelligence at DSM
Competitive Intelligence at DSM is organised within BIND, the business intelligence network DSM. At DSM some 35 people with a master's or bachelor's degree in business and/or chemical technology are involved across the company. Their functions concern BI management, research and analysis. An interesting part of the presentation was the market barometer in which the BI group forecasts two quarters ahead, based on strong supply chain indicators.

Competitive Intelligence at Cisco
The competitive intelligence at Cisco is driven by sales intelligence and is based at a CI portal with all the relevant information and intelligence about the complete global competitive arena. James Crowther explained that Cisco has a global team of 12 people dedicated to the CI global activities and led by CI Team Cisco. Each team member is dedicated to one of Cisco's key competitors. If new competitors enter the competitive arena, the dedicated Cisco team investigates everything about this competitor. This reconfirms the statement I have seen about Cisco's competitive intelligence: "We spend a lot of time thinking through what is publicly communicated by competitors, working with our sales forces, our customers, with people who are funding new businesses and start-ups as they emerge. That's why CI is fundamental to how we drive our business".

Competitive Intelligence at Belgacom
Belgacom is the national telecom operator in Belgium. Belgacom didn't start out the traditional way from data to intelligence to action. Luc Rooms stated that the real start was the action management wanted to take, based on an intelligence focus on markets, company position, competition and environment. Data and information gathering on the intelligence activities was second, resulting in actionable intelligence. The prime target is to facilitate decision-making for group strategy at strategic level and for marketing at tactical level. Belgacom opts for a decentralised CI approach to be close to the business. Internal co-ordination is

guaranteed through a virtual committee at Belgacom. In the production of the right intelligence, three levels are important: group level scope, strategic business unit level scope, and the tactical business unit level scope. At the business unit scope Belgacom uses the "allaire-approach" for market definition, a portfolio approach for short and long term, related to the narrow and large scope. The presentation closed with the statement: "Questions are never indiscreet. Answers sometimes are", explaining the sensitivity of the actionable intelligence at Belgacom.

Competitive Intelligence at Danone

At LU-Danone Benelux, active in the biscuits market, intelligence is a centralized capability called "market research consumer intelligence". The company is one of the few FMGCs in the Benelux countries with a well-established intelligence function. As this became a strong competitive market with numerous new participants such as Pepsico, Kelloggs, Masterfoods, Unilever, Heinz, Nestle and others, LU-Danone changed their vision into a broad market vision from a "share of market" into a "share of stomach" perspective. The consumer intelligence mission is: "Increase the company's performance through better decision-making, based on maximum insights in markets, trends, competition and the trade environment". Criteria for success are: collection of the relevant information, a strong network and knowledge base, the position of the consumer intelligence function in the organisation and the dissemination which is seen as a critical success factor. Michel ten Donkelaar is director of consumer intelligence and a member of the management team, and coordinates the global intelligence capability.

Finally, I have been able to express my vision of the future of competitive intelligence. Companies should add to the day-to-day and short-term focus of the operations defined as "economic companies" versus a management style such as "living companies". In "economic companies", organisations continue with competitive portfolio management at operational and tactical level where pricing strategies, outsourcing and off shoring are the key themes combined with a strong focus on corporate governance and merger and acquisitions. The aim is to produce wealth for a small group of institutions and individuals, managing for profit. The future should focus much more on sustainable and long-term competitive advantages by innovation, where building renewed dominating market positions, building alliances and creating virtual networks are the key themes. Then the real shift can be realised from "economic companies" to "living companies", which fulfil their potential as ongoing communities with a management style for growth and long-term survival.

Strategic competitive intelligence can play a key role in the timely identification of social, economic and political discontinuities, finding new markets, technologies and lines of business and uncovering real added-value and unique merger and acquisitions opportunities.

How much longer will management let the organisation struggle with data and information?

"It is not enough to aim, you must hit".

Here I will show senior management how to get more out of the organisation's data, information and knowledge flows. It's not about additional investments in IT or business intelligence systems solutions but about people and how to obtain real intelligence from the organisation's data and information flows. People are the key to success; only people make an organisation more intelligent and alert. But they have to be shown what and how to do this.

In most organisations, management is managed by information instead of having the ability to manage information themselves. Although hundreds of billions of Euros are still being invested in information technology all the year round, it remains a huge problem to deliver information to the right person, at the right time, in the right format. Since the mid 1990s, the sector has attempted to improve the structure, accessibility and delivery of data and information, marketed as business intelligence (BI) solutions. But how do you know whether you have real intelligence or just more processed information? The answer is simple: "information costs money, intelligence makes money".

What are the key indicators for identifying real intelligence within organisations, i.e., the intelligence that makes money? To do so we must first explain the meaning of intelligence. To get real intelligence in companies, management needs to facilitate the transformation process from data, information and knowledge into intelligence. The majority of companies, however, are still in the data and information phase. Why? In order to create an intelligent and alert company, organisations must integrate the three areas of business intelligence, competitive intelligence and organisational intelligence into enterprise intelligence. I will explain this in greater detail. The first area is business intelligence, the objective of which is to structure, access and disseminate internal data and information flows in organisations. Since the mid 1990s, the software industry has implemented numerous business intelligence solutions designed with the aim of deriving some "intelligence" from the vast flows of internal data and information. The second area is competitive intelligence, where the objective is to collect, analyse and disseminate both internal and external information and knowledge for transformation into intelligence to be communicated to senior management, who can act on it. The third area is organisational intelligence, also called human intelligence. Organisational intelligence is the key factor to successfully creating intelligence within organisations. It is one of the greatest cultural challenges to get people to take ownership of information and the consequences of changes therein. Technology plays a supporting role in helping people to work together more effectively and efficiently.

Within an intelligence-enabled culture, the appropriate processes and tools need to be put in place to support collaborative or team-based decision-making. Getting this process right starts before any product, tool or vendor selection is made. Its basic requirement is that the organisation understands the nature of the information flows; responsibilities need to be clarified and understood. Once deployed, the technology needs to support and encourage collaboration and information exchange with the aim of keeping experience and reduplication of labour to a minimum. Underpinning all this means that data, information and knowledge really become the most important company asset in "creating the intelligent and alert organisation".

To create the highest leverage from the company's information assets, knowledge workers must be able to share and re-use information regardless of format or location. Information which can't be found and can't be retrieved is useless. For many years I have successfully implemented intelligence processes in many companies across Europe. A frequently-asked question is: what is the ROI, return on investment, of competitive intelligence? The ROI of competitive intelligence far exceeds information and knowledge management. For the ROI of information management I have made the following initial calculation, based on three assumptions:

1. Time wasted in collecting information: The time a knowledge worker spends collecting information is 30 percent of his/her time per day. Based on an average all-inclusive salary of 60,000, – Euros this is 20,000, – Euros per year/per knowledge worker.

2. Knowledge deficit/enriching information: The amount of this gap can be calculated at another 5,000, – Euros per year/per knowledge worker.

3. Opportunity cost: the assumption is an average revenue per knowledge worker per year of 150,000, – Euros/1600 hours per year means 95 Euros per hour. Cost are estimated at 12,000, – Euros per year/per knowledge worker.

The facts and figures are indicative; however, this means total cost per knowledge worker per year of 25.000, – to 37.000, – Euros. The cost to a company with 250 employees amounts to 6 – 10 million Euros per year. The average investment in a competitive intelligence capability in a company with 250 – 500 employees amounts to around 100,000, – to 120,000, – Euros.

I have identified three strong indicators of real intelligence within companies. The first indicator is that the company always seems to be a step ahead of the competition. Companies which are ahead of competitors always have a good basis culture of human intelligence competences and can access information and intelligence that is not yet stored in electronic databases and is not available to the competition.

The second indicator is that the intelligence professionals deliver real and different insights and foresights about future competitive dynamics. The third indicator is that senior management has a thorough understanding of intelligence, regularly uses it to plan and to make better decisions, and sees intelligence as a management discipline to continuously and consistently feed the strategic management processes. For these senior managers, executive teams and CEOs, the next quote should in fact no longer apply: "If generals can't do without good intelligence, why does senior management think it can?"

Case: Cisco
Cisco was founded in 1984 and is currently world leader in networking equipment. Total revenues were US$ 22 billion in 2004 with 37,000 employees in 67 countries. R and D spending averages 17 percent of total revenues per year. In 2001 Cisco faced huge problems because of the bursting of the Internet bubble. Revenues fell by 40 percent. Market capitalization in May 2001 amounted to US$ 135 billion compared to 11 key competitors with US$ 156 billion.

1. The Strategic decision to implement Competitive Intelligence in 2001
Because of the downturn in 2001, the Executive Board of Cisco decided to implement competitive intelligence (CI) in the organisation with the aim of responding more effectively to the changes in international markets.

Reason:
▶ With no foreseeable growth in spending and fierce competition in key markets, Cisco realised that it must compete effectively to win new business and protect its customer base;
▶ As a result of this increased competitive pressure, Cisco had to fundamentally rethink its understanding of its competitors and the strategies it used to sell to customers;
▶ Complicating matters further, Cisco had to find a way to efficiently disseminate CI to its 10,000 sales people worldwide.

2. Mission
Cisco's CI mission is: "to identify the key competitors in the international markets, evaluate their threat in terms of technology, sales, marketing, channels and finance delivering competitive sales tools and competitive sales support".

> *"Since many of our markets were either stagnating or declining, we realised that the only way for us to grow was to take market share away from our competitors. In order to do that we needed to educate our 10,000 sales force about our competition".*
> (Director Strategic Marketing Cisco)

3. Action
A. Creation of a CI Team charged with the task of collecting, developing and dis-seminating CI information to support 10,000 sales people;
B. Development of a CI portal to support Cisco's sales force with CI informa-tion;
C. Content and functionality are designed around how the sales force needs to use CI in the sales processes, with the explicit goal of supporting daily deci-sion-making.

Cisco determines that a CI portal which collects all competitor information in one place is an effective way to supply this information quickly and efficiently to its distributed sales force.

Cisco ensures its sales force can use the portal's information by heavily tai-loring design and content to how sales personnel use competitive intelligence. It means that all competitive information is available about:

▶ Who they are
▶ What they sell
▶ How they sell against Cisco
▶ How they sell against the competitors
▶ How their products perform versus Cisco's

All relevant information which the sales force has at its fingertips has been organ-ised through the web. Examples are: CI Home Page, Focus on Competition pro-grammes, Competitive Hotline, Competitive Sales Guides, Competitive Voice-mails, Request for Competitive support, E-Sales.

4. How is Cisco's CI organised?
Cisco's CI Team has 12 full time employees who are responsible for shifting through thousands of internal and external data and information points to find nuggets of information that could help the sales force to win contracts. These nug-gets are melded together into several resources that the sales department can use in its presentations, sales pitches and negotiations with prospective customers.

> *"A sales person never goes to our CI portal and has to ask "what does this mean for me or my sales" We have done the thinking for him. All they have to do is to absorb the information and to drop it into their presentations".*
> (Director of Competitive Intelligence at Cisco)

5. Results of CI efforts

The results of the implemented CI process at Cisco are the following:

▶ Raised sales awareness and understanding of Cisco's competitive landscape, providing a more holistic perspective of its competitors;
▶ Increase of Cisco's market share in all technology groups;
▶ Total cost of initial development: US$ 100,000, – to 300,000, -
▶ Total initial development time: 6 months
▶ Annual cost of system maintenance: US$ 75,000, – to 150,000, -
▶ Research staff required for ongoing maintenance: 12 FTEs
▶ IT staff required for ongoing maintenance: not applicable
▶ Corporate IT commitment for development: not applicable
▶ Yearly maintenance cost before and after the CI portal have decreased with 50%
▶ First year gain from competition in 2002: 10% market share

Over the period 2001 – 2005 the ratio of market capitalization changed dramatically in favour of Cisco:

2001 Cisco versus Key Competitors US$ 135 versus US$ 156 billion; 2005 Cisco versus Key Competitors US$ 182 versus US$ 93 billion

"Competitive Intelligence at Cisco is fundamental to how we drive our business".

Case: Fierce competition in food retail in the Netherlands

Albert Heijn is the leading food retail chain in the Netherlands. The image of Albert Heijn (AH) has been high quality, luxury supermarkets and premium prices. In 2002, the market share decreased in certain product categories such as detergents, beer, drinks on the one hand, and on the other hand the quality of other supermarket chains increased and even the discount formulas Aldi and Lidl introduced fresh vegetables. So Albert Heijn lost ground also through the country's worsening economic climate. Since 2001, they were losing 0.5 to 1.0 percent market share. In the summer of 2003 the Board of AH took the decision to fight back by reducing consumer prices on thousands of products, starting in October 2003. Reactions from the market were fierce: from the competition, from the fast-moving consumer goods producers as well as from members of parliament. Producers such as Peijnenburg and Unilever challenged AH in court because of the downtrend in consumer prices and because of copying packaging for AH's own brands at the expense of the premium brands. The fast-moving consumer goods producers accused AH of lowering the prices, leading to less room for innovation. Unions and industry experts calculated a loss of 40,000 jobs in the sector in the period 2004 – 2005. Since the start of the price competition by AH, AH's market share increased to an all-time high by the end of 2005.

As a consequence, the share of AH's own brands increased at the expense of the premiums brands from companies like Unilever, P&G, Heineken, Grolsch, Campina and all the others.

> *"Leadership is action, not position".*
> (Donald H. McGannon)

What has happened and why should the fast-moving consumer goods sector, FMCGs, blame themselves and not the retailers like Albert Heijn and others? There are several reasons for this. The first reason is that senior management in the FMCG-sector has for many years accepted that 90 percent of all new product launches would fail. It's the management of "trial and error", leaving the management of well-known brands to young marketers with job titles such as product manager, brand manager or marketing manager. The second reason is that the retail brands have gained similar positions to the A-brands from the perspective of reliability, superb quality, taste, availability and image. The only difference between the retail brands and the A-brands is the price difference of 20 percent on average. Consumers experience this quickly and move towards the retail brands. Especially at times of a downturn in the economic climate, consumers feel this in their pockets. The third reason is that images no longer influence the consumer, and retail brands are increasingly usurping the position of A-brands. The fourth reason is the fact that since the 1990s the management within the FMCG-sector has not introduced sufficient innovation in order to secure their leading position over time. Innovation in food retail now comes from the retailers themselves who are much closely involved with consumers owing to improved research and information technology.

The FMCG-sector has responded by shaking up their portfolios. Heinz is returning to their core activity and selling off the local brands. Unilever sold its perfumes and deep-freeze division. Sara Lee is planning to sell off around 40 percent of the business. After closing down production lines, and even entire production facilities, the FMCG-sector has been forced by retailers to fine down their portfolios. By concentrating on core brands as a category the FMCG-sector hopes to combat retailers with their own private brands, and is putting more emphasis on practical, Mediterranean and healthy foods.

Research into Competitive Intelligence

In 2005-2006 a study was conducted by SCIP US, the Society of Competitive Intelligence professionals, among 520 competitive intelligence professionals. It's important to note that 75 percent of all respondents were located in the USA.

Management summary

For many organisations, competitive intelligence (CI) is a relatively small function, funded and supported to varying degrees by other departments throughout the organisation. CI can be located in many different parts of the business, but often operates either as a separate competitive intelligence or business intelligence department, or as part of marketing or market research. Most CI units support several types of business activities, use an assortment of competitive intelligence tools and techniques, and supply intelligence to multiple levels of management through a variety of competitive intelligence deliverables.

Most survey respondents allocate their limited resources among the various components of the competitive intelligence cycle (planning, collection, processing, analysis, dissemination), with the majority of their time spent on analysis and secondary data collection.

▶ Internal employees are the most important primary sources of information; publications and web sites are the most important secondary sources.

▶ Competitor analysis and SWOT are the most frequently used analysis methods.

▶ E-mail has surpassed hard copy reports, personal delivery, and presentations as the most commonly used method for acquiring and disseminating CI. Competitive intelligence practitioners have many delivery options, and they need to know how to determine the best method for selecting specific deliverables.

▶ Many tools and technologies are internally available to help collect information and report intelligence. Almost half of the survey respondents are confident they use the most appropriate technology.

Survey participants appear more concerned with improving their skills and increasing the impact of their analytical products than obtaining additional funding or technology. When asked what changes would help improve their organisation's competitive intelligence processes over the next 12 months, the top responses involved accessing, integrating, and sharing information, and better educating themselves and their management about competitive intelligence.

The results of this survey imply that competitive intelligence is on a positive trend and CI is at a key juncture in its quest to gain acceptance and provide value to organisations:

▶ Awareness is high and CI visibility has increased in many organisations. Most CI practitioners create exposure to senior management through distribution of their deliverables. They present an excellent opportunity for CI practitioners to demonstrate the value competitive intelligence provides to the organisation.

▶ More organisations are assessing the effectiveness and value of their competitive intelligence activities, but all should employ objective measures.

▶ For most CI practitioners, developing a mission statement and formal competitive intelligence procedures and objectives should be a top priority.

▶ Competitive intelligence is often a relatively small function with limited budget and resources, but it receives additional support from other parts of the organisation. Making the best use of these additional resources is a challenge for many CI professionals.

Research results in more detail

Competitive intelligence professionals work in a wide variety of environments where change is a constant factor. At the departmental level, almost half of the respondents reported one or less full time equivalent (FTE) employees supporting CI. Competitive intelligence is a part-time function for many respondents, but almost half spend at least 75 percent of their time on it. In most companies, additional help for the CI effort is available in other parts of their organisation.

Participants reported generally modest competitive intelligence budgets. More than half have less than US$100,000 (excluding salaries) and only one in eight has US$500,000 or more. In about a third of the respondents' organisations, CI is a stand-alone competitive intelligence or business intelligence unit, an increase from the 10 percent reported in previous research. This implies an increased functional independence and opportunity to support multiple departments. For 22 percent of the respondents, their competitive intelligence function reports into marketing or market research; it is equally likely to report into strategic planning, information services/info centre, or business development – mergers and acquisitions.

People who work in competitive intelligence must be flexible, as the nature of their work requires dividing their time among several responsibilities. CI professionals typically spread their limited resources among the various components of the CI cycle – planning, collecting, processing, analysing, and disseminating intelligence – with the majority of time spent on analysis and secondary data collection. Many CI professionals also manage the CI function, and spend time allocating resources and overseeing projects and budgets. They also develop and nurture relationships with management, internal clients, outside suppliers, and others.

Supporting business decisions is the ultimate goal for many competitive intelligence functions, and the survey indicated that most CI practitioners support several key types of decisions, including those involving strategy and business development.

Respondents reported generating a wide assortment of intelligence products for internal clients, many using sophisticated analysis. Company profiles are the most common (produced "sometimes" or "frequently" by 86 percent), followed by competitive benchmarking and market or industry audits. Two-thirds report using some type of early warning alerts and more than half develop customer or supplier profiles and technology assessments.

Collecting information that can be turned into actionable intelligence is a critical phase of the competitive intelligence process, because without quality information there is little possibility of meaningful intelligence. In this study, survey participants indicated that most forms of primary and secondary sources are important to their CI practice – especially publications, Internet web sites and company employees. As one might expect, there was a good deal of difference in responses from respondents with larger or smaller competitive intelligence budgets and staffs. Secondary sources continue to be a main source of information for many competitive intelligence professionals, often viewed as more important than primary or people sources. The most accessible and least costly (and unfortunately usually the least valuable) were viewed as the most important.

Competitive intelligence professionals can apply many analytical techniques to turn information into actionable intelligence. But CI practitioners generally prefer to use only a few techniques, and those preferences have not changed much over the years. In this survey, CI practitioners indicated they use two analytical techniques, competitor analysis and SWOT, frequently and others occasionally.

By its nature CI often contributes to more than one internal group, and the survey responses reflected that. As expected, most respondents serve a wide variety of internal clients with CI content and multiple deliverables. Serving several different internal employees with limited resources requires a certain amount of finesse, and solid direction and processes.

Disseminating competitive intelligence to a wide and diverse internal audience often requires several different delivery methods. Respondents to this survey favour delivery methods that can reach large numbers of clients at once, such as printed reports/alerts and presentations/staff briefings. But e-mail tops all other methods. E-mail is also the primary method others in the organisation use to send competitive information into their competitive intelligence unit.

Many technologies on the market today support competitive intelligence. Some help collect information, while others make analysis easier or more accurate. Other technologies report intelligence or assist in developing and maintaining internal contacts with clients and information sources. When asked what internally available technologies supported CI activities, most respondents used those technologies that help them collect information (such as search/text retrieval software) and report intelligence (intranets and web or teleconferencing). Almost half are confident that they have the most appropriate technology.

Participants appear more concerned with improving their skills and increasing the impact of their analytical products than obtaining more funding or technology. When asked what changes would most help improve their organisation's CI process over the next 12 months, the top responses involved accessing, integrating, and sharing information, and better educating themselves and their management about competitive intelligence.

The survey respondents selected the ability to better integrate multiple sources of information as their most desired change. This indicates that the respondents do not feel "information starved," but want the ability to better handle the information they already have. It may also indicate the need to spend less time on information handling. Interestingly the respondents do not seem to want to purchase new technology (ranked ninth) as a solution although technology may be the best way to address this need.

The need for more training for individuals involved in intelligence ranked second among the changes that would improve competitive intelligence processes. Based on the number of one-person departments and less than full time practitioners, this need for training is not particularly surprising. For larger CI organisations, this ranking may be driven by the belief that better skills and more competitive intelligence knowledge are required to improve organisational excellence.

Respondents were asked to consider what changes have taken place in their overall competitive intelligence operations or processes during the last twelve months. The results indicate that competitive intelligence is on a positive trend, and at a key junction in its quest to gain acceptance and provide value to organisations. The downsizing and budget cuts that followed 9/11, and the earlier economic downturn, appear to be over for most respondents' organisations, and many competitive intelligence units are now stable or growing.

Most respondents have regular contact with their senior management through their deliverables, and many report high levels of CI awareness and increased management visibility. This positive environment presents an excellent opportunity for practitioners to improve CI's overall standing and to lay the groundwork for additional budget, headcount, or resources by demonstrating the value competitive intelligence provides to their organisations.

Some companies may be trying to provide more tools to competitive intelligence staff (possibly in lieu of more budget or resources). Outsourcing of research or analysis is present and increasing for some respondents, although only a minority indicated increases in their organisations. For many, additional help is available in other parts of their division or elsewhere in the organisation, and about two-thirds of respondents indicated that at least some of their company's personnel participate in competitive intelligence activities.

When asked how their organisations measured CI effectiveness, the majority of respondents used customer satisfaction surveys, but a minority reported using more objective methods such as return on investment (ROI). Even fewer respondents applied measurements to the value of their CI function and 30% reported having no formal or standard measurement processes.

Slightly less than half of survey respondents indicated their organisations have the fundamental organisational characteristics that typically indicate acceptance of a function by an organisation. Just over a third reported their competitive intelligence function has a mission statement, and less than half said they have formal competitive intelligence procedures or written key objectives.

Historically, there has been a high correlation between having these organisational characteristics and high levels of competitive intelligence awareness and participation. This survey again showed those relationships, as CI functions that have mission statements, objectives, and formal CI procedures are much more likely to have high levels of company-wide competitive intelligence awareness.

More than half of the respondents reported that most or all of the personnel in their organisation know the competitive intelligence function exists, a good indication of effective CI outreach and marketing. This awareness is directly correlated with the size of the respondents' organisations.

Overall, approximately one-fourth of survey respondents reported that all or most personnel participate in competitive intelligence activities, indicating active networking and information gathering throughout the organisation. On the flip side, more than one-third reported that few or none participate. Those with small participation numbers are not fully accessing the internal competitive knowledge of their employees, and competitive intelligence practitioners may not be benefiting from the value that this information can bring to their process.

A large, diverse group of 550 competitive intelligence professionals completed the survey, resulting in 520 usable responses. Respondents work in many different industries, which reflects SCIP 's diverse membership and the increased use of competitive intelligence across most types of organisations. No single industry had more than 17 percent of all respondents, and when combined, more than half of the respondents work in four industry groups (education, pharmaceutical/biotech, CI or strategy consulting, telecommunications/Internet).

Survey participants work all over the world, and all global regions are represented in the survey results. Similar to the distribution of the SCIP membership, slightly more than three-quarters of the survey respondents work in North America.

Survey participants work for a variety of organisation sizes. Nearly a quarter work for small organisations (annual revenue less than US$10 million), slightly less than a third work for mid-sized companies (US$10 million – $1 billion), and just under half work for companies with annual revenue greater than US$ 1 billion.

Participants represent many levels of competitive intelligence experience and all major CI constituent groups (practitioners, vendors, consultants, and academics). Almost 40% are in the "trenches" doing the work, with titles of analyst, researcher, collector, or technical staff. Another 40% are filling a managerial role (manager, department manager, director). Because many of them work for companies with small competitive intelligence budgets, some of them probably fill dual roles as competitive intelligence analyst and manager.

Intelligence lessons from the military

"Leadership involves remembering past mistakes, an analysis of today's achievements and a well-grounded imagination in visualizing the problems of the future".
(Stanley C. Allyn)

For many years I have been asking myself the question why the business world hardly adapted to the lessons we can learn from the military. The management discipline strategy originated in the military and it has now been accepted in the world for almost 50 years. However, this is not yet the case with intelligence as management discipline. Of course there are large numbers of companies which have excellent competitive intelligence competences in place, and others again which have some kind of marketing or technology intelligence capability in place. In most cases the success of these intelligence efforts depends on where the competitive intelligence function is located in the organisation. It should be as high up as possible in the hierarchical structure of the organisation, and this means at senior management level.

"The best solution for the question of where to place the office of competitive intelligence is on a par with functions that report directly to the CEO".

Imagine that during the preparations for going to war or during a fight or conflict the intelligence, officers report to a captain, major or colonel. Yes, of course in operations, but should it also be the case in tactics and strategy? In the military this is not the case and intelligence officers report to the highest ranks, that is, to generals. But to whom do the researchers and business analysts who are active in the marketing intelligence department usually report? To the marketing manager or marketing director. Do they see the whole competitive landscape in which the company is operating? They do not. Another development sees many marketing research and marketing services departments transformed into marketing intelligence departments. Unfortunately this is no more nor less than just re-labelling.

I learned an excellent lesson from the example of the Statistical Office of Winston Churchill during the Second World War. We all remember the movies of WWII with the huge mock-ups of the battlefield and the maps showing the movements of troops and equipment. The staff regularly reported to Churchill on the victories and losses. However, we all know that most staff, in organisations too, don't like to bring bad news and are inclined to be overly optimistic about critical developments and major threats. So Winston Churchill decided to establish a "Statistical Office" just a few hundred metres away from the central staff. The objective of this "statistical office" was to enable the staff to bring him the bad news, to bring him "the brutal facts", and to inform him of the real threats and risks Britain was facing. Could you imagine in business competitive intelligence professionals who would tell senior management and CEOs "the brutal facts" facing the company, either at present or in the future? The main reason that this probably doesn't happen is the huge egos of some members of the board. In 2005, Marcel van Berkel of the DSM company in the Netherlands made this great statement: "If Generals can't without good intelligence, why should CEOs think they can?"

So I think it would be useful to give the reader some relevant lessons from the military.

1. The C3I capability in the military. C3I stands for Command, Control, Communications and Intelligence. The critical success factor in the military in time of war is to destroy the C3I capability of the enemy. It confirms that the military relies strongly upon their intelligence capabilities and that intelligence seems to be a "pre-condition for survival". In the business world it should be no different, because we have to foresee in time the potential movements of our competitors in the marketplace. But how many companies do have in place a structured way to identify "early warnings" in time?

2. Reconnaissance in force: tactics in time of conflict. Information-gathering is ranked extremely high as a factor for waging war successfully. Many armies owe their success to flexible, rapid and creative intelligence-gathering teams, which enabled them to act quickly in a pro-active than in a re-active way.

3. Know your enemies and know yourself and in a hundred battles you will never be in danger. This famous statement was made by Sun Tzu, the legendary general who lived 500 years B.C. The statement is highly applicable in the business world of today. Coaches and sports trainers work in accordance with this principle, because in every competition or game they try to anticipate the way opponents act and think.

4. General Rommel. This general was very successful during WWII. He had a very clear view of how to manage his forces. We will highlight four of them:
   ▶ Explain to the key people within the force the strategy, and the role of the key players in this strategy. Explain, in addition, the consequences of implementing the strategies;
   ▶ Ensure up-to-date information and knowledge for the force and educate and train them accordingly;
   ▶ Know what keeps the people busy in practice and know about the problems they are facing in day-to-day operations. Do not rely on structures of planning and control, get out of your ivory tower and your "own world". By acting this way, encourage an attitude of openness to change and adapt strategies to new situations created by the dynamics in the environment;

▶ Keep contact with your people beyond the next layer and find out what keeps them busy. Be genuine and honest, or your people will soon realise you don't believe what you are telling them.

These four approaches resemble the way in which 21st century management in the 21st century should approach things.

5. General Patton. In the legendary WWII movie "Patton", there is moment where the general is sitting on top of his tank; he says: "Rommel, I read your book". The explanation of this statement is that General Patton had studied Rommel's past successes and knew exactly how Rommel would enter the fight in Northern Africa. So Patton was very well prepared and had generated foresights into how Rommel might act. How many CEOs today judge their counterparts in the competitive arena as an "open book"?

6. Similarities with the military. As described earlier, there are three key similarities between the military and in business: First "reconnaissance", which in business means foresights about the key drivers of change; Second "intelligence", which in business means the structured and consistent way of scanning the periphery; Third "war", "war games" or "strategic war mapping", which in business mean thinking of the disruptive and quite unexpected issues of relevance that might impact on the company – "scenario planning and analysis".

7. OODA loops, meaning Observing, Orienting, Deciding and Acting. In the military this is a closed loop. In business and in some governmental intelligence agencies we spend less time in using the eyes and ears, which means we lose the ability to observe. We overspend heavily on equipment such as x-rays, metal detectors, sensors, and face and eye scanners. This leaves less capacity to observe from the side, which should enable us to see the big picture. As an example, I like to ask management: "How do you use the eyes and the ears of your sales force?" Is it structured, is it consistent, have you explained to them the potential benefits for the organisation?

8. Principles of war and intelligence. *The Marine Corps Way* by Jason Santamaria, Vincent Martino and Eric K. Clemons, describes the principle of war as "Hit the other fellow, as quick as you can and as hard as you can, where it hurts him most when he isn't looking". In terms of competitive intelligence this means:
   ▶ when he is not looking = surprise
   ▶ hitting, as hard as you can = focus
   ▶ hitting, as quick as you can = tempo
   ▶ hitting, when he isn't looking = vulnerability

This is reminiscent of that statement by Frederick the Great: "To be defeated is forgivable to be surprised is not". One of the purposes of competitive intelligence is not to be surprised by the changes in the external dynamics. But we know that there are examples of numerous companies, which have been overtaken by surprise by the changing external dynamics in the business environment. Unfortunately, there will be many more such casualties in the near future.

9. What can we learn from the US Marines? As already mentioned, *The Marine Corps Way* gives us a key message that acknowledges the increasingly central role that information plays in armed conflict in the 21st Century:

> *"A structured and a formalized approach to the management of information, known as Information Operations".*

I refer to the diagram, explaining that in US Marines operations everybody is involved in all aspects of the operation, from start to finish where information and intelligence is the key issue to survive. In the business world I often try to explain that competitive intelligence is a pre-condition for existence.

Three Approaches in surprise strategies

I.   Stealth   - Denies the counterpart any knowledge of impending action

II. Ambiguity   - Acting in such a way that the counterpart does not know what to expect

III. Deception   - Convincing the counterpart that we are going to do something other than what we actually going to do

Source: The Marine Corps Way

What can we learn from the US Marines?

Key Message:

Acknowledging the increasingly central role that information plays in a 21st Century armed conflict:

Structured and a formalized approach to the management of information.

Known as "Information Operations"

Source: The Marine Corps Way

What can we learn from the US Marines?

IO Cell
➤ Dedication of personnel and resources
➤ Full-time IO Officer
➤ Diverse group of individuals with different backgrounds
➤ Individuals are not fully dedicated but is part of core responsibility

IO Plan
➤ Based on commander's guidance
➤ Selection of information based activities
➤ Formulation a preliminary plan for employment
➤ Extensive coordination and participation with others

IO Implementation
➤ Execution of the operation
➤ Monitoring the effectiveness of efforts
➤ Fast response to changing events
➤ Making the appropriate adjustments

IO is from Start to finish involved in all aspects of the operation

Source: The Marine Corps Way

---

10. After Action Reviews or AARs. Companies like ExxonMobil, GE and others use AARs as an approach to evaluate their decision-making processes. As we all know, there is nothing more difficult than taking the right decisions. AARs are originally from the Pentagon. The aim of AARs is to learn from both successes and failures by asking your management the following four key questions:
   1. What was supposed to happen?
   2. What actually happened?
   3. What were the differences and WHY?
   4. What can we learn from it?

One of my clients has around 150-200 AARs in one page format in the competitive intelligence portal with key words and a search engine easily accessible for all management teams. Can you imagine how invaluable this simple tool of information and knowledge sharing is? Maybe it's too simple, which may explain why it's hardly ever used.

Government intelligence agencies
> *"In politics there is nothing that is planned in advance".*
> (Franklin D. Roosevelt)

Many writers have informed us that Weapons of Mass Destruction (WMD) were never found in Iraq. Despite the lack of the right intelligence, the Bush administration decided to invade Iraq in March 2003. US governments rely heavily on the information from their intelligence services. Examples include the crises in Korea,

Cuba, Vietnam, Afghanistan and Iraq. The US has two important organisations amongst others active in intelligence: the CIA, Central Intelligence Agency, with 25,000 employees and NSA, National Security Agency, with 40,000 employees. In 2006, the US spent 44 billion dollars on intelligence. The maxim is " he who knows most will win in the end" and so the US will maintain political and economic superiority. It is expected that the huge investment not will decrease in the next few years.

The intelligence efforts, before the decision to invade Iraq, may have been insufficient. Intelligence analysis has concentrated on obvious information gaps caused by the pressure of the political policy-makers. We may conclude that the US lost credibility because of the insufficient intelligence results related to Iraq.

A similar situation occurred in early 2006 with respect to Iran. The US had been lobbying Europe about Iran's potential nuclear ambitions. On several occasions the CIA made extremely impressive presentations to the politicians of European countries. Of course, there were many questions to which the right answers were not given. Once again, the information was based on yawning gaps in human intelligence provided by people who not been in Iran for a decade. In addition, there is a mistrust of the CIA within the US itself. The CIA was founded in 1947 by Democrats from the Ivy League University world of Princeton, Harvard and Yale. Because of its history, the conservatives in the US will never fully trust the CIA.

The main focus of NSA is best practices involving the tapping of phones, fixed lines and wireless, email and other sources. NSA is able to tap electronic sources worldwide. It had been done in Bosnia at the time of Mladic, Karadzic and Milosevic in the 1990s, in Rambouillet and Dayton at the time of the peace negotiations between Serbia, Croatia and Bosnia. In February 2006, it came to light that NSA had also been tapping US citizens. The decision to tap the domestic population can only be approved by court order.

Why have so many intelligence agencies around the world made so many mistakes over the last couple of years? They have plenty of funds and access to the most modern electronic equipment. Israel lacked the right intelligence in 2006 about the size of the Hezbollah armed forces and the number of rockets they had. Five weeks of war in Southern Lebanon didn't bring the expected success. In Afghanistan, the US, UK and NATO lacked intelligence, and were surprised by the swift recovery of the Taliban forces in 2005-2006. In Somalia, the US has been supporting local and regional warlords for over 20 years, ever since the 1980s. In 2006, all of the sudden the local mullahs assumed control, supported by Al Qaeda. After the election in Gaza, the US was surprised by the victory of Hamas. And of course, we have the result of the biggest failure in intelligence, the WMD in Iraq.

Why did those failures occur? My knowledge and experience suggest that intelligence agencies still overestimate the information they can gather from electronic sources. Western intelligence agencies have invested billions of Euros in putting in place the full range of electronic equipment. This is similar to the situation in the Dutch intelligence agency AIVD, which also relies heavily on electronics, so-called "sigint" and to a much lesser extent on human intelligence, so-called "humint".

In competitive intelligence in the business world we always put the puzzle together from pieces derived from numerous relevant sources of information. Increasingly, we use experts, researchers, business analysts around the world, and above all published sources of journalists. The chief advantage of using journalists as sources of information is that they have done their homework. Most of the time they are knowledgeable about the local and regional situation, they do their research and they also have information on other non-commercial issues which are of high interest. They publish work on new developments, cultural changes and the minds of people.

The best sources for this kind of information, which should also be used by the intelligence agencies, are the numerous articles in the pages "opinion" in quality newspapers and magazines around the globe. I'd like to give you an example from a quality newspaper in the Netherlands, NRC Handelsblad, where excellent articles have been published for country intelligence purposes. In just one edition opinions are given by:

▶ Ahmed Rashid, author of the book "Jihad, the Rise of Millitant Islam in Central Asia"
▶ E.J.Groeskamp, author of the book "Terra Cognita, the last journey around the world"
▶ Dominique Moist, of IFRI, French Institute of International Affairs
▶ Vladislav Inozemtsev, Director of the independent Centre of Post-Industrial Research in Moscow

I gave some intelligence examples of what we can learn form the military. I also gave some bad examples of intelligence obtained from government intelligence agencies. We must learn from both.

I repeat: If Generals can't do without good intelligence, why should CEOs think they can? On average, the CEOs of major international companies occupy their position as CEO for seven years. In the top 25 Dutch companies listed on the AEX on the Amsterdam Stock Exchange, the CEO retains his position for 3.5 years. Why the rapid turnover in CEO's? Is it down to poor performance, is it difficult to lead companies in the right direction, is it because of the fast-changing dynamics in the business environment or is it a lack of vision and any a clear strategy? Nowadays most companies have a wide range of management control mechanisms in place. Examples are:

▶ The Supervisory Board
▶ Accountants

▶ Audit Committee
▶ Corporate Performance Management
▶ Management of Key Performance Indicators
▶ Risk Management
▶ Balance Score Card
▶ Six Sigma

> *"If you would take, you must first give, this is the beginning of intelligence".*
> (Tao-Te-King)

But it seems that all these mechanisms are not enough, because most companies regularly face trouble.

Frequently-used important arguments are bad economic climate, downfall of the economy, stable markets, competitive pressure and less customer interest. The legendary General Sun Tzu stated, 500 years before Christ, "Know your enemies and know yourself and in a hundred battles you will never be in danger". Based on the above overview of mechanisms, one might conclude that companies know themselves. But do they know their enemies, or, in other words, do they know their competitors? The majority of companies are still hierarchical and bureaucratic. Management thinks they know their competitors. Jack Welch of GE told his managers that they should ask themselves every morning when they wake up the simple question: "Why is the competition doing better than we are?"

However, most managers hardly know the simple answers to the following questions:
1. Who are our competitors?
2. What are the objectives of our competitors?
3. What are the strategies of our competitors?
4. What are the strategic intentions of our competitors?
5. Why and where do they compete?
6. Why are our competitors better than we are?
7. How do their products and services compare to ours, and where is the edge?
8. Who will be our new competitors in 1-3 years' time?
9. Where do our competitors hurt us?
10. What have we done to hurt them?

Most managers struggle to answer those questions. But how will you ever be able to compete if you don't keep a constant eye on your competitors? These questions deal with your direct or immediate competitors. But what does management know about "secondary competitors"? This is about different products and services solving the same problems in a similar way. And what does management know about "tertiary competitors", which is about different products and services solving or eliminating the problem in a different way? Having the answers now and having them 1-3 years from now is another challenge.

Several times, I have quoted the question: "If Generals can't do without good intelligence, why do CEOs think they can?" We can learn a lot from intelligence and the military.

OODA LOOPS

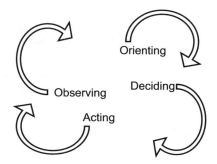

- We spend hardly on the eyes & ears, losing the capability to observe
- We spend heavily on equipment (e.g. x-rays, metal detectors, sensors, face scanners)
- Do we observe from the side and looking at the big picture?

Source: US Airforce

Principles of War

There's only one principle of war and that's this:

"Hit the other fellow, as quick as you can, and as hard as you can, where it hurts him most, when he isn't looking"

Hitting,

➤When he isn't looking	= Surprise
➤Hitting, as hard as you can	= Focus
➤Hitting, as quick as you can	= Tempo
➤Hitting, where it hurts him most	= Vulnerability

➤Which is identical to competitive intelligence

Source: The Marine Corps Way

OODA Loops, as I said earlier, stands for Observing, Orienting, Deciding and Action, and is a closed loop. In the military they take the time to observe. In business, we hardly take time for observation; we rely heavily on equipment and technology, which makes us less able to see the bigger picture.

Similarities with the military

Military   **Business**

↓   ↓

Reconnaissance   - Studies on "Key Drivers of Change"
Intelligence   - Environmental scanning
War games   - Scenario planning

"Management should finally start to prepare the organization for success in
an unpredictable future"

Source: The Marine Corps Way

We can translate the principles of war into the principles of competitive business practice: surprise, focus, speed and hitting companies where they are most vulnerable. Comparisons with warfare show us that continuously watching the key drivers of change, environmental scanning and scenario planning are the important tools in preparing the organisation for success in the unpredictable future. With the support of intelligence management, one is able to foresee the future events.

In the military they have defined three strategies for surprise: stealth, ambiguity and deception. A fine example of a deception strategy is the case of Boeing, who announced to the world and Airbus that they would also produce a bigger Jumbo Jet 747 as the response to the A380, and then doing something different, by developing the Dreamliner.

Finally, the Information Operations or "IO". In the military, information, and thus intelligence, plays a crucial role in 21st-century armed conflict. IO is a formalized approach to the management of information. IO consists of an IO Cell, an IO Plan and an IO Implementation. From "start to finish" IO or Information Operations is fully involved in all aspects of the operation within the US Marine Corps.

All I have described here, from OODA Loops to the IO, is highly relevant for and applicable to our day-to-day business; it is called competitive intelligence. Although we can learn and benefit a lot from this example, we persist in our reliance upon equipment and on information technology. These are good supportive tools but the essence of IO or intelligence is people. Investing in intelligence within company's means investing in people. There is no doubt that investing in competitive intelligence, that is to say, in people, will pay dividends.

The most famous example of a company which invested heavily in people is General Electric under the leadership of Jack Welch. The market value of GE was, at the time Jack Welch started as CEO in 1981, around 12 billion dollars. Bt the time he left, in 2001, the market value had increased to 400 billion dollars. Key factors in this success were a clear strategy to be number one or two in the market, cost cutting, investment in growth and in change. In addition Jack Welch proved himself a successful leader and manager of people. Even though he let some 130,000 people go, he created substantial employment; over 98 percent of all employees valued Jack Welch because of his leadership and his strategic direction of the company. People are trained to be pleasant; but managers should tell their employees where they are wrong. People deserve no less, according to Jack Welch. Famous is the explanation of the 20-70-10 percent of employees, that you have to get rid of the 10 percent of your employees who do not perform. It's better for GE and for themselves. Jack Welch's key role has been leadership and looking/developing management talent. According to Jack Welch, the most important task of a CEO is to develop talent. It's similar in sports. You are looking for the stars and the weaker players should be replaced. Famous, too, are the thousands of work-out meetings across GE year after year. The aim was to demolish bureaucracy and hierarchy and reward people who took risks and who went the extra mile. The most important task for leaders and managers is the management of people.

It's amazing how much talent nurtured in GE has moved to a CEO position in other companies. The HBR of May 2006 made an overview of these 20 companies: Albertson's, Allied Signal, Comdisco, Conseco, Fiat, General Dynamics, General Signal, Great Lakes Chemical, Home Depot, Intuit, Iomega, McDonnell Douglas, Owens Corning, Polaris Industries, Primedia, SPX, Stanley Works, Terra Lycos, 3M, TRW. No single company has ever produced so many CEOs.

Many examples in competitive intelligence are from the larger companies. This doesn't imply that competitive intelligence only applies to big businesses. It is also relevant for small and medium-sized businesses. However, the big companies are more conspicuous in the media, at seminars and conferences as platforms to share best practices and to learn from each other. Both kinds of businesses need each other: the small need the big companies and the big need the small. The statement below explains this.

> *"Dividing industry into big and little is artificial. Industry is both. That makes it industry. 95 percent of US industries employ less than 500 men each. Today's big industries were small within our lifetime; many of today's small industries will become big before our lifetime ends. Large industries make small industries necessary, and small industries make the large ones possible. Wipe out large industries and you wipe out three-fourths of the small ones. Wipe out the small ones and the large ones cannot go on. They work together. Each has a part in the nation's job".*
> (William J. Cameron)

Part II

Establishing a competitive intelligence capability

Introduction

"Restructuring is an ongoing exercise. It should never stop. In this fast moving world, companies need to adjust and rethink their organisational set-up and their strategies all the time in order to survive and gain on the competition in the long run".

In part I, I listed many objectives of competitive intelligence and the focus towards the future of the company in its fast changing dynamics in the business environment. However, the ultimate goal is to stay ahead of your rivals in the marketplace and to anticipate new market opportunities. Nowadays, we have available an ocean of information which is doubling every 18 months. Many organisations have trouble dealing with the information overload. Management frequently reacts with the attitude that they think they have enough information to take the right decisions. Certainly, competitive intelligence is not the solution to having all relevant information in place. But information overload makes it difficult to see what's really going on. Then we have the problem, in many cases, that management think they know, but in fact don't know.

Take the example of mergers and acquisitions. Numerous studies tell us that at least two-third of all mergers and acquisitions fail. The quantitative data and information delivered by accountants, lawyers, strategists and risk managers is given greater importance than qualitative information, and in most cases the necessity intelligence is lacking.

Accounting still has much too strong an influence on mergers and acquisitions, on strategy, decision-making and evaluation of companies. Is it correct to use accounting data and information as the platform for prognoses, prediction, trends analysis, discount cash flow projections and extrapolation? I don't think so. What about customers and non-customers? Are customers not the pre-condition for the existence of any profit-making organisation? What is being done to take customers into account when the decision is made to acquire or to merge?

Competitive intelligence can become the critical success factor when real strategic decisions have to be made. But when do we ever talk about strategic decisions? What do we mean by strategic decisions? Are those decisions important? We should stop confusing 'strategic' with 'important'. Competitive intelligence professionals can truly contribute to the company by bringing in strategic intelligence beyond the information that is already known. For this we use the intelligence-based executive decision model (see diagram at page 170).

What we assume we know	
1: What-we-know-we-know	**2:What-we-know-we don't-know**
• Define what information is needed and find out what information is already regularly collected, who does what?	• Find out how information that would be important can be gathered. Allocated to a small team or a dedicated person to investigate. Define deadline.
3:What-we-don't know-we-know	**4:What-we don't-know-we don't-know**
• Run an out of office activity with sales people, purchasing people, managers, and other people with a lot of interfaces to the environment. Don't forget management	• Involve top management and board of directors in defining different scenarios on where the world is moving in the medium to long term. Repeat 1-2 times per year.

Source: Joharis Window (1996)

I once read an interesting statement by Jan Herring about information and intelligence:

> *"Information costs money, intelligence makes money. The question is not whether intelligence is valuable, the question is how to make intelligence valuable".*

So senior management has to ask themselves if they want to have competitive intelligence inside the company beyond the traditional filters of information by managers in the positions of marketing, strategy, R and D, technology, risk management, etc. Because there is only one place competitive intelligence can be successful, and that's at senior management level.

> *"The best solution to the question of where to place the office of competitive intelligence is on a par with functions that report directly to the Board".*

The competitive intelligence director will challenge management on the following aspects: he will divorce himself from his own predispositions, assumptions and the large anti-management biases; he will add positive energy and inspiration to what senior management has to accomplish; he will be listening critically, and will ask questions like "What if"? He will contribute to the strategy process because he has in-depth knowledge about the complete competitive arena; he will forecast collateral damage on future decisions; he will quickly analyse the impact of bad news; he will identify the blind spots in strategic management, and will make suggestions as to how to overcome the limitations in recommendations;

he will be able to criticize management decisions, because he is able to foresee negative unintentional consequences; he will identify unforeseen events and will make the recommendations as to how to overcome these; he will see new business opportunities and facilitate 'making it happen'.

Strategic is the most overused word in business. It means "This is important"

The aim of true strategy is to master the market environment by understanding and anticipating the actions of other economic agents, especially competitors.

Source: HBR/S05

No doubt such a person, male or female, will come up against the egos of senior management and CEOs. Senior management must be open to having a kind of "watch dog" next door. Imagine the case at the time of the merger between Daimler Benz and Chrysler in 1998: was there one person at senior level in Stuttgart, Germany, who told CEO Jürgen Schrempp that the planned acquisition of Chrysler was a bad idea? Probably that person would have been promoted to a location far removed from Daimler Benz's headquarters.

> *"Competitive intelligence involves breaking out of established patterns in order to look at things in a different way".*

Establishing a competitive intelligence competence is not that easy because it can clash with the big egos. That's the most critical issue. I am not talking about marketing intelligence or market intelligence that has been implemented in companies with the filter of the marketing manager or marketing director. The majority of efforts in this kind of department mainly concern the market, customers and sometimes competition. Recommendations of importance hardly reach senior management. That is not surprising, because marketing has changed over the past 15 years into downstream marketing instead of upstream marketing.

Case: War room at Ford USA
What happens if a new manager from outside the company has been appointed at the board of a company? You might assume that this person will repeat his or

her successes from the previous position. This is always a key topic in competitive intelligence. A good example is Alan Mulally, appointed CEO of Ford USA in 2006. Alan Mulally's previous job was as CEO of Boeing. After September 11, the aircraft sector faced huge problems. Mulally cut over half of the workforce to 50,000 employees, reduced the product portfolio of models from 11 to 4 and succeeded in reducing the production of Boeing aircraft by 50 percent.

In 2006, the total sales of Ford dropped from US$ 46.3 billion in 2005 to US$ 40.3 billion, a decrease of 13 percent. Ford's total losses in 2006 were been US$ 12.7. Over the next ten years Ford, as well as GM and DaimlerChrysler, will face another huge problem; improved fuel consumption of their cars. President George W. Bush announced, in his State of the Union on January 24 2007, that the fuel consumption of cars in the US must be cut by 20 percent by 2017.

Mulally is planning to do the same at Ford. He cut the workforce by over 80,000 employees and hopes to have Ford back in profitability again by 2009. To restructure Ford he devised an interesting strategy, which is highly relevant and has been done in the sphere of competitive intelligence: establishing a war room.

At a board meeting in the autumn of 2006 he invited his management team to follow him downstairs to his secret "war room". This war room is just a room; but the four walls are covered with cards with graphics and diagrams in the codes red, orange and green based on the emerging situations in the company. The layoff of the 80,000 employees has the code green. Products and markets have various colours: red, orange and green. This is Mulally's way of making visual Ford's battleground, with the intention of constantly seeing changes in the competitive landscape of the automotive sector in order to act.

Such a war room with the complete battlefield of the company and the sector is very much to be recommended, not only in crisis situations. How does management hope to compete unless a constant eye is kept on the rapid and dramatic changes in the competitive environment?

I recommend to the management of every company to establish such a war room to protect management from blind spots, complacency and arrogance. Success breeds failure. It enables management to act quickly on external changes, because the most important decisions are not taken inside your company but outside your company. Another example of blind spots is Youtube, which has been acquired by Google in October 2006 at a cost of US$ 1.6 billion. Youtube was been founded early in 2005. Neither Google, Yahoo nor Microsoft anticipated this development, and all were blind-sided. Don't forget: the outside world and management must establish a competitive intelligence regime in order to avoid failing to see new opportunities in time.

"When you hire people who are smarter than you are, you prove you are smarter than they are".
(R.H.Grant)

Competitive intelligence goes far beyond marketing intelligence and deals with all aspects of the business in the fast changing environment in the competitive arena. It's not about the past or the present. It's about the future. It's beyond information that is already known, about significant insights and foresights, about early warnings, about the full understanding of the patterns, events, business recipe and strategic issues, about supporting evidence in difficult situations, asking the questions "What if?" It's about mobilizing the knowledge people in quick assessments for current and future decision-making. A way of looking differently so as to uncover the common ways of thinking and identifying the unusual patterns as they occur.

I once read a good example of how to look at problems in a different way. In World War II Britain was hard-pressed and had suffered many losses of aircraft. One possible option was to wait and see and hope for better luck. The British and US military joined forces to find out what could be done. The planes that did come back were badly damaged and one obvious option was to increase survivability and to reinforce those areas of the planes that were damaged. However, the losses of aircraft continued. Then one night in a brainstorming session one man suddenly realised that, because they couldn't examine the planes that didn't come back, perhaps the answer was to reinforce the undamaged planes that returned, rather than those that were. The result was a dramatic and consistent reduction in the number of aircraft lost throughout the rest of the war.

Competitive intelligence moving in

In the mid 1980s the business world became aware of competitive intelligence. Benchmarking 'ruled the roost' in those years. In the 1990s, competitive intelligence received the attention of top management, and an increasing number of companies developed resources dedicated to this new field. Competitor analysis and intelligence became much more important, although they became a subject of increasing importance in the various marketing departments.

Important contributions to the field were made by management gurus like Levitt, Kotler, Ansoff and Porter, who have written numerous books about the importance of external orientation for every business, small, medium or large.

In most companies external orientation is the domain of marketing departments. They deal with customers, markets and competition, and have access to the internal data and information and use external market research, ad hoc or continuous monitoring by third parties as Nielsen, IMS, GfK, Gartner, Forrester, Datamonitor, etc. A great majority of companies can access the same information and information sources as their rivals can. So the analysis of the information will be of great importance. I have listed below the analysis tools most frequently used by marketers:
▶ PEST analysis
▶ SWOTI analysis

▶ Market segmentation analysis
▶ Competitor positioning analysis
▶ Five forces analysis

> *"To meet the great tasks that are before us, we require all our intelligence and we must be sound and wholesome in mind. We must proceed in order. The price of anger is failure".*
> (Elwood Hendricks)

Most such analyses are carried out on the tactical level and in most cases do not have any strategic level beyond the yearly marketing plan. What is missing is the identification of specific management needs for the mid and long term beyond the marketing function. What is needed is to have alternative information sources and to identify the need-to-know information required for decisions which will impact on the company over the next 1-3 years. Analysis tools capable of generating strategic intelligence are:

▶ Key Intelligence Topics
▶ Competitive intelligence brainstorming and assessments
▶ Early warning
▶ Scenario planning and analysis
▶ Strategic war mapping
▶ Trend analysis
▶ Forecasting based on business foresights
▶ Strategy under Uncertainty

I will describe some of the most applicable analysis tools and techniques later in chapter 18 of part II. I hope to have made clear that marketing intelligence has a more finite scope than competitive intelligence. Another aspect of influence is market research. Over the past 5-6 years I have seen many market research departments transformed into marketing intelligence or market intelligence departments. To my view this is a mere re-labelling of the same operations. Market researchers love their methodologies and techniques, unlike the management discipline of competitive intelligence. So, please, do not confuse market research with marketing intelligence, and leave competitive intelligence out of it.

> *"Positioning competitive intelligence as marketing intelligence and placing it within a marketing department is the kiss of death".*

Another aspect is the need to overcome internal assumptions, corporate taboos and myths, too much reliance on internal data- crunchers and a reluctance to tell management the brutal truth.

In competitive intelligence it is crucial to ask the right questions and to ask ourselves if we really know what we know but which may not be so. I have listed at page 148 four dimensions: what we know, what we'd like to know, what we think we know and what we don't know.

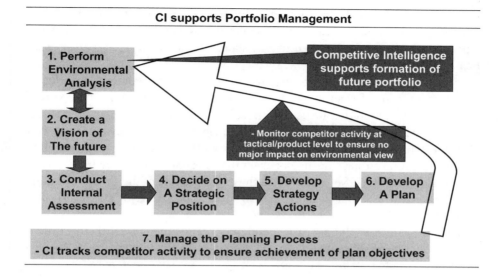

CI supports Portfolio Management

1. Perform Environmental Analysis

Competitive Intelligence supports formation of future portfolio

2. Create a Vision of The future

- Monitor competitor activity at tactical/product level to ensure no major impact on environmental view

3. Conduct Internal Assessment → **4. Decide on A Strategic Position** → **5. Develop Strategy Actions** → **6. Develop A Plan**

7. Manage the Planning Process
- CI tracks competitor activity to ensure achievement of plan objectives

Case: Corus

> *"It's not what we don't know that gives us trouble, it's what we know isn't so".*
> (Will Rogers)

This statement by Will Rogers really applied in the case of Corus, the merger of UK-based British Steel and Hoogovens in the Netherlands. I will briefly describe what happened at the time of the merger between these companies. When I worked on this case, based on an extensive research-based article in NRC, October 2002, I couldn't believe my ears and eyes.

In 1999, Hoogovens CEO, Fokko van Duyne, sensed that his counterpart CEO, John Bryant of British Steel, favoured a merger between the two companies. The former CEO of British Steel, Brian Moffat, had not succeeded in finding a suitable European partner for a merger. The Executive Team at Hoogovens took the initiative, opening discussions of a possible merger with British Steel. At the time, British Steel too was open to talks with the Dutch. In 1997 and 1998, British Steel was in profit, to the tune of 409 million and 276 million respectively. In 1999, British Steel made a loss; since the merger in 2000 up to 2005 the merged company Corus made only losses.

The management of Hoogovens observed only limited due diligence, thinking themselves sufficiently well informed with regard to British Steel. They didn't make the effort of visiting British Steel's plants in the UK to check and see their performance. Later, the facts came to light: "British Steel's production facilities had seen no investment since the middle ages".

The Board of British Steel told the Dutch management of Hoogovens they wanted to have the same strategy as Hoogovens based on a focus on R and D and "specialties". "We really believed them", stated one member of the Supervisory Board of Hoogovens.

The management of British Steel saw Hoogovens as the leader in the industry and saws a means of improving their own loss-making activities. The Board of Hoogovens was proud that British Steel, with much bigger sales, regarded Hoogovens as the leader within the sector. This contributed tremendously to the "complacency" which already existed in Hoogovens, which at that time was an arrogant company with no strong external focus on the external business environment.

The Board of Hoogovens calculated the exchange rate of the British Pound at 2.50. However, the actual exchange rate in 1999-2000 was 3.50. The Board speculated on a depreciation of the British Pound down to 2.50.

Last but not least there was a "gentlemen's agreement", which the British management were subsequently unable to recall. The management of Hoogovens were forced to conclude, in 2002: "collectively, we have been naïve".

> *"The truest characters of ignorance are vanity, pride and arrogance".*
> (Samuel Butler)

What can be learnt from this dramatic merger of Hoogovens and British Steel, resulting in the new company name Corus? In my view this represents a violation of all aspects of competitive intelligence:
- ▶ no or limited due diligence;
- ▶ speculation is not a word we use in competitive intelligence;
- ▶ no thorough analysis of the real intentions and ambitions of the management of British Steel;
- ▶ no analysis of the blind spots in strategies;
- ▶ arrogance and complacency;
- ▶ very naïve management;

Andrew Grove, former CEO of Intel, wrote in 1996 entitled "Only the Paranoid survive". The management of Hoogovens should have been more paranoid!

However, some years later I read an interview with Philippe Varin, CEO of Corus, in the FD of August 31 2006. The question the journalist asked was: "Competition also cuts cost. What is the operational margin of Corus compared to competition?" CEO Philippe Varin answered as follows:
- ▶ "The last time we measured this was in 2005. At that time we were lagging behind our European competitors by 4.5 points (EBIT)";
- ▶ "Because of all the changes in our sector, the merger between Mittal and Arcelor, we don't have access to the right data";
- ▶ "Qualitatively, we probably haven't improved compared to 2005".

We might conclude that since then not much has improved at Corus. If a company is unable to compare some basic key competitive financial ratios such as EBIT over a period in excess of nine months, something must be seriously wrong. I was amazed to hear no reaction to this response by Philippe Varin of Corus from the financial press or from analysts in financial institutes. In competitive intelligence, paranoia drives us constantly to ask "WHY".

The role of information technology

"Competitive intelligence is not a database".

Competitive intelligence is not an information technology solution. It is a strategic supportive capability to help us to structure and order the vast streams of data and information. For years, the IT sector has offered business intelligence solutions, but this is software and not analysed information. Competitive intelligence is not a database. There are a variety of IT-based tools available to support the competitive intelligence activities and to share information. Such tools include web-based portals, intranets and groupware like Microsoft Exchange, Microsoft Sharepoint and Lotus Notes. These IT tools should never be the end objective for the establishment of a competitive intelligence capability, and should only be used to enable us to create a kind of shared information platform.

In some cases companies call their competitive intelligence activities business intelligence, because business intelligence covers the intelligence of the whole business. In such cases competitive intelligence is seen as an intelligence activity in respect of competitors. It is a basic misunderstanding to see competitive intelligence as just an intelligence activity focusing on competition. However, intelligence focused on competitors is called competitor intelligence.

Unfortunately, the IT world has adopted the term 'business intelligence' for many software solutions. They still don't bring one ounce of intelligence. Intelligence is created by people and not by implementing business intelligence based software. Since the mid 1990s the IT world has been promising us that their business intelligence solutions will increase "intelligence". Briefly stated, the aim of business intelligence software solutions is to better understand the internal data and information flows, better structuring and ordering of the enormous streams of information and ensuring appropriate access to it. Questions business intelligence tries to answer are the crucial facts of evidence out of the vast volumes of internal data. Almost every organisation has installed one or more business intelligence solutions. Most are difficult to use as well to understand because of their complexity. An additional problem in many organisations is that much of the data and information is out-dated and therefore no longer reliable. Another problem is that many business intelligence software solutions are not integrated, which means that different solutions run on different systems in different company functions. Since 2001-2002 the sector has succeeded in improving its software by developing more user-friendly solutions, clear performance indicators communicated by attractively designed dashboards. These improvements could lead to a more strategic use of business intelligence, however they do still have a mainly internal focus.

> *"Most number crunching tools, often referred to as business intelligence tools, are typically considered inappropriate as they focus on quantitative information. The focus of competitive intelligence is on actionable intelligence from qualitative information and processes".*

Since 2002 I have been addressing and chairing National Business Intelligence Congresses as well as congresses of the Butler Group in the Netherlands. I have presented at these events my vision on topics such as strategic information management, business and competitive intelligence, strategic intelligence, etc. The audience is interested in these and has commented favourably over the years. During breaks and lunches I have spoken with many participants at these events, amongst them CIOs, CFOs, IT specialists, controllers, business consultants and directors. They all agreed with me on the strategic importance of competitive intelligence for senior management, however, they all showed only interest in the short term. They agreed on the importance of "outside in", but were unable to act. In most companies in Europe the aim of strategies focuses on cost cutting and improvement in efficiency rather than on innovation. I call this "strategy of exploitation" executed with the management style of managers whom I call "shopkeepers", i.e., those who mind the shop. The opposite is "strategy of exploration" executed by entrepreneurs, who always have themes on the agenda such as innovation and business development. Competitive intelligence is best covered by the "strategy of exploration": because of its infinite scope, competitive intelligence is unending. To me this is one of the key reasons why competitive intelligence is difficult to understand and above all difficult to accept because of its completely different aims and scope.

> *"You can only win the 'war' with ideas, not with spending cuts".*
> (Klaus Kleinfeld, CEO of Siemens)

The key elements in competitive intelligence

"In many cases certain people and external forces are blamed for failure. This means management can avoid redefining their basic assumptions. Potential failures are seen as the evidence of inadequate execution of the strategies rather than acknowledging that the wrong decisions have been made".

The aim of competitive intelligence focuses on the immediate future. A good starting-point is a brief overview of the history of the organisation and its successes in the past in the competitive arena. It is recommended that this be done also for the present. How has the organisation performed, what have been the successes and failures, how does the competitive landscape currently look and where do we want to go?

In the diagrams you see that competitive intelligence is part of the strategy process towards the input for the development of the future portfolio: an important role with a specific focus on strategic intelligence. The other important role of competitive intelligence is to monitor the tactical and operational changes in the competitive environment, which enables management to act appropriately.

There are not many banks which have a competitive intelligence regime in place. They desperately need it. Consider the banking world with the highly paid analysts as an example. The leading financial information provider Bloomberg did researched the ability of analysts to forecast stock prices. The research was conducted over two years, from August 2004 – 2006, in 350 financial institutions with over 2,500 analysts. The findings were dramatic: at Merrill Lynch 34 percent of forecasts were correct, at UBS and Credit Suisse the percentages were 29 and 26 and in number ten on the list, Citigroup, the percentage was 16.

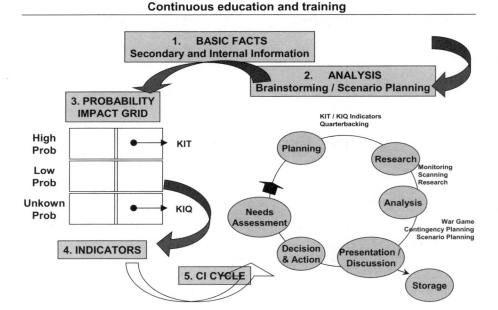

In the diagram on page 153 you see the six major steps in developing strategies and especially the vision for the future. It's certainly not a matter of predicting the future, but well-applied competitive intelligence enables management to foresee the future events. In phase 7 you see the crucial role of competitive intelligence as it also leads the planning process and the monitoring of competitive activities. A competitive intelligence regime within a company is able to do this, because competitive intelligence is future-oriented and is the continuous activity of bringing in outside information.

Of course, you may ask whether getting outside information in from the dynamics in the company's business environment is the task of marketing and other company departments. Indeed, marketing departments should do this, but they do not. In most companies marketing is a downstream activity focusing on existing markets, current customers, branding, promotions and advertising. But upstream activities are essential to marketing. Innovation, business development, unmet customer needs, and new channels are key themes in upstream marketing, which I call intelligence or evidence-based marketing. However, research has found that marketing departments are not keen on planning, research and analysis; where they do carry out research, in most cases this is traditional market research which also, in most cases, has been outsourced to third parties. You have probably seen in many companies the numerous customer satisfaction research studies which provide handy rankings but don't you tell anything about WHY. In 2005 Jack Welch, former CEO of GE, and Suzy Welch, former chief editor of

Harvard Business Review, published one of the best selling management books in the US in 2005, entitled "Winning".

One of the key statements they made was: "Customer satisfaction measurement can be obtained by traditional surveys, but those are rarely enough to give you the gritty data you need for a real read of the customer. Find out if each customer would recommend your products and services".

So, if marketing is not able to bring the outside world in, in a structured and consistent way, who else should do this within the organisation? Sales people will not do this, nor will strategists. If you want to continue the business as it is, management can of course do this by gathering the pieces of information, unstructured and ad hoc. Business as usual, then, and don't get angry if you are overtaken by future events, new initiatives on the part of rivals, new regulations, new players in the market or new and disruptive technologies. The most important decisions are not taken inside but outside the company.

Case: European beer market "Beer industry has been asleep for years"

This was the newspaper heading on February 24 2005. We have been looking at each other instead of looking at the changing drinking needs of the consumers. We are lagging behind developments. Beer has become a mass product, which has been under pressure from other beverages such as cocktails and wine. In addition, management has been looking too much towards other promising prospective markets such as China and Russia. The sector has forgotten all about the 'goose that laid the golden eggs", Europe. Innovation should be the new saviour for the productive development of the brewing industry.

Competitive intelligence can play this crucial role but management and employees in companies need to be taught how to do this by responding to the following questions:
1. What kind of data and information does the management of the company need?
2. Where is this kind of information available?
3. What are the most important information sources?
4. How does information from these selected information sources to be brought in, in a structured way?
5. How do we separate need-to-know information from good-to-know information?
6. How do we balance need-to-know information with the real information needs?
7. How do we organise data and information entry?
8. How do we identify real information needs?
9. What about the existing knowledge? How do we make it accessible?
10. How do we manage the sharing of tacit knowledge?
11. How do we divide tactical information with strategic information?

12. How do we transform information and knowledge into intelligence?
13. Do we continue to send out hundreds of emails daily which someone thinks could be relevant?
14. How do we create an alert?
15. How do we create early warnings?
16. How do we ensure that the key company departments communicate with each other?
17. How do we ensure that the key company departments share key information?
18. Do people understand strategic information management?
19. What are the most applicable intelligence methodologies and techniques?
20. What kinds of analysis tools are best suited to run a successful competitive intelligence regime?
21. How do we organise potential intelligence assessments?
22. How do we create a culture of competitive intelligence?
23. What kind of pitfalls might await us?
24. What can we learn from other companies: best practice and worst practice?
25. How can an IT solution be of support?

From my experience with the implementation process of competitive intelligence within numerous companies throughout Europe, I have discovered how difficult it is for many managers to deal with information and strategic information management. In addition, I have faced many difficulties with management teams regarding the transformation of vast streams of information into competitive intelligence. Even in the numerous international Master Classes on competitive intelligence that I taught since 2003, I saw how difficult it is to manage information in the right way and to extract intelligence from properly. This implies that people need continuous training in competitive intelligence. The diagram at page 158 gives some insights into what I mean by continuous training and education.

The diagram gives an overview of some key topics in training in competitive intelligence. First of all, it is important to find out information about the basic facts. Secondary information sources are relatively easy to generate information from. A real challenge is to gather the information from inside the company. In most cases the information is available, however, it is difficult to track and in addition difficult to access. As a next step, we have to interpret the available information and to make an initial analysis. Then we shall be able to assess the probability of the potential impact. If the impact is likely to be profound, we may make an additional effort with a KIT, Key Intelligence Topic. If we don't have any idea, we should come to a KIQ, Key Intelligence Question. From both the KIT and the KIQ we are able to derive indicators to be used as input into the competitive intelligence cycle: needs assessment (1), planning (2), research (3), analysis (4), presentation and discussion (5), leading to the final decision and action to be taken.

Types of Competitive Intelligence

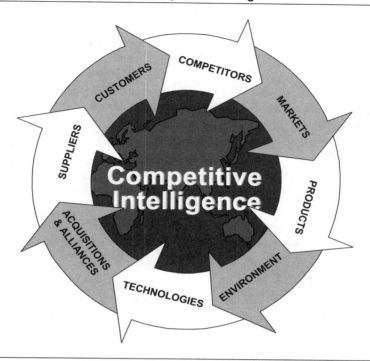

Case: IBM

"We get up every morning and think about killing IBM".

A competitor of IBM made this statement in 1990. At the time Lou Gerstner came into IBM in the early 1990s, competitive intelligence took off within the business units. IBM found out that many business units used a silo approach to intelligence-gathering during this period. In the late 1990s, the company restructured their intelligence activities towards a corporate intelligence capability, challenging their way of thinking. In 2006-2008 the company changed their intelligence efforts into three areas of excellence as shown in the diagram below.

The evolution of CI at IBM		
Early 1990s	**Late 1990s**	**2006 – 2008**
• Isolated in BUs • Silos approach in intelligence gathering • Lou Gerstner	• Need for synergy • Centralized approach • Corporate CI Team	• 3 Centres of Excellence • Virtual & cross functional teams • 12 senior executives responsible for 12 key competitors

Source: IBM

As can be seen from the diagram above, IBM took another two important decisions: They created around the three centres of excellence virtual and cross-functional teams so as to derive maximum benefit from information and knowledge-sharing throughout the company. They have identified 12 key competitors and made 12 Vice-Presidents responsible for them as centralized intelligence hubs.

Competitive intelligence in IBM has been defined as follows: "CI is the process of enhancing marketplace competitiveness through a greater understanding of our rivals with the aim of obtaining insights into the environment in which you choose to compete".

Interestingly, IBM identified four key threat levels which originate from environmental factors driving competitiveness (1), alliances and partnerships (2), overall firm-based factors such as finance (3) and new offerings of specific attributes which bring competitive advantages to rivals (4). Based on these threats IBM classified them into four levels:

1. Current and near term threats: fast growing with strong competitive differentiation;
2. Established threats: mature companies with medium to strong competitive differentiation;
3. Longer term strategic threats: young and new market entrants;
4. Diminishing threats: mature companies with falling competitive strategies.

The key challenges are how to sustain competitiveness as market dynamics evolve, to understand what are the key attributes of market competitiveness and how to maintain or re-invent competitive differentiation of these attributes. For these three challenges IBM uses three definitions of competitiveness. Firstly, the competitiveness which represents the overall competitive threat of a company within the market. Secondly, the revenue, which represents the maturity of the company. Thirdly, the bubble-size which represents the growth rate and gives indications of the level of success of the firm's chosen strategies in the marketplace.

IBM also expressed some final thoughts, in which the key factor is obtaining a broad overview of the competitive landscape. They recommend the following "don'ts" and "do's" and some traps to avoid when addressing the question of competitive intelligence:

▶ Don't think only of the obvious competitors, but think of how competitors' core skills could be dealt with;
▶ Don't just think in market shares, revenues, growth or finance, but recognize quantitative and qualitative assessments;
▶ Don't think in terms of "single" lines of business, but think about the "whole" business and acknowledge blurred boundaries;
▶ Don't just think about threats now this minute, but look to the future and beyond the "usual bad guys";
▶ Don't fall into the trap of "hotline" mode to respond to answering competitive questions, but feed and shape the need for the right information and become trusted and pro-active;
▶ Don't fall into the trap of becoming data-addicted, but deduce the data needed from the potential business needs;
▶ Don't fall into the trap of the "Stockholm Syndrome"("my competitor is the most dangerous in the world), but respect the competition, while retaining the IBM sales confidence;
▶ Don't fall into the trap of chopping and changing, but continue to work on selected competitors.

The case of IBM offers a good example of how a major multinational company manages its competitive intelligence competences. At IBM competitive intelligence is fully integrated in the daily operations, is part of the strategy process and is fully accepted by top management.

"Intelligence is an inescapable part of every decision we make in business today".

Frequently, management's first reaction to the subject of competitive intelligence is "that's about competition" or "about competitor analysis". That is incorrect, as may be seen from the example of IBM and many others. Competitive intelligence is much more and goes far beyond traditional competitor analysis. Consider all the aspects competitive intelligence deals with:

▶ identifying opportunities for competitive advantages;
▶ discovering the causes of competitive shortcomings;
▶ exploring and filling knowledge gaps;

▶ sharing of know-how in problem solving;
▶ creating new knowledge and permanent learning;
▶ shaping strategies that will drive sustainable advantages;
▶ challenging conventional wisdom and questioning assumptions;
▶ creating a provocative look at the competitive environment;
▶ meeting the unique information needs because every business is unique;

Competitor analysis cannot provide these answers. To remain competitive, a company needs to support its current position and orchestrate its future position. By doing this an organisation can become a real winner, with sufficient flexibility to create and maintain sustainable competitive advantage. This means that competitive intelligence deals with all aspects, which influence the current and future competitive position.

Case: Dutch politics

A good example may be taken from Dutch politics. Both the decisions were crucial decisions for the future. The first was the election of the new leader of the Liberal Party VVD. Although the whole nation knew that Mrs. Rita Verdonk was very popular among Liberal Party voters, the party leaders and other members of the party decided differently. After Summer 2006, the party leaders decided to organise elections for the new leader only among the party membership, completely ignoring the factors in the external political situation in the Netherlands. By a very small majority, the members of the Liberal Party elected Mark Rutte as the new leader. In the national parliamentary elections in November 2006, the Liberals took a drubbing, losing six seats in parliament. Another embarrassment was that Mrs.Verdonk got more votes than Mr.Rutte, compounded by the fact that after the election the party leadership announced that no mistake had been made.

With this decision they scored an own goal and will probably find themselves in Opposition for the next few years, from 2007-2010.

> "The state is made for man, no man for the state".
> (Albert Einstein)

In contrast the Labour Party adopted a very clever strategy. After the elections in November 2006 it was expected that the Labour Party would be asked to form a new government with the Christian Democrats (CDA) led by Prime Minister Jan Peter Balkenende. In 2002, both parties were also involved in coalition negotiations with the aim of forming a coalition government. They failed because they didn't understand each other well and because of a huge lack of trust. In 2003, Labour party leader Wouter Bos, previously been with Royal Dutch Shell for ten years, decided to prepare himself better for the potential coalition negotiations in 2007, or earlier, in the event of a potential fall of the Balkenende administration in parliament. To support him in the coalition negotiations in January 2007 Mr. Bos decided not to appoint his second in command in accordance with hierarchy, but rather to have the best intelligence-based person as his second in the coalition negotiations. This was Jacques Tichelaar, number 13 on the candidate list of the Labour Party. How did Mr.Tichelaar gather his intelligence to prepare the Labour Party for successful negotiations?

▶ Identifying the potential "breaking points" within other parties in parliament with a special focus on the Christian Democrats CDA;
▶ Already in 2003, Mr. Tichelaar became the so-called "spy" on the Christian Democrats,
▶ Focus of his intelligence efforts:
   1. identifying the atmosphere within the Christian Democratic Party
   2. identifying the individuals influence
   3. identifying the atmosphere within other political parties
   4. being present as guest at all conferences of the Christian Democratic Party.

This example of the Labour Party is an excellent one which demonstrates how intelligence can contribute in such a difficult situation as the formation of a coalition government. I assume that Mr.Bos, during his time with Royal Dutch Shell, had become aware of the great contribution information and knowledge-based intelligence can have at both the organisational and individual levels. This example is comparable with that of IBM, who decided to appoint twelve vice-presidents for twelve key competitors.

The diagram at page 161 shows which areas of intelligence cover competitive intelligence activities.

Characteristics of CI
• Future focused
• Pro-active
• Continuous monitoring
• Direct linked to decision making
• Linked to strategic management
• Perspective in stead of precision
• Qualitative information
• Analysis & interpretation
• Knowledge sharing
• People's business
• External developments translated towards the internal organization
• Published & non-published information

This diagram at page 161 shows the related areas of competitive intelligence: markets, products and services, the environment, technologies and R and D, mergers, acquisitions and alliances, supplies, customers and competitors. The placing of the chief emphasis depends on the activities of the organisation. But simply being active in market intelligence or competitor intelligence doesn't bring the in-depth business insights which are needed for successful competition. Many organisations do have a market intelligence or marketing intelligence activity in place; but this lacks the perspective which competitive intelligence should bring. In addition, there is the current a trend to re-brand market research, marketing services or market support as marketing intelligence. But the main focus of these intelligence activities is market and competition. The biggest problem is that the intelligence is limited within the marketing department, where intelligence is reported to a marketing manager or marketing director.

Positioning competitive intelligence within marketing intelligence or within a marketing department is the kiss of death. Evidence for this is given in the diagram at page 165, with an overview of the key characteristics of competitive intelligence.

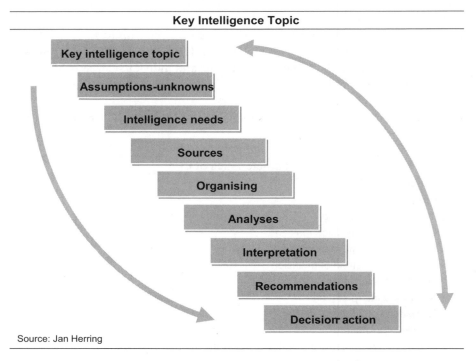

Key Intelligence Topic

Key intelligence topic
Assumptions-unknowns
Intelligence needs
Sources
Organising
Analyses
Interpretation
Recommendations
Decision action

Source: Jan Herring

A good example of how Royal Dutch Shell sees competitive intelligence is the further strengthening of the characteristics: the 'seven guiding principles of competitive intelligence' (CI):

1. CI is a line responsibility
2. CI supports decisive action
3. CI covers the entire competitive environment
4. CI is not about the past, but the future
5. CI is not founded on the Internet, but created by people
6. CI is about the brutal truth
7. CI is done legally and ethically

"Error is not a fault of our knowledge, but a mistake of our judgement giving assent to that which is not true." In Shell, the competitive intelligence activities are not executed by staff. Decisive action means that we are talking about actionable intelligence. It's about the entire competitive environment and not just small parts of the business environment. All aspects of the external business environment are involved. The aim of competitive intelligence is about the future, future events which can be foreseen and not about the past or history. Although a vast majority of managers frequently consult various Internet websites for information, this is not intelligence. The result of intelligence is making your interpretations, doing your analysis, making the appropriate recommendations and action. This result is not always what management likes to hear; it may not confirm or conform to their assumptions. Competitive intelligence is a critical analysis with a potential result which may not always be pleasing to management. Especially in the case of mergers and acquisitions, where competitive intelligence might conclude that the decision to acquire or to merge is inadvisable. This is the brutal truth and it might lead to potential conflicts with the sizable egos of key decision-makers or with the board of management. In such cases, it should never be forgotten that the competitive intelligence professionals are acting in the company's interests. Finally, competitive intelligence is always done legally and ethically. SCIP, the International Society of Competitive Intelligence Professionals, uses a Code of Ethics which might be applicable in cases of doubt:

▶ To continually strive to increase the recognition and respect of the profession;
▶ To comply with all applicable laws, domestic and international;
▶ To accurately disclose all relevant information, including one's identity and organisation, prior to all interviews;
▶ To avoid conflicts of interest in fulfilling one's duties;
▶ To provide honest and realistic recommendations and conclusions in the execution of one's duties;
▶ To promote this code of ethics within one's company, with third-party contractors within the entire profession;
▶ To faithfully adhere to and abide by one's company policies, objectives and guidelines;

Carrying out competitive intelligence endeavours in accordance with this Code of Ethics will never put you in danger or discussion. As one of the initiators of the competitive intelligence discipline in companies, I was amused in the late 1980s when the Dutch National Intelligence Agency in the Netherlands paid me a visit to discover what I was planning to do with intelligence for organisations and companies. At that time I was also frequently asked for interviews by television, radio and other media to explain competitive intelligence. I quickly learned that you should always require to see a copy before it is broadcasted. This helped me avoid CIA or KGB content, so dear to the hearts of journalists.

Case: Boeing looking for a new enemy

I already described how Boeing misled Airbus with the development of their new aircraft Dreamliner. Airbus announced in the late 1990s that they were developing the biggest passenger aircraft with a passenger capacity of 600-800. Boeing responded with the announcement that they were developing a larger plane too, based on the Jumbo 747. However, Boeing also had another vision and started at the same time developing the successful Dreamliner, which will be "in the air" in 2007-2008. In 2005, Airbus found out about the Dreamliner and Boeing's new strategy. Airbus continued to struggle with the test flights of the A380 and faced huge problems of late delivery. The number of new orders also suffered.

"Your worst enemy is always a man of your own trade".

Another strategy adopted by Boeing was to seek a new target: the EU subsidies for the Airbus. Boeing confronted the EU with the subsidies accorded to Airbus, which were seen to be in contravention of WTO. This battle, initiated by Boeing, lasted for two years and in the meantime Boeing continued to restructure, in addition the strong focus on the development of the new Dreamliner. Clearly, this was a highly intelligent competitive strategy which misled Airbus dramatically.

At the end of my many presentations to boards of management throughout across Europe, I always used the famous categories of companies devised by Peter Drucker, to act or not to act and how competitive intelligence can prevent management from trading on past successes, and avoid complacency and arrogance:
1. Companies that make things happen
2. Companies that watch things happen
3. Companies that wonder what happened

Boards of Management like these very well-known categories; but in recent years and still today many companies are wondering what has happened to them. Some examples: KPN Qwest, DAF Trucks, US Car industry, US Consumer electronics industry, Polaroid, Belgian Sabena Airlines, Swiss Airlines, Dutch Fokker Aircraft Industries, Arthur Andersen, Enron, Parmalat, Dutch Ahold, British Steel/ Dutch Hoogovens (now Corus), Levi's etc.

"The fundamental qualities for good execution of a business plan are, first, naturally – intelligence-. Then discernment and judgment which enables one to recognize the best methods to attain it. Then singleness of purpose and lastly what is most important of all "stubborn will". His thought and faith must be communicated to those he leads. He and they must form as one at the moment of executing the plan. That is the essential condition of success".
(Ferdinand Foch)

II.1 KITs: Key Intelligence Topics

"What keeps management awake at night?"

KITs are important or strategic issues of high concern to the management of an organisation. In most cases they are crucial and therefore very important for the focus, on a case-to-case basis, of competitive intelligence efforts in a structured way. Examples of key intelligence topics can be:
▶ Analysis of new potential competitors beyond the business horizon;
▶ New disruptive technologies impacting on the company in 2-3 years' time;
▶ Innovation from new market entrants;
▶ Emerging future trends;
▶ Identifying future unmet customer needs;
▶ New entrants from India, Russia and China into the European market;
▶ Other events likely to influence the future existence of the business;
▶ Consequences of a merger related to the competitive positioning.

A key intelligence topic analysis has nine steps which must be taken in a structured way as shown in the diagram at page 166.

I will describe the nine steps necessary for a key intelligence topic in more detail.
1. Key intelligence topic. An important aspect is to define the key intelligence topic, frame it, timeline it, define the urgency and the strategic impact and define the kind of decision we are intending to take.
2. Assumptions/unknowns. What do we think we know, what are our assumptions, what are our doubts and where are potential blind spots?
3. Intelligence needs. What kind of information do we need, how do we get the information, where are the pieces of the information puzzle located, what does the big picture look like?

Intelligence based Executive Decision Model

Executive Decision Model	Tips for Successful use

Executive Decision Model

1. Situation Description (facts/data):

   _____

   _____

2. Analysis/Explanation/Interpretation (impact):

   _____

   _____

3. Options (pathways to a solution):

   _____

   _____

4. Recommendations (If I were you, here's what I'd do.)

   _____

   _____

5. Negative unintended consequences:

   _____

Tips for Successful use

1. Keep it one page, one side.
2. Use positive, direct, power language.
3. Provide at least three options, one being doing nothing.
4. Put yourself in the boss' shoes when you decide which of the options you're going to select as your recommendation.
5. Forecast collateral damage.

Source: James Lukaszewski

---

4. Sources. What kinds of information sources are indicated? The first dimension is internal versus external information. In most organisations we can obtain the necessary information from internal sources. So we should ask ourselves the question: who within the company might possess the information we are looking for? Which company departments might be of help to us? The second dimension is secondary versus the primary information sources. Secondary sources are those sources such as all kinds of publications, Internet information, and the widely available commercial on-line databases such as Datastar, Dialog, Reuters, Bloomberg, etc. Primary sources are information from people, generated by interviews and dialogue. The third dimension is hard versus soft information. Hard information is quantitative data, figures, statistics, research; soft information is indicative and qualitative. The successful generation of information is mainly a matter of creativity.

5. Organising. How will the information gathering be organised and how can a joint effort be realised? Information assessments are a very effective way of collecting information in an organised way. At this stage it is also of prime importance to share the information among the people involved.

6. Analysis. This is one of the most important aspects of a key intelligence topic as well as of competitive intelligence as a whole. However, analysis is difficult

to conduct and few people are able to produce a successful analysis. A further aspect is which analysis tools can be used in the best way?

7. Interpretation. Another key aspect in a key intelligence topic is how we deal with our interpretations. It's all about seeing, seeking, using and sharing the information along the four ways of approach, as described in the diagrams on page 174.

8. Recommendations. Approaching a key intelligence topic without making the appropriate recommendations makes a KIT useless. We are able to make the right recommendations because we have been through the complete situation step-by-step and have put together all the pieces of the puzzle. If we still lack some crucial pieces of information we should define the gaps. Good recommendations can be made on thorough analysis, realistic assumptions, options analysis and by developing potential scenarios. In practice, many times we make recommendations based on a lack of good information. Moreover, recommendations are often made as summaries of key findings. This is not intelligence.

9. Decision. In management decision-making is the most difficult task. But structured key intelligence topic processing makes it possible to make informed decisions because of the combination of at least 75-80 percent of the available information and knowledge, the right interpretations and the appropriate analyses. The result is an excellent intelligence analysis for decision-making.

> *"Unless a decision has generated into work, it's not a decision. It's at best a good intention. While the effective decision itself is based on the highest level of conceptual understanding, the action commitment should be as close as possible to the capacities of the people who have to carry it out".*

To show how a key intelligence topic can be executed, I describe in the diagrams on page 172-173 the key intelligence topic of the US government before the war in Iraq in early 2003. We are all experts and we all have our opinion as to whether the decision of the Bush administration to start the war in Iraq was correct. The case description has been complied from information and analysis in the Financial Times in February 2004.

Bad decisions can often be traced back to the way the decisions were made. The alternatives were not clearly defined, the right information was not collected, the cost and benefits were not accurately assessed, and there was a lack of intelligence. But sometimes the fault lies not in the decision-making process but rather in the minds of the decision-makers. The way the human brain works can sabotage the choices we make.

> *"Don't fall in love with your decisions. Everything is fluid. You have to constantly, subtly make and adjust your decisions".*

KIT Comparison to decision to invade IRAQ

---

1. Key Intelligence Topic: - Does Iraq has WMD?
2. Assumptions-unknown:
   Assumptions - Iraq has the capability to produce WND
   - Iraq has the infrastructure capabilities
   - Iraq is a treat to global stability
   - Is Iraq able tot translate these intentions into reality
   Unknown   - Does Iraq has WMD?

3. Intelligence needs: - We have to know the information based
   facts Iraq has WMD
   - If yes, what is the intention of the Iraqi
   government?
4. Sources: - Unscom 1991 – 1998
   - Iraq dissident groups
   - Watching by satellites
   - Public sources

KIT Comparison to decision to invade IRAQ

---

5. Organizing: - Getting access to Unscom sources
   - Intelligence Sharing between Allies: US, UK, France,
   Israel, Germany

6. Analysis: - CIA en MI are leading in appropriate analyses
   - Wrong information rather than good analysis
   - Pressure of policy makers

7. Interpretation: - Lack of actual information; CIA didn't have a
   single source in Iraq
   - Incompleteness of the information
   - No increase in intelligence
   - Sharing between the allies
   - Disagreement among intelligence agencies
   about the important claim relating to Iraq's
   effort to acquire more than 100.000 high
   strength aluminum tubes, cited as
   evidence of Iraq's nuclear ambitions by Colin Powell

KIT Comparison to decision to invade IRAQ

8. Recommendations: - "Our analysis will be shown to be the best and most reasonable analysis that could have been done with the information we had in those circumstances"

9. Decision – action: - US National Intelligence Council on the eve of the war:
"Since UN inspections ended in 1998 Iraq has maintained its chemical weapons efforts, energized its missile program, and invested more heavily in biological weapons; in view of most agencies, Bagdad is reconstituting its nuclear weapons program".

   - Early March 2003 President Bush started the war in Iraq

KIT Comparison to decision to invade IRAQ

Lessons Learned:
- ⟍ Incompleteness of information
- ⟍ No hard facts
- ⟍ Lacking human intelligence
- ⟍ Lack of sharing intelligence among allies
- ⟍ Raw intelligence has been channeled to policy makers: this is seen as irregular and unprofessional
- ⟍ Decision has been made on obvious gaps

Source:
KIT analysis based on "The sources seem to have been the problem ......
our analysis will be shown as the best that could have been done"
FT, February 3 2004

Case: Creating your future competitors

Companies always look for new opportunities for growth and sometimes they do this by creating their own new competitors in the near future. Are they forced to do this or is this a kind of naïve management? I will describe three examples of companies, which create their own future competitors.

The first example is the German machinery equipment industry sector. Germany is famous for its very high quality machinery equipment, with many players in SMEs. In the last couple of years much machinery equipment has been exported to the Far East, especially China. Now the German and European markets face increasing imports of similar machinery equipment. For the German industry this means pressure on prices and margins because of the low cost-efficiency of Chinese imports.

> *"The Chinese have a burning ambition over the next 20-30 years to become an aircraft manufacturer, sending already thousands of aerospace engineers overseas to study".*
> (Thomas Enders, co-CEO of EADS)

Seeing-Seeking-Using-Sharing disconfirmed information

SEEING information
- Know what you are looking for and train your eyes: asking the critical questions will force you to pay attention to areas you are typically unaware of
- Develop an outsider's perspective: a person or group to tell you things you don't see from your vantage point - having more information at hand is critical

SEEKING information
- Challenge the absence of disconfirming evidence: receiving recommendations without contradictory information is a red flag – a maverick who argues another point of view –
- Under search in most contexts, however over search in crucial contexts: think about an implication of a error – over searching is then a wise strategy –

Source: adapted from HBR 1/2006

Seeing-Seeking-Using-Sharing disconfirmed information

USING information
- Unpack the situation: don't over emphasize on one focal event and discounting other relevant information – think about the full context of your situation –
- Assume that the information you need is in your company: around 60 percent of the information needs are within the organization

SHARING information
- Everyone has unique information, but ask for it explicitly – if not asked people will never know that the information might be of value to you –
- Create structures to make information sharing happen: a small team can be made responsible for assembling information from numerous sources

Source: adapted from HBR 1/2006

The second example is the decision by Airbus to build an assembly plant for the A320 in Tianjin, China. The reason for this is that Airbus aims to acquire a strong foothold in China's vast market in the long run. Until 2025 China will need over 2,000 new planes. Airbus states that an assembly plant is less technology-intensive than other parts of the aircraft-production process and will in addition not involve technology-trade issues. However, Airbus might create China's own commercial airliner industry in the long run. The Chinese government have already made clear that China hopes to develop her own aviation industry. The CEO of EADS, the French-German European Aeronautic Defence and Space company and owner of Airbus, stated in an interview in October 2006: "The Chinese have a burning ambition over the next 20-30 years to become an aircraft manufacturer, sending thousands of aerospace engineers overseas to study". How naïve can management be?

> *"Your suppliers have supply chains and their suppliers have supply chains, so people don't know what's from China".*
> (Beaumont Vance of Sun)

The third example describes China's supply chain risk by Sun Microsystems. Many companies heavily rely on components from China. Increasingly, China is selected because of cheap labour, cost and stability of manufacturing and the lack of labour unrest. The dependence on China is growing: "every single computer in the world right now has at least one critical component that is made in China". What will happen if China closes its borders or some other type of catastrophe occurs? Aon's 2006 political and economic risk map rates China as "medium-risk" on a scale of six levels ranging from low to high risk. Significant exposures to terrorism, economic perils or foreign exchange risk for companies doing business with China are not expected. Potential risks are identified concerning the possibilities of war, legal and regulatory actions, political interference and supply chain vulnerability.

Sun's risk management department has listed the potential risks and ranked them by severity and probability. Next, they ascertained to what extent each risk is mitigated in terms of insurance, alternative sourcing etc., resulting in "residual risks". The residual risk numbers are used to determine their strategies, based on a similar tool to identify terrorist risks by the CIA. Sun uses software which sorts through text, audio and video files in order to reveal key trends in risk drivers with the aim of predicting events. The system tracks non-political risks, government sanctions or embargo-related activities.

This example of Sun Microsystems doesn't give the insights in creating potential new competitors. However, there is no doubt that we create with the suppliers of components and beyond towards the Electronic Manufacturing Suppliers Providers (EMS), Contract Manufacturers (CM), the Original Brand Manufacturers (OBM) and the Original Design Manufacturers (ODM) our new competitors for the future. The example also gives a useful overview of how risk management and competitive intelligence interface.

However, companies have also begun to realise that there is a downside to being lean and mean. It can leave their supply chains with little flexibility if there is a disruption.

> *"The current emphasis on risks has put a lot of pressure on top management. Everybody realises that even an innocent scenario can become a nightmare if not properly managed. Senior management has no choice but to lead the process implementation of competitive intelligence, driving intelligence awareness through every level of the organisation. The real danger is that, still, senior management aren't up to this challenge".*

II.2   Information and information sources

> *"Information is disintegrated if you don't have your objectives to focus on".*

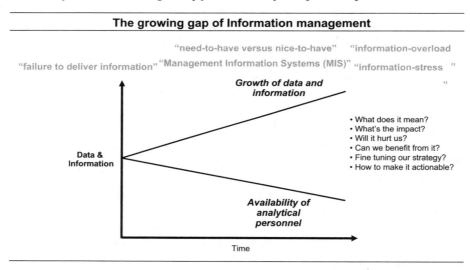

The growing gap of Information management

"need-to-have versus nice-to-have"   "information-overload"

"failure to deliver information" "Management Information Systems (MIS)" "information-stress "

Growth of data and information

Data & Information

• What does it mean?
• What's the impact?
• Will it hurt us?
• Can we benefit from it?
• Fine tuning our strategy?
• How to make it actionable?

Availability of analytical personnel

Time

We have to take into account that the volume of information in the world is doubling every 18 months. Unfortunately most organisations are in an information overload and management faces in their daily operations information stress. But information is the lifeblood of our organisations: how are we to survive in the information age making distinctions between the good-to-know information versus the need-to-know information. We all have the attitude that we should collect as much information as possible because we are afraid of missing some piece of information vital to us and vital to the organisation. Organisations have spent billions of Euros on information technology in order to make the internal streams of data and information structured, ordered and accessible. Since 1990, we have estimated these investments in information technology at around 16,000 – 25,000 billion Euros. But management in the business society still suffers from a lack of availability and access to the right information. We are drowning in information yet we still desperately need to have the right information.

In business we frequently hear that around 50 percent of all IT investments fail. How can we turn this around, how can we manage to have the right and needed information in our organisations? Another strategic issue in information management is how to get the right external information into our companies in a structured and consistent way. In the diagram below we see the overview of sources versus the information and dimensions in business information.

What are we talking about?

Sources		Information	
• **Primary** →	first hand	• **Qualitative** →	in context
• **Secondary** →	via via	• **Quantitative** →	focused on figures
• **Internal** →	internal info.+ external info.	• **Internal** → about own company	
• **External** →	external info.	• **External** → about environment	
		• **Hard** → facts, explicit	
• **Published** →	paper +electronically	• **Soft** → rumours, intuition	
• **Non-published** →	knowledge in heads of people		

Research methods

Desk research →	published & non--published (telephone)
Field research →	Non-published (face to face, telephone, observation, written, internet)

II.3   Information Audit

"Information is the lifeblood of our businesses".

The diagram "what are we talking about?" presents an overview of the aspects of information and the aspects of information sources. By conducting an information audit you will be able to identify exactly the information needs as well as the future scope of the information needs. An audit makes the information needs transparent and also makes it possible to identify gaps in the organisation's information needs. However, organisations change and re-organisation and restructuring take place at least every 2-3 years. But an audit is not a 'one-off' process. The business environment changes, organisations change and the information needs and streams change. So an information audit should take place regularly, based on the changing dynamics within the company's business environment.

Turning your internal information into the intelligence needs of today

The information audit should take place across the organisation and its outcome will be: identification of the information needs;
▶ an inventory of the available information and its value;
▶ identification of current expertise and current knowledge;
▶ identification of information gaps;
▶ a review of the use of external information and how it might be used more effectively and efficiently;
▶ a review of internal information sources, their values and what could be improved;
▶ a mapping of information streams and current bottlenecks within those information streams.

Today, information and knowledge are recognized as the core assets of any organisation and are potentially the source of an organisation's key and future competitive advantage. A good and thorough understanding of these assets and how they can be used to stimulate creativity and innovation are the key benefits of conducting an information audit. Management will make economically rational decisions if only they can accumulate sufficient information. The aim of the information audit is:
1. Making better use of intellectual assets;
2. Making better use of external information;
3. Avoiding of information inefficiencies and duplication;
4. Avoiding information overload and information stress;
5. Saving time and costs through efficiency and effectiveness.

The information audit results are a perfect basis for identifying the future information and strategy-based intelligence needs of the organisation.

The information sources of intelligence are not secret sources. Many people think that the main sources used within the intelligence agencies CIA, KGB, MI6, etc., are secret sources of information. Not so. Take the example of NATO. Up until the late 1990s NATO's intelligence sources were mainly based on classified information collection; only a small proportion was gleaned from Open Sources. In the years 2000-2001 NATO made a major shift towards making better use of Open Sources. In the diagram "Relevance of Open Sources" you will see the shift towards much greater use of Open Sources with the aim of plugging the gaps in intelligence-reporting.

Relevance of Open Sources

Change from classified sources to open sources

National Approach   NATO Approach
Information Requirements   Information Requirements

Classified Collection / Open Source

Open Source Collection / National Intel Contributions

Intelligence   Open Source
collection   collection
to fill gaps in unclassified   to fill gaps in intelligence
knowledge   reporting

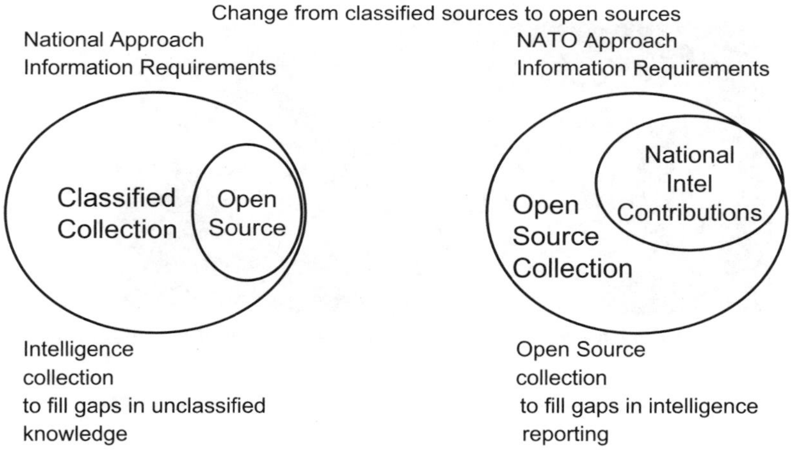

Source: NATO Open Source Intelligence Reader

II.4   Strategic Audit

"Consensus is good unless it is achieved too easily, in which case it becomes suspect".

The strategic audit is a systematic approach to define the requirements of the in-company competitive intelligence function. The challenge is to develop a competitive intelligence activity, capability or regime that accomplishes the key objectives and strategies of the organisation by identifying the key drivers of the way the company really competes within the competitive arena. The strategic audit may also be seen as a competitive intelligence needs assessment, which aims to:

1. Identify which markets, customers, competitors, products and services, technologies and legal issues should be monitored;
2. Identify possible future events which will have a potential impact on the strategic position of the company;
3. Identify the strategic input needed and expected by senior management;
4. Identify which analytical alerts, analysis tools, emerging early warnings might be applicable;
5. Identify the organisational needs, responsibilities and future competitive intelligence portfolio in the founding of the competitive intelligence capability;
6. Set competitive intelligence goals in line with the strategic business plan.

Providing a framework for a future focused competitive intelligence regime

In carrying out the strategic audit it is essential to understand the overall mission of the organisation as well as the specific strategies of the individual business units. The start of the strategic audit will be to identify also the strategic plans for the whole organisation as well as to identify the business plans of the specific business units involved in the founding of the competitive intelligence capability. Also, senior management must be interviewed; they must be asked the key questions about how the company competes in the marketplace, what are the strategies for the different markets, the key success factors and what are the differentiating factors in the competitive positioning.

To make the necessary shift towards a much greater focus on intelligence, it might be helpful to see the diagram "An ocean of information towards intelligence". In the strategic audit we go through this overview of what will really be needed in order to select the areas of relevance for the organisation. In addition, this offers a perfect overview of what a future competitive intelligence portfolio should look like.

An ocean of information towards intelligence

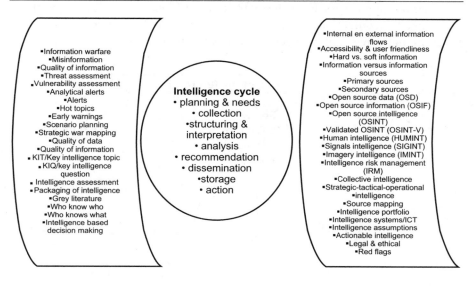

- Information warfare
- Misinformation
- Quality of information
- Threat assessment
- Vulnerability assessment
- Analytical alerts
- Alerts
- Hot topics
- Early warnings
- Scenario planning
- Strategic war mapping
- Quality of data
- Quality of information
- KIT/Key intelligence topic
- KIQ/key intelligence question
- Intelligence assessment
- Packaging of intelligence
- Grey literature
- Who know who
- Who knows what
- Intelligence based decision making

Intelligence cycle
- planning & needs
- collection
- structuring & interpretation
- analysis
- recommendation
- dissemination
- storage
- action

- Internal en external information flows
- Accessibility & user friendliness
- Hard vs. soft information
- Information versus information sources
- Primary sources
- Secondary sources
- Open source data (OSD)
- Open source information (OSIF)
- Open source intelligence (OSINT)
- Validated OSINT (OSINT-V)
- Human intelligence (HUMINT)
- Signals intelligence (SIGINT)
- Imagery intelligence (IMINT)
- Intelligence risk management (IRM)
- Collective intelligence
- Strategic-tactical-operational intelligence
- Source mapping
- Intelligence portfolio
- Intelligence systems/ICT
- Intelligence assumptions
- Actionable intelligence
- Legal & ethical
- Red flags

The outcome of a strategic audit is the knowledge of where to focus the organisation's strategic information needs, both internally and externally. As already explained, the dynamic changes in the external business environment are of strategic importance. Every manager is always looking for new opportunities in the outside world, yet at least 95 percent of organisations lack a structured way to seeing in time opportunities in the market place and space. We all are active in the strategic management processes and as a result we define our strategies and make our strategic choices for the near future. But what if all of a sudden new issues loom on the horizon and take us off our guard? In such cases, "strategy as active waiting" might be of relevance. I describe 'strategy as active waiting' below.

II.5 Strategy as Active Waiting

"Competitive intelligence serves, in effect, as the CEOs Chief of Staff".

Management always likes to discover the ultimate strategic opportunity. How can we take the time and make pro-active decisions on potential discoveries in the business environment? How can we innovate in time with the aim of making the best of new business opportunities? In most companies this is difficult; we have developed our strategies and made our strategic choices. We have learned not to change our strategies too quickly, but to give them time to bring results. But we still have no supportive solution to enable us to sniff out new business opportunities before the competition does. It's like looking out of the window into the fog. What might happen and if it does how can we be there in time?

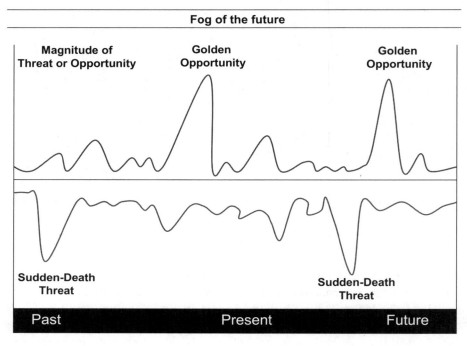

Fog of the future

Source: HBR/S05

The purpose of a business is to create and capture value and sustain it in the future. Golden opportunities arise when several windows of opportunity open simultaneously. Volatile markets face a steady stream of small and medium-size opportunities. On the other hand we know that business opportunities are rare, their timing is almost never under control of an individual company, but it's very important to be ready if they come. The challenge is to act smart during a long period of 'business as usual', because volatile markets have many variables which are individually uncertain and which interact to create unexpected outcomes. In order to see opportunities in good time, management should be aware of two key factors during the 'strategy as active waiting' process:

1. volatile markets lie outside company control;
2. to enable a 'strategy as active waiting process', there is an urgent need for continuous and consistent monitoring, scanning and tracking: this is the battlefield of competitive intelligence.

"Curiosity is free-wheeling intelligence".

First example: Remember the early 2000-2002s when the senior management of the European telecom sector predicted that 3G mobile technology would revolutionize their business sector? Most of the key players in the European telecom sector such as Dutch KPN, British BT, France Telecom, Deutsche Telecom and many other mobile phone companies jumped on the 3G bandwagon. They all thought they "could not miss this TGV of new 3G technology". Most were somewhat undiscerning in their forecasts and most had a strategy of active shaper of this new technology. However, many examples from business teach us that in markets there are only a few shapers and many followers. The telecom players all wanted the role of shaper of the industry. The sector as a whole proclaimed it had made bids of around 100 billion Euros in 2001 for licensees, based on their predictions. In 2005 the telecom sector came to the conclusion that 3G was more evolution than revolution, and that consumer adoption, technical and economic benefits had lagged behind the initial projections and forecasts. During the period 2002-2004, the telecom sector had to make huge efforts, restructuring and laying off thousands of employees, in order to recover from the 3G disaster.

Many variables influence the nature and timing of an opportunity. I have listed some of them here:

▶ Technology revolution
▶ Customer's evolving needs
▶ Government policies
▶ Changes in capital markets
▶ Rivals' priorities
▶ Technical innovations
▶ New knowledge, insights and business foresights
▶ Emerging future events, other relevant topics

Without a doubt, this is precisely one of the key areas focused on by competitive intelligence; you can imagine how competitive intelligence might have prevented the telecom sector from bidding on this highly uncertain and potential revolutionary new technology, 3G.

Second case: Taking into account the variables listed above, consider the Chinese car market. Interaction between variables frequently creates new customer needs. In China, increasing numbers of the population are seeing their income rise. The government is investing heavily in new roads and infrastructure. The huge middle class in China has new aspirations, such as better housing, image/luxury goods from the West, and displays a lively interest in acquiring their own car. Financial institutions open up and offer consumers financial products and services such as mortgages, loans, credit cards and easy credit. New opportunities emerge because of exogenous factors.

In the diagrams below on 'strategy as active waiting' six questions have been listed which might help us foresee opportunities in good time. Again, a competitive intelligence capability is the perfect solution to both support and feed such a strategy process of active waiting.

Strategy as active waiting

Six questions that might be of help:
1. What is the anomaly and why does it exist?
   - ❑ Discrepancies, shifts, assessments and analysis

2. What changed in the external environment to give rise to the opportunity?
   - ❑ Changes in the regulatory, market, technical or social context

3. Is your company under pressure to manufacture a golden opportunity?
   - ❑ Often, excuses declare an opportunity "golden" for the wrong reasons

Source: HBR/S05

Strategy as active waiting

4. Why is the Euro 20 billion bill still on the ground?
   - ❑ Ask yourself, why hasn't someone jumped on it already?

5. How quickly will competitors move?
   - ❑ A competitor's management turmoil, strategic myopia, resource constraints might lost a year but won't last forever.

6. Can you get big fast?
   - ❑ Scaling up quickly. Many companies aren't up to the task.

Source: HBR/S05

II.6   Why competitive intelligence may fail

We must also take into account the fact that competitive intelligence may fail. It needs a structured approach and can't be done on a temporary basis. It's not about just collecting information, because then it's better to employ other people whose profession is that of information provider. It's also not looking at the past and present but especially at the future, less at threats and much more at exploring opportunities. Professionals active in competitive intelligence need to be irritating, even a little paranoid, and should not be charmed by nice stories and nice assumptions.

In the diagram below you will see some of the key reasons for the failure of competitive intelligence.

Why competitive intelligence efforts may fail

- Too much collecting of data; almost anyone in an organisation collects data
- In many cases marketing research, marketing services are transformed to marketing intelligence
- But intelligence is forward-looking and decision-relevant
  - "What will the competitive environment look like when we launch our new product next year?"
  - "How significant will this emerging technology be in our industry?"
- The only KSF is the ability to establish an ongoing dialogue with senior management about upcoming decisions
- So information and intelligence that is relevant and useful
- Don't get involved with requests for backward-looking data
- Setting up another information unit, simple labeling it intelligence, is quickly seen as duplicative

---

Competitive intelligence needs the acceptance of senior management, who must be open to the brutal facts, the blind spots, identifying the gaps in the company's strategies and open to the new business opportunities provided by competitive intelligence professionals. An isolated intelligence function somewhere in the organisation or linked with some department or company function will die sooner or later, especially in the next round of cost cutting. Inevitably, these next rounds of restructuring will come.

> "Competitive intelligence must be on a par with other functions that report to the Board".

Competitive intelligence must be organised around senior management at the highest level of the organisation. Could you imagine that intelligence officers in the military should operate at lower levels in the organisation? This is the case when intelligence is required to support the operations. At the top level of military organisations, intelligence officers are the most important group: professional intelligence staffs are close to the decision-makers: the generals. This is why competitive intelligence professionals should be at the highest level in companies "on a par with the other functions that report directly to the Board".

I therefore recommend that competitive intelligence should start "with the guys at the top".

II.7 Competitive intelligence as driver for innovation

"60 percent of innovation comes from outside your industry boundaries. Systematic innovation requires a willingness to look at change as an opportunity".
(Peter Drucker)

The above statement by Peter Drucker is so very true. Peter, who died on November 11 2005, is regarded as the most famous management guru of the 20th century. He wrote some 45 books on management. Innovation is one of the key drivers for long-term revenues, profitability and business value. Most organisations face enormous problems in creating innovation. But innovation is the pre-condition for long term shareholder value. The most important success factor of innovation is top management, who should be fully involved with the management of innovation. Unfortunately in many organisations this is not the case. In our competitive intelligence-driven innovation practices I have identified ten reasons why successful innovation faces difficulties:

1. lack of latching on to new ideas as people are too busy in their day-to-day operations
2. lack of vision for the future in the majority of companies
3. a management culture which is too often rooted in the past and the present
4. lack of involvement of top management, who should be the key drivers of growth; this is the root of the problem. They are more interested in growth by mergers and acquisitions.
5. new products, services and innovative processes are too often "one-offs"
6. lack of a structured approach to new ideas, new markets and new technologies
7. too strong a focus on short term issues, which makes it difficult to see "the wood for the trees"
8. process shortcomings because of individual problems and political aspects
9. insufficient planning, lack of coordination and cooperation, failure to carry out responsibilities, the setting of unrealistic targets
10. the 'not invented here' syndrome

Information and knowledge make a substantial contribution towards innovation and growth. There is a wealth of excellent information and knowledge outside, which in most organisations is hardly used. Competitive intelligence-driven innovation can make huge contributions in respect of innovation and growth. Applying this can be achieved by asking yourselves the following ten questions to which you should give realistic answers.

> *"If a company is interested in finding the future, most of what it needs to learn is to learn from outside the industry sector".*
> (Gary Hamel)

The challenge is to give the answers to the following ten key questions which explain why innovation and growth in your company will succeed or otherwise:

1. Do you make a distinction between the information needs to optimise the daily operations versus information and knowledge to enhance innovation and innovative strategy development?
2. Do you have a systematic, consistent and formal process in place to collect customer, market, competitor, technology and competitive intelligence?
3. Is the competitive intelligence, beyond traditional marketing intelligence, you are collecting looking forward beyond your traditional strategic planning horizon? If you fail to plan, you plan to fail!
4. Does the intelligence combine hard issues like knowledge-based facts and figures and trends with soft issues like early warning signals, business insights, business foresights including options and scenarios on predictions and what might happen?
5. Do you also involve colleagues inter-departmentally within the organisation, from business units and specialists, in the collection of the necessary information?
6. Do you have a process in place to cross fertilise these various forms of intelligence-gathering with the aim of enriching the perspectives and scope of the company and identifying the real opportunities at an early stage?
7. Has an internal information-sharing platform been established to collect, discuss and disseminate the collected information and analysed intelligence?
8. Are there regularly organised assessments such as exchange forums, management workshops, etc., to make sense of that information and intelligence and examine how to exploit and explore it at the next stages?
9. Has the company entrusted a key driver, next to the champion, to orchestrate and explore the information and intelligence for innovation, strategy development, customer value creation and finally new business creation?
10. Has there been set up a system to recognize and reward people for information, knowledge, intelligence and other insights all of which lead to the innovation needs and potential new business opportunities?

> *"If you fail to plan, you plan to fail".*

If you are able to answer these ten questions, or at least seven out of the ten in the affirmative, then you may well have a good basis for real innovation and new business creation.

Competitive intelligence can play a crucial role in the management of innovation, because competitive intelligence supports the tracking down of the right information and knowledge which is of key importance towards innovation. Planning is very important and the SMP portfolio mapping can be an excellent support tool.

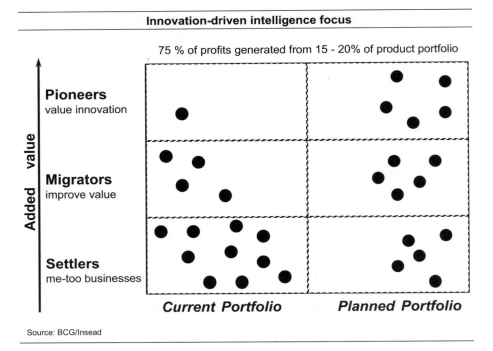

Innovation-driven intelligence focus

Source: BCG/Insead

The above shows how we can execute an intelligence-based portfolio planning analysis, where we separate the current portfolio of the company versus the future planned portfolio. In this portfolio analysis for the future I divide the portfolio into three categories of products and services.

First we have the "settlers". In most companies the settlers generate around 70-80 percent of total sales and represent only 15-20 percent of the profitability. Many initiatives in innovation are in the area of settlers, which do not generate business value in the long term. Second in the portfolio analysis we have the so-called migrators. Migrators are products or services within the portfolio which generate less sales but whose profitability is substantially higher. Third we have the pioneers in the portfolio who generate substantial sales at the highest profitability. Most companies have a portfolio of 60 percent settlers, 30 percent migrators and only 10 percent pioneers. The challenge of intelligence-driven innovation is to create innovation in the sector migrator and above all pioneer sectors, leading to a better balance in the sales portfolio, which creates additional profitability. Innovation should be planned in the long term towards a ratio of around 50 percent settlers, 30 percent migrators and at least 20 percent pioneers.

Case: Unilever-P&G

What is wrong with Unilever, which has now for several years lagged behind its key competitors Nestle, Danone and Procter & Gamble? Numerous initiatives have been taken with the aim of improving its performance. First was the reduction in the number of brands from 1600 to 400. Second was "the path for growth", which was not realised during the planned period of five years. Third came several rounds of cost cutting, the closing of many plants and the integration of marketing and sales. In 2006 Unilever sold its frozen food division and in the autumn of the same year, restructured its R and D activities. The company had around 64 departments active in R and D across Europe which were restructured into six "global centres of excellence".

> *"Unilever's competitors not only seem to have the ability to demonstrate speed, but they also have the ability to accelerate quickly to capture new opportunities".*

The general problem with Unilever is that it doesn't bring to the market differentiated new products because of its bureaucratic organisational structure. Establishing six "global centres of excellence" is again a form of centralisation and in my view more inward-looking rather than outward-looking. Unilever should follow the example of Procter & Gamble (P&G) and create and develop genuine innovative products. New in P&G's innovation strategy is the concept of "Connect + Develop". The Connect + Develop approach is a concept for external relationships with a strong focus on ready-to-go innovations. Through the "C + D" relationships, P&G is continually searching for products, packaging, technologies and commercial opportunities that can be reapplied to P&G brands and rapidly introduced to better serve consumers.

P&G challenges everybody in the world with the question: "Do you have a new product, technology or process that addresses an unmet consumer need? Can you offer a significant new benefit to one of P&G's existing product categories?"

"Will you become part of P&G's global innovation network?" Examples of "Connect + Develop" are the successful products Bounce, SpinBrush, Olay Skin Care and Swiffer Duster.

This is an excellent example of looking "outside in" in creating and building innovative products based on innovative minds within their global business relationships network.

"Coming together is a beginning, keeping together is progress, working together is success".
(Henry Ford)

The last comment on Unilever is the remark made by CEO Patrick Cescau in the FT in June 2006, quoted by Tom Peters in his seminar of December 2006 at Nyenrode University. Patrick Cescau said that Unilever has a very divers team of Board of Directors with only one female member, yet women purchase 85 percent of all Unilever products. Tom Peters dislikes the idea that leaders don't represent their prime target groups. In this context Peters also referred to one of the key articles in the Economist in 2006: "forget China, India and the Internet: economic growth is driven by women".

Scientific citation
Establishing a competitive intelligence capability is a perfect way to support this kind of portfolio planning by collecting the right information and knowledge in order to identify the new innovative business opportunities at an early stage. How can we do this? Below I will show four diagrams of how to track emerging technologies and making forecasts of these new technologies. The basis for forecasting emerging technologies lies outside the company by monitoring, scanning and tracking in a structured way secondary sources of information and knowledge. I will describe the scope, the secondary sources, a case approach and the forecasting.

Forecasting emerging technologies

Scope:
- Research tells us of the positive correlation between scientific publications and patents

- Science & Technology databases are of impact in many fields of innovation

- Technological forecasting: exploratory and normative

- Exploratory: project the present state of technology into the future assuming a certain rate of technological progress

- Normative: backward from the future to the present by relevance trees and foresight. (e.g. national objectives for social, military and industrial development)

- National foresights: large scale Delphi analysis(1000s)

Forecasting emerging technologies

Secondary sources:

- Science citation index and Engineering index by subscription

- US patent database with all patents since 1790 – today, is full text and free of charge

- European and Japanese patents, to be searched via internet (not so unique as US patents)

- Free database search tool and very unique is www.scirus.com

- Commercial on line databases

Forecasting emerging technologies

Case approach:

- Definition and analysis of the key words
- Define the time frame of the analysis
- Use the search tool www.scirus.com to select the scientific citation: going through the database of LexisNexis on keywords tracking the citations in:
  - US patent and Trade Mark Office USPTO
  - European Patent Office EPO
  - Japanese Patent Office JPO
  - Patent Cooperation Treaty PCT
  - World Intellectual Property Organization WIPO
- Analyse the relation between scientific citation and patents using the regression model
- Results : positive correlation

Scope. Research tells us of the positive correlation between scientific publications and patents. So we must match up both areas. Science and technology databases are of importance in many fields of innovation and there are thousands of public databases in the world available nowadays. The challenge is to use them but we have to do this in a structured way. In addition of course there is the forecasting methodology. This can be exploratory: projecting the present state of technology into the future assuming a certain rate of technological progress. It can be normative: backwards from the future to the present by relevance trees and foresight. Foresights can be small or large scale Delphi analysis, which depends on the strategic impact we try to achieve.

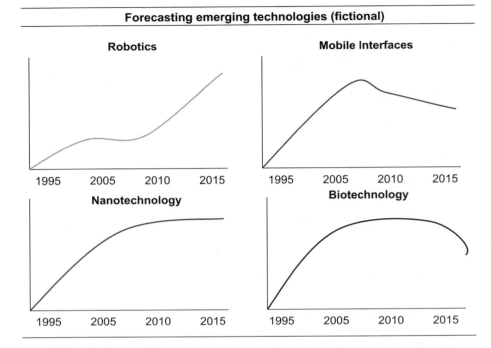

Secondary sources. Scientific and engineering publications can be scanned in commercial on line databases and the Internet. The best results can be achieved by citation. The same can be done with the various patents databases: I have listed the most important in the diagram of the case approach.

Case approach. The first step here is a key word analysis of the relevant issues of the technologies, engineering and patents. The second step is to define the time frame. New technologies do not emerge only in one year's time: it might be several years ahead of us. So we have to go back in time to be able to identify the first publications on relevant technologies. Through the years the number of publications, the perspectives and the scope will have increased. Sometimes we have to go back 15-20 years to find out about the very first publications. The third step is to use the applicable search engines which enable us to scan materials about the relevant technologies, engineering and patents. A very useful search engine is the search tool www.scirus.com. Patents can be scanned in the specialised patent databases of USPTO, EPO, JPO, PCT and the WIPO. As a result of the scanning we can analyse the relations between scientific citation and patents by weighting and using the regression model.

Results. The results of the analysis can be projected in forecasting curves as shown in the fourth diagram on robotics, nanotechnology, mobile interfaces and biotechnology.

"Which technologies will revolutionise business over the next 10-15 years?"

This statement is of importance in showing how new technologies will be applicable to the business. There are numerous initiatives in innovation and new technology which are not always applicable in the business world. Very good inventions have been created in the past and will be in the near future for which there is not always market acceptance, because customers don't accept it. A good example is the thousands of new products in the fast-moving consumer goods industry which are introduced in retail. Around 85 percent of these product introductions and/or line extensions disappeared 3-6 months after their introduction into the market place. Another example is the newly introduced DaimlerChrysler Smart-for-Four car. Based on the successful concept of the Smart City car for just two persons, DaimlerChrysler thought that the line extension with a new Smart car for four persons could be successful. The lifecycle of the Smart-for-Four was only two years: it was launched in 2004 and production was halted in early 2006. The same happened to the new Volkswagen beetle and the DaimlerChrysler PT Cruiser. Both cars are still available on the market, but have very limited success.

It is necessary also to look at the market opportunities and unmet customer needs at an early stage. With innovation and technology development this can be achieved by combining technology intelligence with competitive intelligence into competitive technology intelligence (CTI). The diagram below shows the combination of both with CTI as the umbrella of the creation of new business value.

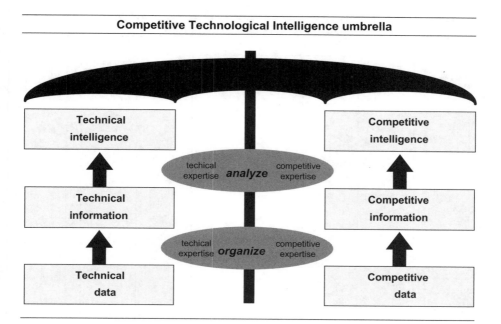

Link between Competitive and Technological Intelligence

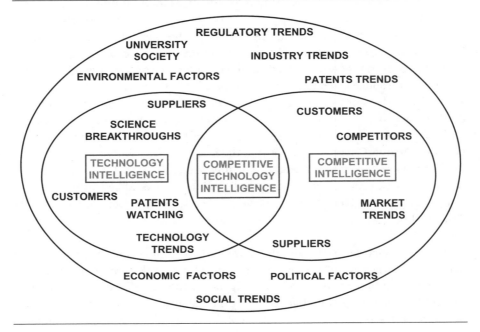

Downsize risk assessment form

Key assumption	Basis of assumption	Confidence in assumption High/med/low	What would have to happen to make outcome attractive ?	What is the risk of this happening? high/med/low	What would be impact if event occurs ?	How far could things be allowed to deviate from plan before action is taken?	What contingency action is planned ?

Source: adapted from Marketing Plans/M.McD.

The diagrams offer a good basis for a successful approach to combining technology intelligence with competitive intelligence and the focus areas of relevance. The downsize risk assessment form can be of help in the identification of the potential risk as well as the potential gaps.

The key questions in the downsize risk assessment form to be answered are:

1. What is our key assumption?
2. What is the basis of our key assumption?
3. How confident are we with our assumption?
4. What must happen to make our outcome attractive?
5. What will be the potential risks if this happens?
6. What would be the impact if it happens?
7. Where are the deviations between our plan and the expected actions? We should analyse the BAR, Before – Action – Review?
8. How does our contingency plan look like?

By going through the questions in the downsize risk assessment form we force ourselves also to consider the potential business outcomes. This is an absolute necessity for innovation and business creation.

Another approach to the identification of innovation and new technologies is the analysis of the combination between:

▶ selecting the winning technologies
▶ the competitive impact of a new technology
▶ the current technology position
▶ the preliminary indications about the coherence of essential current and future know-how

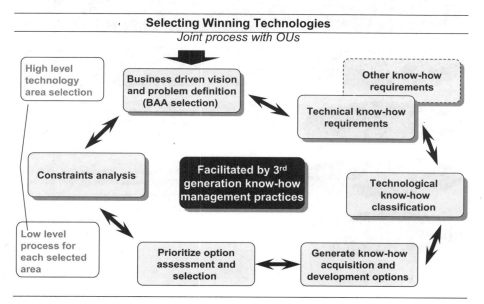

Competitive impact of a technology
*Describes the nature of the advantage offered **by** that technology*

Base technology
- Essential to be in the business
- Widely exploited by competitors
- Little competitive impact

Key technology
- Well embodied in products and processes
- High competitive impact

Pacing technology
- Under experimentation by some competitors
- Competitive impact likely to be high

Emerging technology
- At early research stage, or emerging in other industries
- Competitive impact unknown, but promising

Source: ADL

Current Technological Position

Clear leader
Sets the pace and direction of technological development. Leadership recognized throughout the industry.

Strong
Able to express independent technical actions and set new directions. Capabilities above average, compared to other players.

Favourable
Able to sustain technological competitiveness in general and/or leadership in technical niches. Capabilities comparable to other players.

Tenable
Unable to set independent course; continually in catch-up mode. Capabilities comparable to other players.

Weak
Unable to sustain quality of technical outputs vs competitors; short-term fire-fighting focus. Reliant on suppliers or partners for these technologies.

Source: ADL

Competitive Impact And Current Technological Position

A *competitive impact* vs *current technological position* matrix provides preliminary indications about the adequate of current know-how

Competitive Impact	Current technology position				
	Clear leader	Strong	Favourable	Tenable	Weak
Base	Alarm signals for waste of resources		Industry average	Alarm signal for survival	
Key	Opportunities for present competitive advantage			Alarm signal for present	
Pacing	Opportunities for future competitive advantage			Alarm for future	
Emerging					

Source: ADL

Selecting winning technologies: the diagrams describe the six phase approach to selecting potential winning technologies by identifying the know-how requirements, prioritising the options and making the constraints analysis. One important issue is the fact that the selection should start with the business driven vision. This means that the selection will start from the business needs perspective and not just with technology mapping.

Competitive impact of a technology: in one map the different stages in technology are described from base technology towards key technology, pacing technology and emerging technology. It gives a perfect indication of the stages in technology development.

Current technology position: another map shows an analysis of the current position of the company related to the technology position. Here five different stages of technology leadership are examined; clear leader, strong, favourable, tenable and weak positions.

Current and future coherence: by combining the competitive impact of technologies with the current position of the company in the technology arena, it is possible to identify the precise position currently occupied by the company and what the future position should be. The result of such an analysis is a clear picture of the company in the competitive technology arena because it identifies:
1. Where the company is wasting resources.
2. Where the current opportunities are for competitive advantage.

3. Where the opportunities are for future competitive advantage.
4. What the current situation is within the sector.
5. Where the early warning signals are for survival, for the present situation and for the future.

Case: Shell

Shell started combining competitive intelligence with technology intelligence into competitive technology intelligence in the late 1990s. At a best-practice event held by SCIP Benelux, the Society of Competitive Intelligence Professionals, in 2003, Christiaan Luca showed how Shell has adapted CTI within the organisation. The diagrams below give a good impression of how competitive intelligence with technology works at Shell in technology road mapping. The complete competitive intelligence cycle has been adopted, from issue framing, conducting research from secondary sources, visualisations, research from primary sources, analysis towards finally actions.

Technology Play or Road Mapping

- The Technology Play or Road Map provides a comprehensive overview of the technical and competitive landscape by describing:

    - business needs
    - market dynamics,
    - key players
    - Competencies

- It provides timing and priorities

- In order to make the right strategic decisions

Technology Road Mapping in Shell

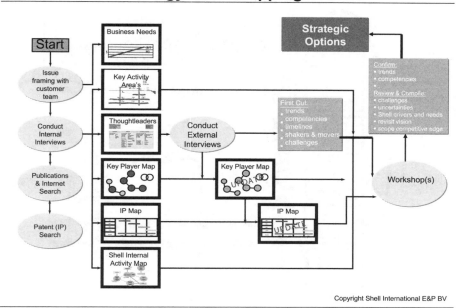

Technology Road Mapping in Shell

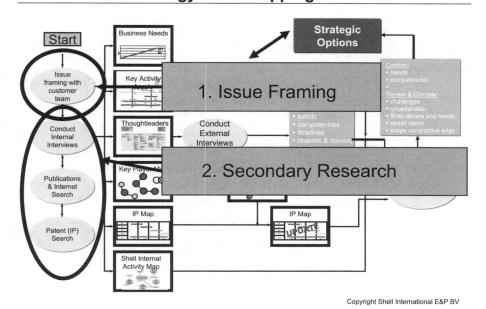

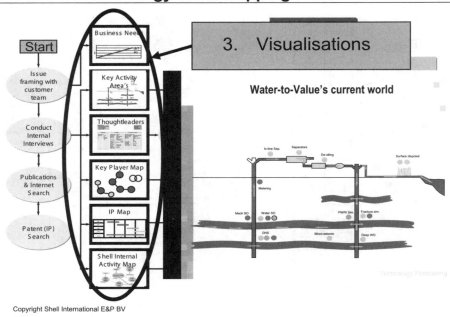

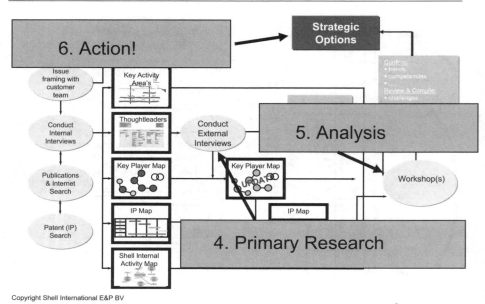

II.8   Trade show intelligence

"Properly organised, a competent well briefed team should be able to gather more useful information than they ever hope to collect in a full year in any other set of circumstances".
(Prior)

In practice, many managers go to visit trade shows without any preparation. Most of them walk around and chat with a few colleagues and competitors also setting out their stall at the event. Often, they may also attend seminars and conferences organised by the trade event organisation during the fair. The reason for going to a trade fair is to check whether others within the sector have presented something new, and check out the stand of the competition. Another reason might be to speak to customers.

In my business career I have attended many trade fairs, both national and international. I am always surprised by the lack of preparation displayed by the management of most companies when they visit such events. Most are not prepared at all. Of course, if the company is presenting themselves with a stand at an event, they will have organised everything down to the last detail. The stand, the presentation, eye catching features, catering, promotional offers, the staff at the booth, instructions to the staff, evaluation after the trade event and the follow-up to customers and potential customers who visited the company's exhibition stand.

Most companies forget how they can gather vital information during trade events like these; often the potential usefulness of visiting rival stands is ignored.

"It's the greatest potential for collecting information in the shortest span of time, for the least amount of money. It's a formal and informal platform for collecting information opportunities insufficiently used in a structured and pro active way".
(CIM, 2/2005)

In the next three diagrams I have described how to visit trade show events in a structured way with the aim of gathering target information about competitors, third parties and the relevant branch organisations. The first diagram describes the resource planning of trade show intelligence. What do we want to know, what do we want to know for our personal development and what do we want to know beyond the current planning horizon? Where can we obtain the information: at workshops, by meeting whom, what is the most effective way of going round the show, what kind of information should our own staff ask for, and what information do we need to gather from third parties?

Resource planning schedule TI

	CI Purposes	Personal Development	Future CI	Fun
Workshops				
Meeting people				
Walking the floor				
Staffing the booth				
Third parties				

Source: CIM 2.2005

The other two diagrams give an overview of the steps to be taken in order to do this in a structured way. I list 20 factors, which might be of relevance.

Increasing the Rate of Return on Trade Shows

1. Rechecking the organization's KITs
2. Determine if the event is appropriate for the KITs
3. Identify every activity and relevant specific information
4. First mine the existing information sources
5. Prepare a time budget for the intelligence
6. Identify how much time to be spend on intelligence
7. Identify the intelligence team
8. Share the plan with as many colleagues as possible
9. Manage the expectations of the intelligence team
10. Book hotel rooms a year before the event

Source: CIM 2.2005

Increasing the Rate of Return on Trade Shows

11. Develop a logistics plan before you get there
12. Contact as many of your information targets before
13. Walk to the tradeshow floor as early as possible
14. Have the team's briefing the evening before
15. Minimize the distance traveled in between
16. Plan the most effective route to the targets
17. Take care of your team
18. The process doesn't end when the show ends
19. Share the collective intelligence results with the management
20. Share the results with others

Source: CIM 2.2005

The Return on Investment, ROI, of trade fairs can be calculated if potential customers make their purchases after the trade show. We need to ascertain that it has been a new customer who has made purchases within a time frame of around six months after the close of the trade show. By doing this calculation, management can assess how effective the fair actually was. The question is, of course, do we make such calculations?

The Rate of Return, ROR, can be evaluated within one week after the trade show. What kind of information have we gathered and what will be its operational and strategic impact on our short and long term company performance? Consider the following:

▶ did our competitors offer special pricing?
▶ will our competitors change their current and future price strategy?
▶ what kind of new activities have our competitors initiated?
▶ how effective will these new activities by these competitors be?
▶ Have they developed new features within their competitive products?
▶ what did they offer to their regular customer base?
▶ Have they developed new services to customers?
▶ how do industry experts or trade magazine journalists regard these new activities?
▶ what third parties presented themselves at the trade event and what could the impact be on our business?
▶ What was new or unique at the trade show and what can we learn from it?

Assessing both the return on investment, ROI, and the rate of return, ROR, gives management maximum business insights into the industry sector and beyond. It also shows management a learning curve of how to improve their trade fair efforts and investments on the next occasion.

II.9   Strategy and intelligence

"Strategic planning does not guarantee strategic thinking, most strategic planning
efforts rely on historic data and numbers generated internally. The essence of
formulating real and differentiating competitive strategies is relating a company to its
external business environment".
(Michael Porter)

Dutch companies don't have a strategy

The Netherlands has vanished. The innovative environment is weak, there is a
lack of researchers and technologists, the connection with the business society is
gone and the investment in research and development lags behind that of other
nations. Innovation is a must. The Netherlands wants to be the best knowledge
society. That's no strategy, everybody wants to win. Does BMW produce the best
car? Everybody wants to produce the best car. Strategy is where you are unique.

Wagenaar of Getronics and Bakker of TNT were asked what their strategy was.
However, they were only able to list the strengths of their company, according to
Michael Porter. What competitive advantage do I want to have? Strategy has nothing to do with being number one, desiring growth, having a vision or learning
from a changing environment. A good strategy has to do with the creation of economic value. It's also important to choose what not to do.

In the US and Europe one of the hottest strategies since 2002 has been outsourcing and off shoring.

Outsourcing will not bring any competitive advantage. Competition can do
the same to get economies of scale. It will bring cost advantages short term, but
hidden cost such as knowledge count for the long term according to Michael
Porter at his visit in the Netherlands in November 2004.

Only a few companies have a strategy. Most managers keep to the ratio and
don't dare to communicate intuition or a vision. They only look at competition.
That's the difference between operational and strategic effectiveness. "You can't
eat strategy". Making a unique choice is strategy. Examples are Ikea, Dell, 3M.
Most companies follow each other in mergers and acquisitions, internationalisation such as the energy companies and the telecom companies in umts.

The environment is extremely dynamic and most companies try to keep three
balls in the air: flexibility, quality, efficiency. For many companies it is all too
much. Take Unilever, for example: cost cutting and fewer brands during 2000-
2005. Result: zero growth. Now it is the time for innovation and marketing. A
unique strategy shared by everybody is the most important aspect. Dutch management is not good at creating a joint shared direction. They concentrate on their
own field, and do not contribute to the overall picture.

Too many companies keep to the traditional industry sectors and this makes
them inflexible. The future belongs to companies with a unique strategy, which

can adapt quickly to the changing requirements of the market and customers. Companies able to do this become part of a connected network of suppliers, customers and partners; a balance between trust and competition with knowledge workers you need to invest in.

Europe must stop trying to compete with low-wage economies. What's needed is the exploration of new markets, innovation, added value and knowledge. That is the strategy for the future, according to Professor Henk Volberda. Sharply defined strategies are vital.

> *"Greatness lies not in being strong, but in the right using of strength".*
> (Henry W. Bacon)

Whatever your strategy, whether it is low prices or innovative products, it will work if it is sharply defined, clearly communicated and well understood by employees, customers, partners and investors. Being big is no guarantee that you will deliver superior business performance over time, yet many still assume it is necessary to be the largest in your industry sector to succeed. Another myth is low cost. You need to pay attention to cost, but you don't have to be the lowest-cost player. Nor do you need to seduce the consumer: you simply have to consistently deliver what you promise.

It's passion for detail that separates the good from the great. All great institution builders, Bill Gates, Estee Lauder, John Rockefeller, showed the ability to move between the daily developments in their business and the bigger picture of where the industry was headed and how this would affect their business.

Initiative has identified three building blocks of high performance: market focus and position, which is all about exploiting growth opportunities; distinctive capabilities, which is all about creating differentiation; and high performance anatomy, which is all about out-executing the competition.

For these companies strategy is not an 'ivory tower' concept, but a living component of their organisation, understood and acted upon at all levels. They approach strategy execution as a series of hills to be climbed, carefully rethinking their strategy at each summit, as the view of the opportunities, threats and challenges become clearer.

The second building block is the mastery of distinctive capabilities. High performers focus on market strategy with a commitment to creating and exploiting a set of distinctive hard-to-replicate capabilities to delivering to the customer.

The third building block is performance anatomy, as the unique way each company translates insights into action. Performance anatomy empowers companies in their goal to out-perform the competition. You can think of it as a pre-disposition to performing at the highest level.

Digging deeper, performance anatomy is comprised of a set of five organisational mindsets top management brings to diverse areas such as leadership and strategy, people development, technology enablement, performance management and innovation. These mindsets drive the important differences in behaviour that set high performers apart from their rivals.

Because they are keenly aware that future performance is not always dependent upon the resources that appear on a conventional balance sheet, high performers also have a sharp focus on intangible assets and often develop innovative models to manage and measure them.

Changing the targets at ABNAmro?

In this context ABNAmro provides a good example of setting objectives and strategies. CEO Rijkman Groenink defined new targets for ABNAmro in 2000 when he became CEO, the so-called TRS target. This TRS target is that ABNAmro should be in the Top 5 amongst 21 listed banks and insurance companies such as ING Bank, Citigroup, Morgan Stanley and 17 others. Only once, in 2005, did ABNAmro almost reach this target of the Top 5, with position number 7. CEO Rijkman Groenink announced in January 2007 that he wished to list additional targets which he could influence. In 2006 ABNAmro was in 15th position out of the 21 listed financial institutes. He asked the question:

> *"If an objective depends more on the external factors than the way we manage our activities, you can dispute whether or not it is still useful".*

An important point is that the payment of shares bonuses to senior management depends on whether or not the bank attains a Top 5 position. In my view two things can be done. Firstly, there is the ambition to better manage the external factors in the business environment. Secondly, there is changing the target. ABNAmro may be expected to choose the easy way of changing the targets and will not opt for the ambition and passion needed for the better management of the external factors. Just think of the payment of shares bonuses. To be able to better manage the external factors the Board of ABNAmro could consider installing a competitive intelligence regime on a par with the Board. This cost them no high investment.

Strategic Planning

"Strategic planning does not guarantee strategic thinking. Most
strategic planning efforts rely on historical data and numbers
generated internally"

"The essence of formulating a competitive strategy is relating a
company to its environment"

Michael Porter

The basic elements in strategic planning are environment scanning, strategy formulation, strategy implementation and finally evaluation and control. The process starts with environment scanning as the basis for the input for the strategic planning process. Competitive intelligence is crucial in this first phase as it is also during the phase of implementation and the phase of evaluation and control. Why? Because the changes in the dynamics in the external business environment are dramatic. Everything changes and organisations can no longer afford to adhere to their strategies in the long run. This means that strategic flexibility is a necessity for survival. Competitive intelligence has an infinite scope based on the changes in the outside world which perfectly fits with strategic flexibility.

"The essence of strategy is choosing to perform differently than rivals do".
(Michael Porter)

The environment scanning focuses on the ever-changing situations with customers, competitors, competition, markets, suppliers, technologies legislation, etc., all of which factors exert a crucial influence on the performance and value of the organisation. Yet in many organisations strategy development is still an activity such as:

▶ A calendar activity, driven at the time the budgets for next year have to be made;

▶ An after-summer exercise on which occasion business and marketing plans are developed with the chapter updates on customers, markets and competition;

▶ A remote area activity where senior management takes a trip to some remote location to discuss strategy, making the SWOT analysis assessment, and where the strategies adopted are those of the most persuasive people, those who think they know it all.

In a majority of organisations this is still the case. The dynamics in the external environment are taken into account on an ad hoc basis and mostly have a limited scope. When the strategy process is over, the strategic plan gets its final hour.

Mission completed; changes in the competitive arena sometimes get attention in between devising next year's strategy. Most major companies hold quarterly reviews.

Case: Philips
In the 1990s, Dutch Philips faced huge problems and the two former CEOs Timmer and Boonstra spent most of their time on cost-cutting and restructuring. In the early 1990s Philips was virtually moribund through inefficiency, ineffectiveness, lack of innovation, low morale among the workforce, and fierce competition. In 2002, Gerard Kleisterlee was appointed as the new CEO. He really fined the company down, back to its core activities and into improved profitability, based on a clear strategy. What happened in Philips during the period 2000-2006?

	2000		2006	
Core activities:	**Sales**	**Oper.margins**	**Sales**	**Oper.margins**
Medical Systems	3.0	5.5	6.8	11.3
Domestic Appliances	2.1	13.5	2.6	15.5
Consumer Electronics	14.7	2.5	10.7	3.7
Lighting	5.0	13.1	5.5	12.7
Semiconductors	5.9			
Components	4.6			
Origin	0.7			
Other	1.8		1.5	
Total	37.8		27.1	

Big does not always mean profitable. Although Philips sales dropped by over 10 billion Euros, profitability of core activities increased from 5.9 percent in 2005 to 8.9 percent in 2006.

The divestment of non-core activities was valued at 6 billion Euros in 2006. The stakes in Taiwanese TSMC and in LG Philips LCD were valued at around 10 billion Euros. The message of CEO Gerard Kleisterlee was clear: "A simple company makes sense". Gerard Kleisterlee was honoured for his years as CEO of Philips by Fortune Magazine as "Europe's businessman of the Year". But the turnaround at Philips could also hold great interest for Private Equity Companies. After all, Philips has hardly any debts, around 6 billion Euros cash on the balance sheet now and another 10 billion Euros worth of stakes in two companies.

> *"There is a tendency among businesses to criticize and belittle competitors. This is a bad procedure. Praise them. Learn from them. There are times when you can co-operate with them to their advantage and yours. Speak well of them and they will speak well of you. You can't destroy good ideas. Take advantage of them."*
> (George M.Adams)

Michael Porter, the management guru, author of many books on the competitiveness of organisations and nations, lists three key elements in the development of competitive strategies:

1. The essence of formulating: this means the process, structured, unstructured, formal, informal, rational, irrational but taking all the steps to arrive at a strategy. The HOW.
2. Competitive strategies: this means the outcome, the course of action of the company's objectives related to the competitive pressure. The WHAT.
3. Relations of the company with its environment: it indicates that the strategy process is done in organisational and environmental contexts. The WHERE, WHEN and WHY.

The best-selling books on management written since the 1980s deal with competition. I have listed the most important:

▶ M. Porter, *Competitive Strategy*
▶ M. Porter, *Competitive Advantage*
▶ M. Porter, *The Competitive Advantages of Nations*
▶ M. Porter, *Michael Porter on Competition*
▶ D'Aveni, *HyperCompetition*
▶ P. Kotler, *Kotler on Marketing*
▶ P. Drucker, *New Realities*
▶ Prahalad and Hamel, *Competing for the Future*

Still many managers struggle with competitor analyses which are in most cases based on some historic and present data and information. This makes competitor analysis one of the weakest analyses in organisations. But how are companies able to compete if they don't keep a constant watch on their competitors and on the ever-changing competitive landscape?

Others argue that competitive analysis, not competitor analysis, is history, and so should Michael Porter be too. On many occasions in client meetings I have heard managements claiming that their company develops strategies on their own strengths and that they don't want to focus too much on competition. The prime focus according to them should be on the market and on customers. Of course, I agree with this, I do not agree that there should be less focus on competition.

It may not be in the company mission statement, or the explicit formulation of their strategies, but much greater attention should be paid to learning all about your competitors in the marketplace, about your rivals who have just one unexpressed objective:

"Never forget that your competitors are after your customers".

They are after your customers, fishing in the same lake as you. They want to capture your market share, they want to expand at the expense of your company and if they do not succeed in their growth strategies the day will come when they will acquire your company or seek to merge with you as equal partners. Mergers based on equal partnership are not true mergers: they are a fairy tale. Just take the examples of Daimler Benz and Chrysler in 1998 and Air France and KLM in 2004.

It was Michael Porter who put competitive thinking on the international trade map. He invented competitive concepts which are still highly applicable in the management of organisations today, concepts such as cost leadership, differentiation, focus and niche strategy, the five forces model and the sector and cluster analysis concerning the competitiveness of nations. Understanding and implementing competitive intelligence can be best shown by matching the two models as shown below:

UNDERSTANDING THE COMPETITIVE ARENA

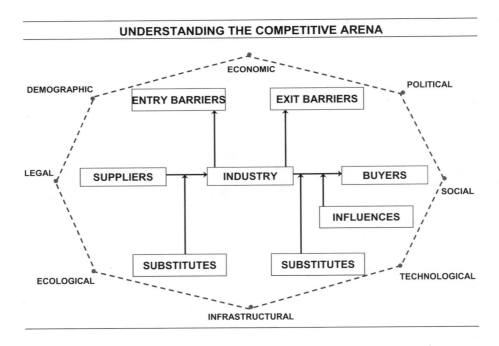

The diagram with the model for understanding the competitive arena shows all the key driving forces in a sector, substitutes, new entrants, buyers and suppliers, combined with the external factors of influence such as economic, political, social, technological, infrastructural, ecological, legal and demographic factors.

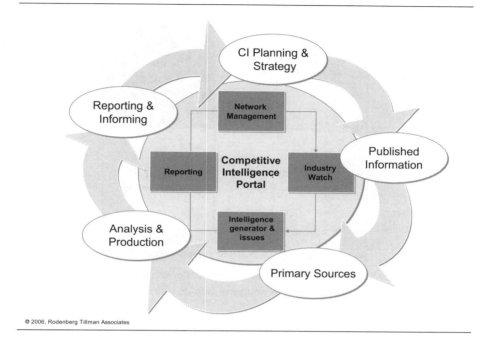

The diagram with the model of the competitive intelligence cycle shows the inner part and outer part. The inner part with the four dimensions network management, industry watch, issues management and reporting with the shared information and intelligence platform in the middle, which can be a business or intelligence IT system, an intranet solution or a web-based competitive intelligence portal.

The outer portion shows the competitive intelligence cycle: competitive intelligence planning and strategy: what are the objectives and strategies we want to achieve with competitive intelligence; the collection and gathering of information from secondary or published information sources; the gathering of information and knowledge from primary sources; the phase of analysis, production and storage; the final reporting and dissemination of the intelligence towards actions.

By combining both activities, the five forces model with the competitive intelligence cycle, maximum flexibility in strategy development will be achieved. At the next diagram, you see the four quadrants of strategy and flexibility.

Strategy and Intelligence

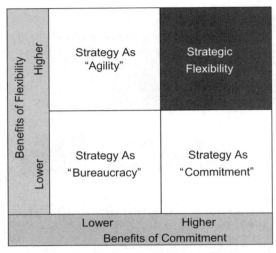

Strategy is about what the company wants to do with the world
Intelligence is about what the world wants to do with the company

Source: CIM J/F 04

Strategy by "agility" is done with a high flexibility rate but a low rate of commitment. Strategy as "bureaucracy" gives both a low rate of flexibility and a low rate of commitment. Strategy as "commitment" gives a high rate of commitment with a low rate of flexibility as well. Strategic flexibility gives both a high rate of commitment and a maximum of flexibility, the ideal platform for competitive intelligence that feeds consistently the flexibility-based strategy development.

During the flexible strategy process four phases are of key relevance as shown in the diagram. This is a closed, continuous loop of anticipating, forming, accumulation and operation. In all four stages of strategic flexibility, competitive intelligence is crucial to:

▶ identifying the drivers of change;
▶ defining the range of possible futures;
▶ applying tools such as scenario planning and strategic war mapping;
▶ feeding of the potential scenarios and strategic war mapping;
▶ defining contingency plans and potential outcomes;
▶ identifying the options on the resources needed as input for the uncertain scenarios and options;
▶ the full engagement of the external business environment;
▶ evaluation of options, assumptions and potential outcomes.

Four Phases of Strategic Flexibility

Anticipate
• Identify drivers of change
• Define the range of possible futures
• "Scenario Building"

Formulate
• Develop an optimal
  strategy for each scenario
• Compare strategies to define
  "Core" and "contingent" elements

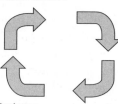

Operate
• Implement the Core strategy
• Engage the environment
• Exercise or abandon options as appropriate

Accumulate
• Acquire the resources needed
  to implement the core strategy
• Access – Take options on the
  resources needed for uncertain
  scenarios

Source: CIM J/F 04

> You can't predict the future
> However you can foresee future events

Finally we have to be prepared in respect of strategic flexibility by having in place contingency plans in case of potential key and relevant changes in the external business environment and which will affect the company. The diagram below gives an overview of the various contingency plans, and the applicable options for the future.

Contingency plans are part of Strategic Management

Present

Defined
Strategies

**Core
Elements**

Contingency
Elements

Future

Industry
Conditions

Option A

Option B

Option C

Option D

Source: CIM J/F 04

The result of having a strategy flexibility process in place means that the organisation is fully prepared to adapt to the key drivers of change as they may occur in the dynamics of change in our external business environment.

II.10   Strategic intelligence

"The aim of strategic intelligence is to place us in the eye of the storm".

As already explained, we use the word 'strategic' in management all too frequently, and basically what we mean by the word 'strategic' is 'important'. The aim of true strategy is to master the market environment by understanding and anticipating the actions of other economic agents, especially competitors in the industry sector and beyond other converging sectors. Strategic intelligence is part of competitive intelligence where strategic intelligence is focused on the longer term and purely future-oriented. Shifts and changes in our dynamic external business environment which are not observed continuously cannot be responded to, and certainly not anticipated. This makes strategic intelligence of key importance in controlling these shifts and changes.

In the diagram positioning of strategic intelligence, we have strategic intelligence positioned at the top at strategic level and looking towards the future. It's not scenario planning which is looking ahead for at least 15-20 years into the future on key events that could happen and could impact on the organisation. Competitive intelligence has been positioned in the middle between strategic intelligence and marketing intelligence.

In the last couple of years I have observed in some companies the establishment of marketing intelligence or market intelligence departments. The main focus of these departments is on markets and customers within the scope of the present and to a much lesser extent the scope of the future. In most cases, competitive intelligence plays no part in the operations. For a practical example I will take the case of ABN Amro Bank (October 2006).

Smart Choice? Marketing Intelligence in Amsterdam.
We are looking for colleagues.

ABNAmro bank has more than 4,500 offices in over 53 countries and is one of the world's largest financial services institutes. The marketing intelligence department leads the way concerning the services, which make the difference: personal contact between the bank and the customer via the various channels in order to achieve the objectives. They were seeking professionals with at least three years experience:

1. Project leader marketing intelligence: projects to increase the marketing and sales effectiveness;
2. Analyst: conducting analyses from the huge databases;
3. Multi-channel communications manager: supervising all the campaigns, actions respecting one-to-one communications and the marketing within the areas of direct mail, call centre, Internet and bank shops;
4. Communication specialist: one-to-one communication via Internet, call centre or direct mail;

5. Operational manager marketing intelligence: to develop a vision and realization of the team objectives and put the department on the map in a pro-active way;

6. Market researcher: based on the methodologies and techniques of research for the private and business market.

Thinking of marketing intelligence, the question is whether this department of ABNAmro will ever succeed in transforming itself from a data and information provider into knowledge-based competitive intelligence. It's fortunate they didn't use competitive intelligence for the activities described before, which would have meant "the kiss of death for competitive intelligence".

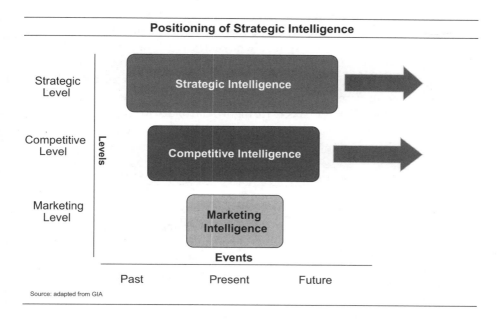

In concluding this chapter on strategic intelligence, I'd like to give the six tasks of strategic intelligence:

▶ Describing all the elements in the competitive environment;

▶ Anticipating the future of the competitive environment;

▶ Challenging underlying assumptions and constantly asking the right questions;

▶ Identifying and evaluating current company weaknesses against future market opportunities and threats;

▶ Applying intelligence to implement and adapt future strategies to the fast changing competitive environment;

▶ Challenge management when certain aspects of company strategy are no longer sustainable in the future.

"The current emphasis on risks has put a lot of pressure on senior management. Everybody realises that even an innocent scenario can become a nightmare if not properly managed. Senior management has no choice but to lead strategic intelligence implementation, driving intelligence awareness through every level of the organisation. The real danger is that, still, some senior managers aren't up to this challenge".

II.11   Competitive intelligence and organisational skills

"Does your company have in place a kind of radar to monitor your external business environment, which indicates and predicts change?

Every manager agrees that the business environment ultimately determines the fate of the organisation. However, only a few organisations in the business world today have a suitable structured system in place. Having a competitive intelligence competency available within the company is not easy. It demands a culture of sharing information, an acknowledgement that shared knowledge, rather than knowledge alone, is power, a recognition by management that every employee possesses knowledge, and that all these aspects are highly valuable to the organisation. These are thus collective intelligence efforts. The diagram below presents an overview of the obstacles related to competitive intelligence within the organisation.

Obstacles related to Competitive Intelligence

PEOPLE
- **inertia to change**
- **too busy - no time to learn**
- **no discipline to act**
- **motivation**
- **constant staff turnover**
- **transferring knowledge to new people**
- **teaching older employees new ideas**

STRUCTURE
- **inflexible company structures**
- **fragmented organizations**
- **functional silos**
- **failure to invest in past systems**

MANAGEMENT
- **the fear of giving up power**
- **the difficulties of passing on power**
- **challenging traditional company style**
- **imposed constraints**
- **lack of understanding about formal approaches**

KNOWLEDGE
- **extracting knowledge**
- **categorising knowledge**
- **rewarding knowledge**
- **understanding knowledge management**
- **sharing between key knowledge groups**
- **making knowledge widely available**

The obstacles have been classified in four key dimensions: people, structure, management and knowledge. People: the most important reason given for not engaging with competitive intelligence is the argument that employees in the organisation are too busy and there is a lack of discipline to act. I have been involved in many processes of implementing competitive intelligence but after the competitive intelligence competency has been established, you quickly see within a short time that the people involved are appointed to other positions in the company. The big advantage of this is that people continue to be active in competitive intelligence in their new positions and the disadvantage is that the newly-appointed people have to go through a renewed training cycle. The result is that it takes several months before new "actionable intelligence" will be delivered to management with increased pressure on the total performance of the competitive intelligence capabilities.

The second obstacle is management. Most important is the fear of relinquishing or delegating power. Another important task is to really challenge the traditional ways the company is performing. Competitive intelligence can lead to seeing things differently and not every manager is able to act this way. The third obstacle is structure. Many companies, especially the bigger ones, face the culture and structure of functional silos, or in other words, don't interfere in other company functions or departments and keep themselves busy with their own stuff. In addition, many organisations are fragmented: many islands with their own way of working and acting. Result: the "left side of the building doesn't know what the right side of the building is doing and visa versa". The fourth obstacle is knowledge-sharing. Although everybody in organisations fully agrees that sharing knowledge is crucial, in daily practice it doesn't happen. In the late 1990s knowledge management was a preoccupation of senior management, and at the EU summit in Lisbon in 2000 the objective for 2010 was that Europe should become the leading knowledge-based economy in the world. This is not the case, either in organisations or within governmental bodies. Collectively we have failed to make knowledge widely available within companies.

In addition, hundreds of thousands of people lost their jobs in the years between 2001-2005 because of cost-cutting. The result was that a vast amount of knowledge disappeared from thousands of companies. But senior management have been proclaiming throughout the last decennia that people are the most important assets on the balance sheet of the organisation, the so-called intangible assets.

"Success in business limits the scope of management and influences behaviour".

Key intangible assets can be defined as:
1. The collective skills, abilities and expertise.
2. The outcome of investments in staffing, training, compensation, communication and other human resource areas.

3. The way people and resources are brought together.
4. The identity and personality of the organisation.
5. Stable over time, more difficult to copy than capital market access, product strategies or technology.
6. Difficult to measure and to copy for competition.
7. Far less attention is paid to intangible assets than to tangible investments.

To give an overview of how to identify the intangible assets, see the overview of the 11 factors of relevance below. Conducting the execution of a capabilities audit will help to boost the organisation's intangible value and can be an excellent basis for the start of the competitive intelligence implementation process.

Organizational capabilities assessment

Organizational Capabilities	Questions	Assess-ment	Rankings
Talent	Do our employees have the competencies and the commitment required to deliver the business strategy in question?		
Speed	Can we move quickly to make important things happen fast?		
Shared, mind-set and coherent brand-identity	Do we have a culture or identity that reflects what we stand for and how we work? Is it shared by both customers and employees?		
Accountability	Does high performance matter to the extent that we can ensure execution or strategy?		
Collaboration	How well do we collaborate to gain both efficiency and leverage?		
Learning	Are we good at generating new ideas with impact and generalizing those ideas across boundaries?		
Leadership	Do we have a leadership brand that directs managers on which results to deliver and how to deliver them?		
Customer connectivity	Do we form enduring relationships of trust with targeted customers?		
Strategic unity	Do our employees share an intellectual, behavioral, and procedural agenda for our strategy?		
Innovation	How well do we innovate in product, strategy, channel, service, and administration?		
Efficiency	Do we reduce costs by closely managing		

Source: HBR 6/2004

• Keep in mind the business strategy
• 0 = worst   10 = best

Case: Dutch Government doesn't know what it is doing

This was one of the conclusions in the report of the Advisory Committee of Economics (REA) to the Dutch Government on "Improvement of Decisiveness" in January 2007. For many years the Dutch Government's four-year plans has featured the objective of improving government decisiveness: better plans, better policies, more decisiveness, less bureaucracy, fewer regulations, less government intervention, more efficiency and more inspiration.

Until 2007 it was always a matter of good intentions, good objectives, many and very thick reports and not much happening. What have been the facts in the past?

1. In restructuring the government the wrong management theories have been used.
2. The pressure to start new policies wins over the execution of existing policies. This means always trying to do new things and less success in executing existing plans.
3. The Dutch Parliament cannot oppose the machinery of government. Because of this, Parliament focuses too much on irrelevant issues and is less able to see the complete picture.
4. Not all Government failures can be corrected by privatisation and the logics of the business world.
5. The Dutch Government is insufficiently aware of what it is doing, who is responsible, and even the size of its own organisation.
6. The government is not a company: public officials react differently to incentives and the free market system.
7. Process management, management rotation systems and performance contracts have been disastrous in the past.
8. Questions are raised about the effectiveness of modern management practices in the business society; by imitating these practices, the public sector deviates much too strongly compared to the private sector.
9. Within the public sector the professionalism of public officials has vanished under meaningless management principles, mainly in favour of process management and financial control.
10. The productivity of bureaucracies is limited; not all products and services of the government should be profitable because of complexity.

Because of these ten factors, Parliament stands aside from controlling the functioning of the government. Members of Parliament ask many questions because of uncertainty and complexity. They lack initiative and in most cases merely react as issues are raised by the media. The Dutch Parliament has a research budget of 500,000 Euros and five employees. The four Planning Institutes of the Dutch Government have a research budget of 55 billion Euros and around 500 employees.

"In politics there is nothing that is planned in advance": Franklin D. Roosevelt. This statement might well apply to the Dutch Government, based on the report of the Advisory Committee of Economics. If the government doesn't know its own organisation, lacks insights into the basic movements within finance and employment, something is radically wrong. Example: In 2005 there were 863,538 public officers, an increase of 22,531 compared to 2001. For years the intention has been to decrease the number of civil servants.

If a National Government doesn't know its own internal organisation, how will it ever become successful in respect of the external dynamics in the nation's environment? Will it be able to create vision, to create successful strategies long term? Will it be able to control the future direction of the nation? For example, what will be the scenario in 2015-2020, 2030-2040? That's what a nation like the Netherlands needs. This is the same with the EU where a clear vision for the future is missing.

II.12   Scenario planning

> *"The only relevant questions about the future are those where we succeed in shifting the question from whether something will happen to – what would we do if it did happen?"*
> (Karl Rose of Royal Dutch Shell)

Scenario planning is different from most other planning techniques because of its focus on ten or more years in the future. It distinguishes itself from other traditional methodologies of strategic planning by its explicit approach towards ambiguity and uncertainty of key future business topics. The current ways of eliminating business uncertainties are:
▶ senior management's intuition and feelings;
▶ good analysis with sufficient resources expecting enough precision;
▶ extrapolation and trend analysis;
▶ keeping to the status quo within the external business environment.

Another method is the "strategy under uncertainty" approach, which will be described in the next chapter. There are several reasons why scenario planning might be applicable. According to Shell there are four important reasons:
1. Success in the future depends not just on a study of the future but on the future success of decisions taken today;
2. In business it is very difficult but also absolutely essential to make valid assumptions about the future;
3. Prepared decision-makers can anticipate the development of situations ahead of competitors;
4. Scenario planning processes help to prepare decision-makers. They may be still surprised by future events, but should never be taken by surprise.

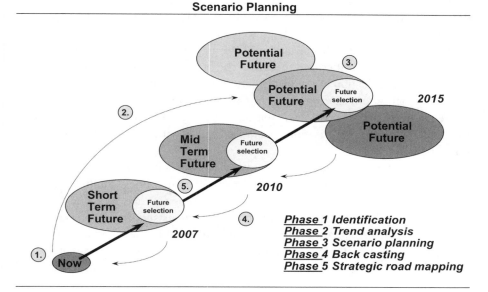

Scenario Planning

Phase 1 Identification
Phase 2 Trend analysis
Phase 3 Scenario planning
Phase 4 Back casting
Phase 5 Strategic road mapping

Competitive intelligence can be the key driver in scenario planning because of its systematic and continuous process of producing necessary intelligence of strategic value for facilitating long-term decision-making. Twelve steps can be identified for the process of scenario planning.

First step: Identifying the relevant issues for the future and creating a group of key drivers. The issues concern the key decisions and factors that might have an impact on the future business. The best way to start is from the external business environment and move inwards into the organisation.

Second step: Identifying the factors such as trends, uncertainties, potential future events and other issues of relevance which might have a future impact on the business seen from the point of view of the external business environment.

Third step: Making the rankings and weightings of importance and uncertainty.

Fourth step: Conducting an influences analysis of how the various uncertainties and potential trends interrelate.

Fifth step: Selection of the potential scenario options by choosing a limited number of key uncertainties around which to build the scenario logistics. Use your intuition and create narratives.

Sixth step: Testing the consistencies. Ensure that the potential scenarios are internally consistent and eliminate those that do not make sense or have become irrelevant;

Seventh step: Flesh out the potential scenarios. Support the scenarios with data and information on potential market size, potential reactions of key players, financial impact, driving forces, key success factors etc.

Eighth step: Study the implications of strategy. Analysis of weaknesses in decisions, plans, opportunities and threats in the future business environment.

Ninth step: Selection of the leading indicators. Identify the leading indicators for early warning monitoring, scanning and tracking.

Tenth step: Discussion of the potential strategic options. Develop the strategies that match with the organisational vision as well as with the dynamic changes in the outside world.

Eleventh step: Reaching agreement and consensus on the implementation plan. Developing strategies is one thing; implementation is another, in most cases even more important. Give the answers to When, What, Who and How?

Twelfth step: Communication which implies the dissemination of the scenarios to ensure implementation will be successful. Identify the target audience and the channels to be used for optimal communication. Informing and communicating the potential outcomes often does not receive the attention it should.

The most famous scenario in the business world was the case of Shell. In the late 1960s the management of Shell asked themselves the key question "What should we do in case of an oil boycott?" With a well-executed scenario-planning model Shell was very well prepared in 1973 when the Arab world decided to impose an oil boycott. Shell was able to act immediately, whilst its competitors such as Exxon, BP, Total, Amoco, ENI, Mobil and all the other key players in the upstream production and exploration of oil hesitated, wondering how to react to this highly unexpected development.

II.13   Strategy under uncertainty

"It's not important that they don't buy your story. It's important that you don't buy theirs."

Strategy under uncertainty is a perfect analysis model which our firm still uses for clients who have to take key decisions today which have huge implications for the future. We learned of this model, developed by McKinsey, through an article in HBR in 1997. The basis is the choices to be made for the near future: the three strategic positions. The first is the managerial decision to become the "shaper" of the industry sector. Shapers of the future play a leadership role in how the sector will operate by setting standards and by creating demand. The second is the decision to become the "adapter" within the sector for the near future. Adapters to the future win through speed, agility and flexibility in recognizing and capturing opportunities in existing markets. The third is the decision of management to take the role of "reserve". By investing sufficiently, the company stays in the game but avoids premature commitments. I always compare this with the Tour the France, the world's most famous cycle race. The leading group ahead of the pack may be seen as the shapers: they determine the speed and tactics of the cycling race. The pack that follows the leading group can be seen as the adapters: they still have a chance to challenge the leaders and close the gap by speeding up. Then there are those who bring up the rear or lag behind the pack, but will finish anyway. At the finish they know what has happened and they might decide to regain ground by being more active the next day.

With reference to companies, here's another quote from Peter Drucker:

> *"There are companies who make things happen".*
> *"There are companies who watch things happen".*
> *"There are companies who wonder what happened".*

Related to the model "strategy under uncertainty" there are four levels of uncertainty. The level of uncertainty implies the level of gathering of the key relevant intelligence and in depth-analysis. The more intelligence has been gathered, the more uncertainty is eliminated. In other words the level of uncertainty could be decreasing, especially at the stage of a range of futures at level III in the diagram.

Case: HD DVD or Blu Ray

Who doesn't remember the battle in the eighties about dominance in the field of video? Sony and Philips lost out to Matsushita with VHS. Now the battle continues with the successor of the DVD. Two parties face each other:

1. the large consumer electronic companies, LG, Sony, Samsung and Philips: they have been developing the Blu Ray format.
2. the Japanese computer companies Toshiba and NEC: they call their technology HD DVD.

The success of the future standard will be determined by the movie industry. Hollywood has already made it clear that they want to have only one format. Four studios expressed a preference for HD DVD: Universal Pictures, New Line Cinema, Paramount and Warner Bros. Total share of the market is 45 percent.

Blu Ray: Walt Disney, 20th Century Fox and Sony Pictures. Also around 45 percent share of the market.

The key difference between the two solutions is the thickness of the protection coverage. Blu Ray has 0.1 mm and HD DVD 0.6mm. The thinner the protection coverage the more data can be on it: this means 25 gigabytes against 15 for the HD DVD. The disadvantage of the thinner solution is the need for new equipment.

The HD DVD can be projected using the same equipment. In January 2007 LG, part of the Blu Ray group, presented equipment capable of playing both DVD solutions. Warner Bros is trying to introduce another new solution: Total HD Disc, which can be played on both equipment solutions, both HD DVD and Blu Ray.

The Three Strategic Postures

Shape the future
Play a leadership role in establishing how the industry operates, for example:
- Setting standards
- Creating demand

Adapt to the future
Win through speed, agility, and flexibility in recognizing and capturing opportunites in existing markets

Reserve the right to play
Invest sufficiently to stay in the game but avoid premature commitments

Source: Adapted from McKinsey/HBR1997

Levels of Uncertainty

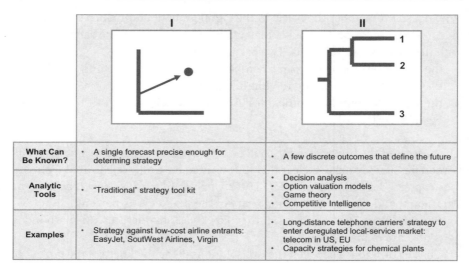

	I	II
What Can Be Known?	• A single forecast precise enough for determing strategy	• A few discrete outcomes that define the future
Analytic Tools	• "Traditional" strategy tool kit	• Decision analysis • Option valuation models • Game theory • Competitive Intelligence
Examples	• Strategy against low-cost airline entrants: EasyJet, SoutWest Airlines, Virgin	• Long-distance telephone carriers' strategy to enter deregulated local-service market: telecom in US, EU • Capacity strategies for chemical plants

Source: Adapted from McKinsey/HBR1997

Levels of Uncertainty

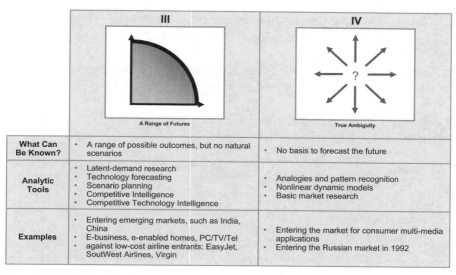

	III — A Range of Futures	IV — True Ambiguity
What Can Be Known?	• A range of possible outcomes, but no natural scenarios	• No basis to forecast the future
Analytic Tools	• Latent-demand research • Technology forecasting • Scenario planning • Competitive Intelligence • Competitive Technology Intelligence	• Analogies and pattern recognition • Nonlinear dynamic models • Basic market research
Examples	• Entering emerging markets, such as India, China • E-business, e-enabled homes, PC/TV/Tel • against low-cost airline entrants: EasyJet, SoutWest Airlines, Virgin	• Entering the market for consumer multi-media applications • Entering the Russian market in 1992

Source: Adapted from McKinsey/HBR1997

At all levels it is of key importance to define the variables, which determine the level of uncertainty. The more intelligence is gathered about those variables, the more uncertainty is eliminated. Take the development of an e-business strategy around the year 2000. At that time e-business was in its infancy and only a few companies had been involved in developing an e-business strategy. In 1998, there would have been uncertainty level IV as shown in the diagram. Hardly anyone could predict in which direction the Internet was going. Around the year 2000, it became clearer, and several organisations perceived how the Internet could be part of their overall company strategy. Level III was reached at that time, but future developments were still unknown. There was a "range of futures".

In order to obtain greater certainty on the possible range of futures, which could impact on the company, the variables must be determined and intelligence must be collected related to these variables. For e-business I have defined five key variables:

1. The development of ICT: information and communication technology could play a vital role here;
2. The role of national governments: the government must also be considered a key variable, although it was not expected that governments would play an initiating role of any importance;

3. The position of suppliers: in e-business it is of course relevant to have your suppliers and other network relationships transparent. They are a key part of e-business;
4. The role of competition: in the development of the company's e-business strategy it is of key importance to identify the plans and intentions of competitors within the sector;
5. Customers: this is a pre-condition, not at least to find out how current and potential customers will experience e-business as a new way of doing business.

Based on our intelligence-gathering efforts, I have divided the level of uncertainty on those five variables over time as follows:

Key variables	1998 – 2000	2000 – 2002
1. Developments in ICT	0	++
2. Role of governments	-	-
3. Position of suppliers	-	0
4. Role of competition	-	++
5. Customers	0	+

o = neutral – = unclear + = clear

Towards 2000 the position as regards the role of the government, the role of suppliers and the role of the competition was still unclear. At customer level, as well as the development in ICT, the key variables were still neutral. The indicators of developing e-business strategies within the business world were still "wait and see what happens". Remember, this was in 1998-2000. Uncertainty level III was still applicable and the outcome could still be a range of futures in more directions than one.

In the year 2000-2001 the situation changed rapidly. In-depth intelligence gathering confirmed fast changes in the competitive landscapes. There were really some shapers within the industry who jumped on the e-business bandwagon. At that time Jack Welch, CEO of GE, was asked how important e-business might be for GE. He replied: "e-business is our first, second and third strategy". Welch explained how important e-business would be for GE. For the majority of companies in the world, GE was at the time the leader in e-business, and remains so in many management themes and solutions in 2007.

This resulted in 2000-2001 in clear e-business strategies and intentions in the sector of ICT, the role of competition and with customers because of the fast penetration of the Internet at private and business levels. In the range of futures at level III, there was greater clarity; e-business strategies were defined as part of the overall company strategy.

Strategy under uncertainty might also be applicable in the automotive sector and in other sectors of industry. Can humankind continue the mass production of cars? What will happen on the Chinese market? Many Chinese also wish to drive cars and regard possessing a car as a symbol of success. But how do we handle pollution? How much longer will the Americans continue to drive their great gas-guzzlers? In 2006 the first sales success of the mighty SUV (sport utility vehicles) came under pressure. Why are former US President Bill Clinton and former Vice President Al Gore so concerned about the global environment and ecology in 2006-2007? Why didn't they do something during their presidency?

The US car industry has been in trouble for over 30 years, because Japan and Korea have taken market share away from them year after year. Didn't they foresee the change in demand for more cars with lower fuel consumption? In January 2007 the Detroit motor show was held once again. Photos of new muscle cars were featured in the media. Are they refusing to see what's really happening to customer demand in the automotive industry? Toyota will become the world's leading car manufacturer in 2007: they have a lot of success with their new technology-driven hybrid cars. Is the automotive sector in the US unconscious? Why do GM, Ford and DaimlerChrysler not change to accommodate future consumer demand and unmet customer needs? If you have watched the decline of the US automotive industry over the past 30 years, you'll find it incomprehensible. But there is more to come, just think of the Chinese cars in the near future. But the future is not tomorrow: it started yesterday.

So we need to ask ourselves some key questions every day: Which technologies will be revolutionised between 2007-2020? When will nanotechnology really take hold? Will the US car industry still exist in 2020?

What do you think when you read the three statements below about business leaders who were sure about future developments in their sectors of industry?

> *"640K ought to be enough for everybody"*.
> (Bill Gates in 1981)

> *"There is no reason anyone would want to have a computer in their home"*.
> (Ken Olson, President and Founder of DEC in 1977)

> *"I think there is a world market for may be five computers"*.
> (Thomas Watson, Chairman of IBM in 1943)

From Intel we know the fast growth of transistors per microprocessor, doubling in volume almost every year. In the early 1980s we spoke of 286 to 386 and 486DX by the end of the 1980s. In the 1990s we moved from Pentium I to Pentium 4 and in the period 2000-2005 towards Xeon and Itanium.

Strategy under uncertainty can be a good approach to the analysis of future developments in breakthrough technologies: future Workspace such as the human interaction with mobile applications, the mobile use of environments, mobile device interaction, ambient awareness and ubiquitous computing.

From 2008 to 2020 new technologies concerning utility computing, hybrid cars, telemedicine, nanotechnology, smart robots, new energy solutions, quantum computing, etc., will find wide acceptance.

To quote Peter Drucker, who died on November 11 2005, and published over 40 books on management: "The future can't be predicted; however, future events can".

II.14   Customer Intelligence

"You can insure your assets, you can replace your building, but you can't replace the customers who don't come back".

In business there seems to be an epidemic absence of customer analysis, leading to a lack of any disciplined systematic process for maintaining awareness of customer needs, interest, purchase decisions behaviours, perception of suppliers and the current state of relationships. If you have your CRM-tools in place, don't rely on them to get the "customer voice" really into your organisation. Starting to understand customer opportunities and threats and focusing on the most appropriate opportunities, companies must try to get consumer involvement inside in order to fulfil their promises to their target customers.

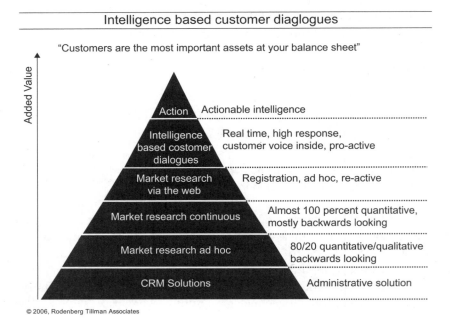

Intelligence based customer diaglogues

"Customers are the most important assets at your balance sheet"

Added Value

- Action — Actionable intelligence
- Intelligence based costomer dialogues — Real time, high response, customer voice inside, pro-active
- Market research via the web — Registration, ad hoc, re-active
- Market research continuous — Almost 100 percent quantitative, mostly backwards looking
- Market research ad hoc — 80/20 quantitative/qualitative backwards looking
- CRM Solutions — Administrative solution

© 2006, Rodenberg Tillman Associates

How can you maintain customer awareness in your company? It is important to conduct a regular review or check-up with all your customers. Traditional market research can no longer accomplish this. Your company should be able to conduct this customer assessment itself, identifying your perceived image, and the key critical success factors from the perspective of your customers purchase decision process and loyalty, because loyalty is the most important indicator as to whether or not your company is still fulfilling customer expectations. Nobody needs to impress upon you the maintenance of good relations with customers. So your company should regularly ask the three key questions:

1. How are we doing?
2. Are we improving?
3. Are we neglecting anything?

Your company needs to start an active dialogue with customers to meet their expectations. Find ways to involve them in your company business decision-making process. Get the voice of the customer inside. You have to identify the real criteria based on which customers decide, find out what makes customers choose to purchase your product; there must be real differentiating factors compared to the competition. The "drivers" are the features that are both important to customers and must be, again, highly differentiating from the product of your rivals. An example of relevant high drivers is given below.

What customers care about

	Differentiation	
High 'Antes'	**'Drivers'**	• **Most tangible attributes don't differentiate**
Features that are important to consumers but are provided by all competitors at similar level	Features that are both important to consumers and highly differentiated from those of competitors	• Intangible, emotional benefits serve as long term competitive differentiation and sustained loyalty
Neutrals'	Fool's gold'	• Challenge is to uncover the relevance of it from customers perspectives
Features that are irrelevant to consumers	Features that are distinctive but do not drive consumers' loyalty to brand	

Relevance (High / Low) — Differentiation (Low / High)

Source: McKinsey

Surprisingly, few companies pro-actively search for ways of improving their product/service. By doing this you create additional customer values and especially loyalty. Loyalty means increased revenues and growth of your share of market.

Asking customers to tell you how you may better meet their requirements and expectations strengthens customer loyalty.

We live in a world of change: purchasing decisions change, competitors' products change, competitors' strategies change, marketing conditions change, dynamics evolve and customers change. Your company must leave behind traditional market limitations, think outside the box and meet the challenge of bringing the customer voice inside.

Customers choose according to image and purchasing criteria

It is important to identify exactly and match up the key criteria by which customers judge your company and what you imagine those factors to be: in a majority of cases, they don't line up.

However, you have to keep in mind that there are hardly any barriers left to switching brands. Nobody but the customer pulls the strings. Creating loyalty by getting the customer's voice inside means that customers pull the strings of your company's offering of products and services.

> *"The true business of every organisation is to make and keep customers".*
> (Peter Drucker in 1953)

The customer voice inside

Getting the customer voice inside leads to fewer hindrances to selecting your company as supplier. Don't take it for granted that your company understands how your customers choose their supplier. Enabling your company to enter into a dialogue with all its customers will be hard to achieve. But imagine if your company were able to make it possible for all your customers to talk to you! It's possible! It's much easier than you think and you should do this in an objective way: "why did your customers choose you?" The most important purchase decision factors influencing customers are similar to the areas of strengths of your company. You can match both by formulating the key four critical success factors. In 95 percent of our businesses only four of these are relevant. In the diagram below an example is given showing how to identify the key critical success factors which really count with customers.

Preparation Phase

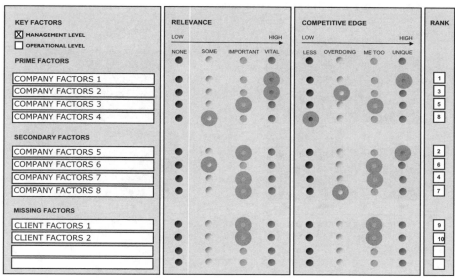

Key Factor Verificator Analysis

Preparation Phase

True Image

Internal	External	Gap

MANAGEMENT GUESSED IMAGE 10/10

COMPANY TRUE IMAGE 7/10 DEVIATION 30 %

MANAGEMENT REALISTIC GOAL 9/10 DEVIATION 10 %

Preparation Phase

Key Factors For Success True Image

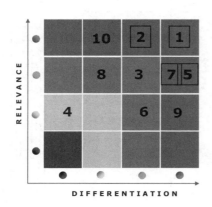
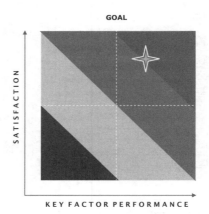

Source: Enertio

Having identified these four key critical success factors and getting the voice of the customer inside, consistently, frequently and objectively, your company will obtain consumer insights. Customers will express their loyalty, describe how they see the relationship, your strengths and weaknesses, and above all their frustrations.

Very few companies have an ongoing process in place to identify the opportunities to serve customers in a continuous and consistent way. Companies who are able to realise this acquire actionable intelligence. Management must answer some key questions:

1. Is our company targeting the right customers or customer section?
2. Does the company have the right mix of strengths for its target customers or does it need to develop new competencies?
3. Does our company have the right mix of strengths compared with competitors?
4. Does our company offer customers the right mix of products and services?
5. What does our company need to do differently to ensure the relationships with its customers in 1-2 years' time?

By doing this you keep your company aware of developments, and this also enables you to build long-term customer relations with the ultimate aim of bringing the voice of the customer inside.

"Vision is what I see and you don't yet see."

In order to realise vision, most companies leave the traditional limitations, try to think outside the box and to bring the voice of the customer inside. Again, vision is what your company doesn't yet see and is all about future customer needs. So try to go beyond your traditional marketing thinking.

Will your company be one of the first to leave behind the traditional limitations of your field? Will your company be one of the premier firms able to meet new customer needs? In other words, is your company one that "makes things happen", "watches things happen" or "wonders what happened"?

Let's go into more detail and bring perspective into customer intelligence. Six Sigma and TQM methodologies have resulted in vastly improved product quality over the past two decades. Human Sigma, like Six Sigma, focuses on reducing variability and improving performance. Six Sigma applies to processes, systems and output quality, whilst Human Sigma looks at the quality of the company employee – customer relationships. In manufacturing value is created on the factory floor. In sales, service organisations and professional firms, value is created when an employee interacts with a customer.

People may think that their behaviour is purely rational, but it rarely is. People base their decisions on a complicated mixture of emotion and reason. Recent research suggests that emotions may play a larger role than analysis.

The customer's voice creates in the end the sustainable advantages

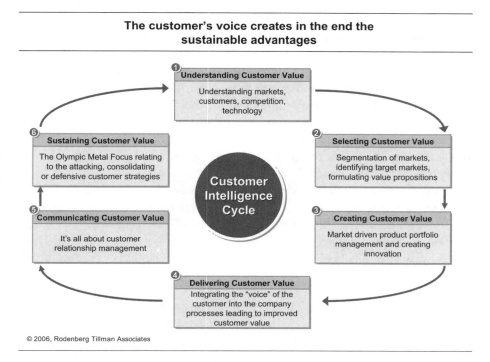

© 2006, Rodenberg Tillman Associates

Customer engagement

Research shows that extremely satisfied customers, people who provide the highest rating of overall satisfaction with a company's products and services, fall into two distinct groups: those who have a strong emotional connection to the company and those who have not. Examining the indicators of customer behaviour, a clear and striking pattern emerges. Emotionally satisfied customers contribute far more to the bottom line than rationally satisfied customers do, even though they are equally satisfied. In fact, the behaviour of rationally satisfied customers looks little different from that of dissatisfied customers.

Imagine you could peek inside the heads of your customers as they think about your company. Would people with a strong emotional connection to the firm show different brain activity from that of other customers? The answer is yes.

> *"Competition whose motive is merely to compete, to drive some other fellow out, never carries very far. The competitor to be feared is one who never bothers about you at all, but goes on making his own business better all the time. Businesses that grow by development and improvement do not die. But when a business ceases to be creative, when it believes it has reached perfection and needs to do nothing but produce, no improvement, no development,... it is done."*
> (Henry Ford)

A Six Sigma approach to measuring and managing the quality of the employee-customer interaction needs to take customers' emotions into account. Based on the work of psychologist Ben Schneider and management professor David Bowen, a method of measuring customer engagement has been developed. It combines traditional measures of customer loyalty with a short array of items that assesses the emotional nature of customer commitment.

Four dimensions assess this customer commitment:
1. Confidence. Does this company always deliver on its promises; did we fulfil your expectations? Are its people competent?
2. Integrity. Does this company treat me the way I deserve to be treated? If something goes wrong, can I count on the company to fix it fast?
3. Pride. This is a sense of positive identification with the company.
4. Passion. Is the company irreplaceable in my life and a perfect fit for me? However, truly passionate customers are relatively rare. They are customers for life and they are worth their weight in gold.

Research suggests that for all kinds of companies, fully committed customers, those who score the upper 15-20 percent, deliver a premium over the average customer in terms of share of wallet, profitability, and revenue and relationship growth. Disengaged customers, those who score in the bottom 20-30 percent, represent a 13 percent discount on the same measures. Business units whose levels of customer engagement are at the top 25 percent tend to outperform all other units on measures of profit contribution, sales and growth by the factor 2 to 1.

Employee engagement

Every dialogue or interaction between an employee and the customer represents an opportunity to build that customer's emotional connection, or to diminish it. Of course, these interactions are not the only way to the customer's heart. Research by Gallup in the USA tells us that only 29 percent of employees are energized and committed at work, 54 percent are effectively neutral, showing up and doing what is expected, and the remaining 17 percent are disaffected. These disaffected employees have a profound impact on productivity, estimated at a loss per year of US$ 300 billion. They destroy customer relationships with remarkable facility, day in and day out.

Performance assessments that acknowledge the importance of emotional engagement, both in customers and employees, provide much stronger links to the desired financial and operational outcomes. Deciding which assessments to use is just the first step. Unfortunately in many companies assessments designed with the right intentions are often deployed in the wrong ways.

Marketing communication claims

In their every day business, companies communicate several claims as a result of surveys. Some examples are. An airline sees itself as the industry leader in on-time performance. A mobile telecom operator claims to be a leader in customer satisfaction by citing an independent study of customers. A retailer announces that it has won an award for being one of the best employers.

High-level averages of company performance may provide good marketing communication claims which make executives feel better about their position in the market place. But because they obscure the considerable variation from location to location within a company, they don't give managers and executives the intelligence they need to improve performance.

Performance roughly follows a normal distribution suggesting that local variability is largely unmanaged. Suppose that instead of assessing your own heart rate, your doctor bases the treatment on a measurement of the average heart rate of your entire city or village. "Average" is simple a summary that represents almost no one. Local managers blame variability from location to location on factors that are beyond their control, and factors shared throughout the company, such as price, product, processes, policies etc., can't by definition explain local variability.

How to realise your company's human sigma

In most companies data about customers remains within the marketing department. Data about employee well-being resides mostly in the human resources department. Financial data is mostly retained by the finance department. But just bringing together these data on a single platform will provide a true picture of the state of health of employee-customer relationships. In practice this means that the responsibility for measuring and monitoring the health of the employee-customer relationships must reside within a single organisational structure with an executive champion who has the authority to initiate and to manage change.

To make it happen. ClientIndicator, the competitive based customer intelligence solution

> *"Customer satisfaction measurement can be obtained by traditional surveys, but those are rarely enough to give you the gritty data you need for a real read of the situation. Find out if each customer would recommend your products or services".*
> (Jack and Suzy Welch in *Winning*)

Early in 2005 I met Thomas Jonsson in Sweden. I was amazed by what he showed me regarding new concepts concerning the measuring of customer satisfaction and customer loyalty. He had developed a great concept that enables management to conduct customer dialogues, ClientIndicator. I am talking about management here, not the guys from market research, who all still favour traditional market research methodologies and techniques.

I always ask myself why so many people in companies cling persistently to their traditional methodologies. It seems to me this happens at all levels of management in organisations. I can write this, because I have visited some 50 companies in the Benelux countries to explain the concept of ClientIndicator. In Scandinavia and elsewhere, numerous companies are already working with this customer dialogue solution.

I already have been active in competitive intelligence for more than 15 years, and have worked within companies with the different intelligence linked company functions: marketing intelligence, market intelligence, sales intelligence, technology intelligence and other relevant company functions. But I have never seen a solution for customer intelligence, but that's what ClientIndicator is. Clearly, I wanted to learn more about this great solution and to add it to the portfolio of my intelligence best practices solutions for our clients.

It's all about asking all your customers the only key and ultimate question that really counts in every sector of business:

> *"Dear customer, did our company fulfil your expectations?"*

In the diagram below you see this question again, expressed slightly differently: "When thinking about us, what image do you see in front of you?" The customer only has to rate the smiley on ten images. As the next step he proceeds to identify the four key success factors and rates them poor-acceptable-good-excellent. If any of the four key success factors have been rated poor, a pop-up appears where the customer is asked to give his/her comments and reasons for the company's poor performance. Now we are talking about customer dialogue, the ultimate way of establishing real time customer contacts. This customer satisfaction-loyalty research takes just 1-3 minutes with average response rates of around 70-90 percent. In the diagram below an example is shown of such a customer dialogue.

ClientIndicator monitoring year round

Choose image:

When thinking about us, what image do see in front of you?

Extremely negative	Somewhat negative	Somewhat positive	Extremely positive

😠 😟 😦 😐 😑   🙂 😃 😊 😄 😁

What is your judgement about our performance concerning;

	POOR	ACCEPT.	GOOD	EXCELLENT
Understanding your market?	●	○	○	●
Deliver creative solutions?	●	○	○	●
Deliver within the agreed time frame?	●	○	○	●
Develop your businesses?	●	○	○	●

Source: Enertio

Professor C.K. Prahalad states that you can only identify customer values starting with the customer and his behaviour. Customer values don't come from the products and services but from the experiences of the customer with these products and services. ClientIndicator gives your company new eyes in the ever-changing customer intelligence landscape. The aim is to monitor continually whether your company is headed in the right direction. It enables you to discover and correct immediately any omissions and dissatisfactions your customers are experiencing. ClientIndicator is a new approach and is applicable as a front line solution or as a strategic customer intelligence solution for inter-active customer dialogue.

ClientIndicator: Four Phases of Implementation

1. Preparation phase: Identifying your company's key customer factors for success. First step is to hold a half-day workshop with senior sales and market management to identify the key customer factors for company success and to identify the self-perceived market image of management. I will use the "key factor verification" to identify the primary, secondary and missing customer factors in a structured way (see the diagram at page 231).

Two-day interview audit with your key customers to determine their views on your company's key customer factors for success and their perceived market image. Also here I will use the same "key factor verification" to identify the primary, secondary and missing factors from the customer perspective.

Finally we hold a half-day workshop with senior management to analyse the results of both previous stages so as to obtain consensus on the key customer factors for future company success.

2. Execution phase: measuring and monitoring of real employee-customer relationships.
   ▶ Internal Employee Image Indicator: to determine the internal images and key company factors for success of the company among front line personnel dealing with customers on a daily basis, e.g. employees of call centres, sales managers, account managers, market managers, marketing staff.
   ▶ Web Indicator: to identify the company image and the key factors for success among visitors to the company website. It will address both customers and prospects which will be identified at the start of the dialogue.
   ▶ ClientIndicator: to expose the company image and key company factors for success to numerous customers, asking the key question "why, dear customer, have you selected our company? From the pricing and quality perspective and from four key company factors for success. After 2 – 3 months ClientIndicator can again identify and monitor the key image question and four key factors for company success in order to find out if the company is still headed in the right direction. Option: here we can extend the ClientIndicator dialogue to find out more about the company's service aspects, company accessibility and customer relations. The result is a "kite" dashboard for real time customer performance from the four perspectives: brand/company image, customer services, customer accessibility and customer relations. Applicable tool will be the Brand Verification Tool.
   ▶ Customer Exit Indicator: to ask the customer why he/she turned his/her back on the company from the price and quality perspective and four company factors for success. Applicable tool will be a modified Brand Verification Tool.
3. Verification phase: verification of fulfilment of the company-based customer objectives:
   ▶ Leakage of image: an analysis of the gap between the company objectives and the fulfilment concerning employees, customers and web visitors.
   ▶ Booster effect to other business units: extensions of the customer intelligence solutions to other business units.
   ▶ Benchmarking analysis of the customer satisfaction results explained in the "zone of excellence and areas for improvement".
4. Achievement phase: companies who have been through the three phases as described above are qualified to become a "Customer Certified Company".

"In business the competition will bite you if you keep running. If you stand still, they will swallow you".
(Semon Knudsen)

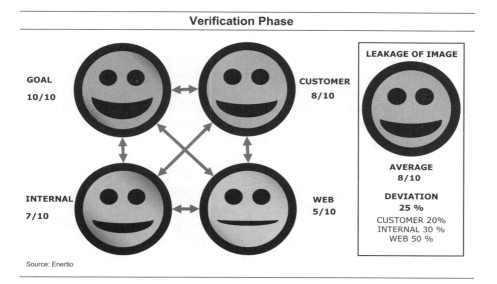

Verification Phase

GOAL 10/10

CUSTOMER 8/10

INTERNAL 7/10

WEB 5/10

LEAKAGE OF IMAGE

AVERAGE 8/10

DEVIATION 25 %
CUSTOMER 20%
INTERNAL 30 %
WEB 50 %

Source: Enertio

II.15   Competitive Intelligence and Scanning the Competitive Periphery

"You can't shut out the outside world without shutting yourself in".
(Arnold Glasgow)

Reading through the Harvard Business Review of November 2005, I was fascinated by Day and Schoemaker's article "Scanning the Periphery". It's a perfect description of how management can prepare themselves for changes in the dynamics of the business environment. It helps management of organisations to foresee changes sooner and understand how they might benefit from it. The diagnostic tool, shown in the range of diagrams, gives you an excellent overview of the pieces in order to see how your organisation is prepared in the current situation as well as for the near future. In our competitive intelligence practices we often see how ill prepared companies fail to take advantage of opportunities in the business environment. Many managers are mainly preoccupied with the present and base their decision-making on data and information from the past and present and also lack the necessary pieces of the puzzle to enable them to see the big picture.

The diagnostic model described in the diagrams in these pages are perfect for assessing how prepared your company is to sense the faint signs of change and to see the early warnings in time.

It enables you to see disruptions before the competition does. Too many managers think they know what's going on with respect to their markets, their customers, the competition, new technologies and legislation and changes of the rules of the game. Porter's five forces model, too, is a great help for identifying changes and dynamics in the business environment in good time. A competitive intelligence capability helps you become an alert company able to see change in time.

The result of the diagnostic analysis has an outcome of four quadrants which identify where your company is. It's good if your company ends up in the quadrants of "focused" and "vigilant". If your company ends up in the quadrant "neurotic" you should narrow your scope and sharpen your focus. However, my assumption is that by far the majority of companies will end up in the quadrant "vulnerable", also based on our best practices in competitive intelligence in the Netherlands, Europe and beyond. A survey conducted among 140 corporate strategists by the Competitive Intelligence Academy in the US confirmed that two-third of the companies surveyed had been surprised by at least three competitive events with high impact over the past five years. In addition 97 percent of respondents stated that their companies lacked an early warning system. We must also take into account that in the US the management discipline of competitive intelligence is far more generally accepted than is the case in Europe and other parts of the world. People, also managers, tend to ignore early warning signals that do not fit in with their assumptions and pre-conceptions. Competitive intelligence is a need-to-have competency to protect management from these pre-conceptions and constantly challenge such assumptions.

Many of you reading this will come to the conclusion that scenario planning and analysis will help companies foresee future change and early warnings. Not so, because scenario planning has a time horizon of 10-20 years on average asking the potential questions about possible events "what if". The legendary example is that of Royal Dutch Shell in the late sixties and early seventies about what to do in the case of an oil boycott to the West. Shell was prepared for the possible eventuality of an oil boycott and ready to act in 1973 because they had done their homework.

Competitive intelligence related to the diagnostic solution of scanning the periphery gives you the answers to numerous questions as described in the diagrams. The nature of your strategy, the complexity of your business environment, the volatility of your business environment, your company's leadership, how your employees access to the data, information and knowledge, the direction of strategy development, the organisation's configuration, and finally the culture, including beliefs, behaviours and values of the organisation. This diagnostic tool, developed and based on extensive research at numerous companies by Day and Schoemaker, is a very welcome solution for diagnosing the actions of organisations in the dynamics of the external business environment.

Scanning the competitive periphery

"It's not the strongest who survives, nor the most intelligent, but the ones most responsive to change".

Charles Darwin

Periphery is:

- The outer part of the field of vision
- The external boundary
- The part of the nervous system that is outside the central nervous system

.... according to Webster

Source: HBR 11/2005

Scanning the competitive periphery

Eight factors of influence have been determined:

I   Nature of strategy
II   Complexity of the business environment
III Volatility of the business environment
IV   Leadership orientation
V   Knowledge management
VI   Strategy making
VII Organizational configuration
VIII Culture

Source: HBR 11/2005

Scanning the competitive periphery

- Companies face environment changes
- How to see these changes sooner?
- How to capitalize on these changes?
- How to avoid the blind spots?
- How to identify the weak signals of change?
- What don't we know that might matter?

Do we foresee changes in the business environment, do we foresee future events, do we have an early warning solution? What do you have?

"Do you have a crow's nest?

Source: HBR 11/2005

Scanning the competitive periphery

Learning from the Past

❑ What have been our blind spots in the past and what's happening in these areas now?

❑ Is there an instructive analogy from another industry?

❑ Who in your industry is skilled at picking up weak signals and acting on them ahead of everyone else?

Source: HBR 11/2005

Scanning the competitive periphery

Learning from the Present

❑ What important signals are you rationalizing away?

❑ What are your mavericks trying to tell you?

❑ What are peripheral customers and competitors really thinking?

Source: HBR 11/2005

Scanning the competitive periphery

Envisioning New Futures

❑ What future events could really hurt or help the company?

❑ What emerging technologies could change the game?

❑ Is there an unthinkable scenario?

Source: HBR 11/2005

Scanning the competitive periphery

I   NATURE OF YOUR STRATEGY

A Focus on your strategy
Narrow (Protected niche)   1   2   3   4   5   6   7   Broad (global)

B Growth orientation
Modest   1   2   3   4   5   6   7   Aggressive

C Number of businesses to integrate
Few   1   2   3   4   5   6   7   Many

D Focus on reinvention
Minor   1   2   3   4   5   6   7   Major (50% of revenue
                                                                     must come from new
Total (add numbers)   products in three years)

Source: HBR 11/2005

Scanning the competitive periphery

II   COMPLEXITY OF YOUR ENVIRONMENT

A Industry structure
Few, easily identifiable   1   2   3   4   5   6   7 Many competitors from
competitors   unexpected sources
B Channel structure
Simple and direct   1   2   3   4   5   6   7 Long and complex

C Market structure
Fixed boundaries and simple   1   2   3   4   5   6   7 Fuzzy boundaries and
segmentation   complex segmentation

D Enabling technologies
Few and mature (simple systems)1   2   3   4   5   6   7 Many converging (complex
                                                                   systems)
E Regulations (federal, state, etc)
Few or stable   1   2   3   4   5   6   7 Many or changing rapidly

Source: HBR 11/2005

Scanning the competitive periphery

II COMPLEXITY OF YOUR ENVIRONMENT

F Public visibility of Industry

Largely ignored　　　　　1　2　3　4　5　6　7　　Closely watched by
media or special-
interest groups

G Dependence on government funding and political access

Low: operates largely　　1　2　3　4　5　6　7　　High: sensitive to
independent of government　　　　　　　　　　politics and the funding
climate

H Dependence on global economy

Low: Affected principally by　1　2　3　4　5　6　7　　High: affected by global
domestic conditions　　　　　　　　　　　　conditions

Total (add numbers)

Source: HBR 11/2005

Scanning the competitive periphery

III VOLATILITY OF YOUR ENVIRONMENT

A Number of surprises by high-impact events in past three years

None　　　　　　　　　1　2　3　4　5　6　7　Three of more

B Accuracy of past forecasts

High: small deviations to　1　2　3　4　5　6　7　Low: results differ greatly
actual forecasts　　　　　　　　　　　　from forecasts

C Market growth

Slow and stable　　　　1　2　3　4　5　6　7　Rapid and unstable

D Growth opportunities

Have decreased dramatically　1　2　3　4　5　6　7　Have increased
in past three years　　　　　　　　　　　　dramatically in past three
years

Source: HBR 11/2005

Scanning the competitive periphery

III VOLATILITY OF YOUR ENVIRONMENT

E Speed and direction of technological change

| Very predictable | 1 | 2 | 3 | 4 | 5 | 6 | 7 | Highly unpredictable |

F Behavior of key competitors, suppliers, and partners

| Very predictable | 1 | 2 | 3 | 4 | 5 | 6 | 7 | Highly unpredictable |

G Posture of key rivals

| Live-and-let-live mentality | 1 | 2 | 3 | 4 | 5 | 6 | 7 | Hostile (aggressive) |

H Susceptibility to macroeconomic forces

| Low sensitivity to price changes, currencies, business cycles, tariffs, etc. | 1 | 2 | 3 | 4 | 5 | 6 | 7 | High sensitivity to price changes, currencies, business cycles, tariffs, etc. |

Source: HBR 11/2005

Scanning the competitive periphery

III VOLATILITY OF YOUR ENVIRONMENT

I Dependence on financial markets

| Low | 1 | 2 | 3 | 4 | 5 | 6 | 7 | High |

J Customer and channel power

| Low | 1 | 2 | 3 | 4 | 5 | 6 | 7 | High |

K Sensitivity to social changes (fashion and values)

| Low: mostly gradual changes from the past | 1 | 2 | 3 | 4 | 5 | 6 | 7 | High: good chance of major disruptions and changes in business models |

L Potential for major disruptions in the next five years

| Low; few surprises expected mostly things we can handle | 1 | 2 | 3 | 4 | 5 | 6 | 7 | High: several significant business shocks are expected, without knowing which in particular |

Total (add numbers) [ ]

Source: HBR 11/2005

Scanning the competitive periphery

IV YOUR LEADERSHIP ORIENTATION

A Importance of the periphery in the business leader's agenda

Low priority   1   2   3   4   5   6   7   High priority

B Time horizon overall

Emphasis on short term   1   2   3   4   5   6   7   Emphasis on long term
(two years or less)   (more than five years)

C Organization's attitude toward the periphery

Limited and myopic: 1   2   3   4   5   6   7   Active and curious:
few people care   systematic monitoring of
                                             periphery

D Willingness to test and challenge basic assumptions

Mostly defensive   1   2   3   4   5   6   7   Very willing to test critical
Total (add numbers)   [   ]   premises or widely held
                                             views

Source: HBR 11/2005

Scanning the competitive periphery

V YOUR KNOWLEDGE MANAGEMENT SYSTEMS

A Quality of data about events and trends at the periphery

Poor: limited coverage and   1   2   3   4   5   6   7   Excellent: broad coverage
often out-of-date   and timely

B Access to data across organizational boundaries

Difficult: limited awareness of   1   2   3   4   5   6   7   Relatively easy: wide
what is available   awareness of what is
                                             available

C Use of database for existing business

Limited   1   2   3   4   5   6   7   Extensive

D Technologies for posing queries to databases

Old and difficult to use   1   2   3   4   5   6   7   State-of-the-art inquiry
Total (add numbers)   [   ]   systems

Source: HBR 11/2005

Scanning the competitive periphery

VI YOUR STRATEGY MAKING

A Experience with uncertainty-reducing strategies

Limited   1 2 3 4 5 6 7   Extensive

B Use of scenario thinking to guide strategy process

Never   1 2 3 4 5 6 7   Frequent

C Number of alliance partners

Few   1 2 3 4 5 6 7   Many

D Flexibility of strategy process

Rigid, calendar driven   1 2 3 4 5 6 7   Flexible, issues oriented

E Resources devoted to scanning the competitive periphery

Negligible   1 2 3 4 5 6 7   Extensive

F Integration of customer and competitor information into future technology platforms and new-product development plans

Poorly and sporadically   1 2 3 4 5 6 7   Systematically and

Integrated **Total (add numbers)** ☐   fully integrated

Source: HBR 11/2005

Scanning the competitive periphery

VII YOUR ORGANIZATIONAL CONFIGURATION (Structure and Incentives)

A Accountability for sensing and acting on weak signals

No one is responsible   1 2 3 4 5 6 7   Responsibility is clearly assigned to project team or dedicated group

B Early warning systems and procedures

None   1 2 3 4 5 6 7   Extensive and effective

C Incentives to encourage and reward wider vision

None   1 2 3 4 5 6 7   Recognition from senior management and direct rewards

Total (add numbers) ☐

Source: HBR 11/2005

Scanning the competitive periphery

VIII   YOUR CULTURE (Values, Beliefs, and behaviors)

A Readiness to listen to reports from scouts on the periphery

Closed: 1   2   3   4   5   6   7   Open:
listening discouraged   listening encouraged

B Willingness of customer-contact people to forward market information

Poor   1   2   3   4   5   6   7   Excellent

C Sharing of information about the periphery across functions

Poor: information ignored   1   2   3   4   5   6   7   Excellent: ongoing
or hoarded   information sharing
                                                                                at multiple levels

Total (add numbers)   ▭

Source: HBR 11/2005

Calculate Your Totals Here

I

II   ▭

III   ▭   Need for
                                     ▭   Peripheral
Total =   ▭   Vision

IV

V   ▭

VI   ▭   Capability for
                                     ▭   Peripheral
VII   ▭   Vision

VIII   ▭

Total =   ▭

Source: HBR 11/2005

The Peripheral Vision Scoring Tool

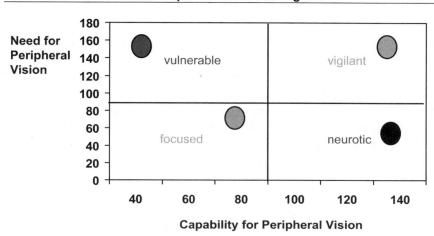

Source: HBR 11/2005

Case: ABNAmro – Antonveneta

Early in March 2005, the Dutch ABNAmro bank showed interest in acquiring the Italian bank Antonveneta. The Italian bank Banca Popolare, the new name of Popolare di Lodi, also showed interest in Antoveneta. For months the potential acquisition of Antonveneta by ABNAmro was in the national and international newspapers. ABNAmro's aim was to develop a third "domestic" market, after the Netherlands and the US. For several years ABNAmro had already had an 8.6 percent stake in the Italian bank Capitalia. From March 2005, ABNAmro bank seemed to have stirred up a hornets'nest. Banca Popolare and its CEO Gianpiero Fiorani did everything to stop the Dutch. The President of the Central Bank of Italy, Antonio Fazio, also got involved, wishing to protect the Italian banking sector from foreign incursions. In 1999 the Spanish Banco Bilbao Vizcaya met its "Waterloo" in trying to acquire Unicredito. The negotiations between ABNAmro and Antonveneta became extremely complicated, with many unexpected developments, influences and changes from the external business environment of the Italian business world. It was only after many months that ABNAmro found out about the personal and friendly relations that existed between Gianpiero Fiorani and the President of the Central Bank, Antonio Fazio. Exactly what happened can be described in another book.

In autumn 2005 ABNAmro finally succeeded in acquiring a majority stake in Antonveneta. In July 2005 I was asked to give my views on this acquisition from an intelligence perspective. The article was published in the Dutch Financieele

Dagblad. My key message was: "ABNAmro could have been smarter". In my article I explained the following:

1. ABNAmro was lagging behind the facts and developments;
   ABNAmro didn't obtain timely insights into the interests of shareholders, supervisors and stakeholders;
2. ABNAmro did not get a clear view of what was really going on in the closed market of the Italian financial sector;
3. ABNAmro ignored the characteristics of the financial sector in Italy: complex structures, chauvinism, national pride, unclear relationships, political intrigues and the closed character of the Italian market;
4. ABNAmro had insufficient insight into the hidden agendas;
5. Obviously, the management didn't learn much from the disaster in 1998 when ABNAmro wanted to acquire the Generale Bank in Brussels. The Board of ABNAmro at that time lacked the key information about how to conduct an acquisition in Belgium from the perspective of national culture.
6. ABNAmro underestimated the capabilities of its rival, Banco Popolare, in the battle for Antonveneta. Banca Popolare had succeeded in obtaining credit facilities from an international banking consortium to enable them to acquire Antonveneta.

The next day the Financieele Dagblad published two "responses from readers". First, the response from ABNAmro, the Director Group Communications, was that ABNAmro was well prepared, had carried out the right analyses, already knew about the efforts being made by Banco Popolare to acquire Antonveneta and had excellent contacts and experience of the Italian banking sector. The response ended by saying that consultants should not advertise themselves too obviously.

The second response came from an individual who wrote that such acquisition targets should be managed like a military operation by having an overview of the entire competitive landscape. In addition he wrote of the potential arrogance and complacency of ABNAmro. In case of failure, he recommended that the management of ABNAmro should conduct a critical analysis to ascertain where it went wrong, including a review by management reflection of their own role. My article of July 19 2005 probably hit the big egos of the Board of ABNAmro.

New facts about ABNAmro. At the time of the acquisition of Antonveneta, ABNAmro always maintained its integrity, at least so they consistently claimed. In the end this was one of the key factors explaining why ABNAmro was successful in acquiring Antonveneta. I have said that ABNAmro had an 8.6 percent stake in Capitalia. To secure its future interests, the management of ABNAmro supported three previous Members of the Board of Capitalia in regaining their former positions. By voting for these three Members at the Shareholders Meeting, their suspension was discontinued. Two of them had been suspended by the Central Bank of Italy. The third Member, Chairman of the Supervisory Board and previous CEO Cesare Geronzi of Capitalia, was sentenced to 20 months in jail for his involvement in the bankruptcy of the hotel group Italcase-Bagaglino. Previously Cesare Geronzi had been suspended because of his involvement in the bankruptcy of Italian Parmalat. I don't think I need spell out any conclusion about ABNAmro's integrity.

II. 16 The scope of competitive intelligence in the organisation

"True wisdom lies in gathering the precious things out of each day as it goes by".
(E.S.Bouton)

Since early in 2000 we have seen how marketing research and marketing services departments have been re-branded as marketing intelligence departments. Is market research the same as marketing intelligence? And what is the level and acceptance of market research within the organisation?

For years market research departments have tried to find a new position within the company. Their ambition is to transform themselves from data providers towards more information and knowledge about markets and customers. Market research still focuses strongly on customer satisfaction and quantitative research using data from research institutes such as GfK, Nielsen and IMS. Marketing intelligence has a broader perspective on markets, customers and competitors. Collecting data is one aspect, but other more important aspects of marketing intelligence are interpretation and analysis within the broader scope of the marketing discipline.

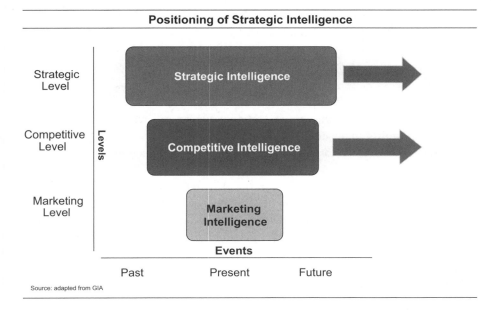

The key focus of marketing intelligence is markets and competitors at operational and tactical level. Usually, marketing intelligence staff report to the marketing director or the commercial director. In such cases, marketing intelligence is generally an isolated function dealing with the present. Other problem in case intelligence is positioned within the marketing department is the filter. The marketing director probably only disseminates the good-to-know information across the organisation. Intelligence is about the brutal truth. Will marketing officers communicate their problems in the market place? Will they communicate their failures? Marketers basically hate research, planning and analysis. But analysis is of high strategic importance in competitive intelligence. This makes marketing intelligence contrary to the realities of the competitive intelligence discipline.

> *"The past cannot be changed, the future is still in your power".*
> (Hugh White)

Does a competitive intelligence regime make organisations more successful? Are organisations that have a competitive intelligence regime in place more or less successful in the long run? I know many companies which have competitive intelligence in place and which are very successful. I don't know companies that have competitive intelligence in place which are unsuccessful. I also know many companies that don't have a competitive intelligence regime, yet which are very successful in their field. Here are some key questions about similar competencies:

1. Does quality management make organisations more successful?
2. Does Six Sigma make organisations more successful?
3. Do balance scorecards, performance management and the monitoring on key performance indicators make organisations more successful?
4. Do IT as well as business intelligence-based IT bring organisations more success?
5. Does a cockpit with KPIs make organisations more successful?
6. Does business development make organisations more successful?
7. Does innovation make organisations more successful?
8. Does strategic management make organisations more successful?
9. Does marketing make organisations more successful?
10. Do customer satisfaction and loyalty make organisations more successful?

All these questions can be answered in the affirmative. In every question the key element is people. People determine the success of Six Sigma, strategic management, business development, marketing, innovation and so on. Having marketing in place does not ensure the right portfolio of products and services. Again, it's the marketing people who determine the success. All this we can classify as intangible assets.

It's the same with competitive intelligence. I have listed similar questions as above, however, these are fully focused on competitive intelligence:

1. Does management see the urgency of the need to develop a continuous and consistent watch on the dynamic changes in the external business environment?
2. Does management want to be surprised by new developments and innovation taking place within their field or beyond in the industry sector?
3. Does management want to stay ahead of competition?
4. Does management want to be faced with unexpected new competitors, new technologies, new legislation or trends?
5. Does management want to be faced with disruptive technologies?
6. Does management want to be faced with medium and long-term threats?
7. Does management want to benefit from new opportunities from the identification of the gaps in their own and competitive strategies?
8. Do management want to be protected from their own blind spots?
9. Does management want to continue to compete without a permanent watch on their counterparts?
10. Does management want to be faced with unforeseen future developments?

All these questions can be answered in the positive and the negative. In order to prevent all those negative questions we invite all management teams in organisations to consider implementing competitive intelligence within their organisations. The model below "how to make intelligence work" is an excellent example of a way in which to make it happen. This model has been used in numerous organisations all over Europe.

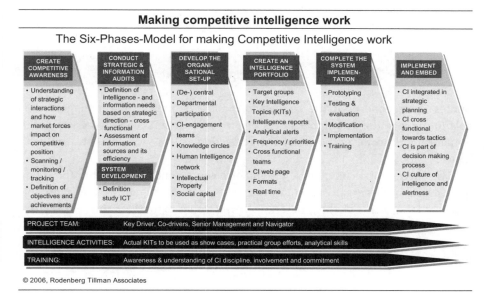

Making competitive intelligence work

The Six-Phases-Model for making Competitive Intelligence work

CREATE COMPETITIVE AWARENESS	CONDUCT STRATEGIC & INFORMATION AUDITS	DEVELOP THE ORGANI-SATIONAL SET-UP	CREATE AN INTELLIGENCE PORTFOLIO	COMPLETE THE SYSTEM IMPLEMEN-TATION	IMPLEMENT AND EMBED
• Understanding of strategic interactions and how market forces impact on competitive position • Scanning / monitoring / tracking • Definition of objectives and achievements	• Definition of intelligence - and information needs based on strategic direction - cross functional • Assessment of information sources and its efficiency **SYSTEM DEVELOPMENT** • Definition study ICT	• (De-) central • Departmental participation • CI-engagement teams • Knowledge circles • Human Intelligence network • Intellectual Property • Social capital	• Target groups • Key Intelligence Topics (KITs) • Intelligence reports • Analytical alerts • Frequency / priorities • Cross functional teams • CI web page • Formats • Real time	• Prototyping • Testing & evaluation • Modification • Implementation • Training	• CI integrated in strategic planning • CI cross functional towards tactics • CI is part of decision making process • CI culture of intelligence and alertness

PROJECT TEAM: Key Driver, Co-drivers, Senior Management and Navigator

INTELLIGENCE ACTIVITIES: Actual KITs to be used as show cases, practical group efforts, analytical skills

TRAINING: Awareness & understanding of CI discipline, involvement and commitment

© 2006, Rodenberg Tillman Associates

In order to make the implementation of competitive intelligence successful according to this model, senior management has to make the following decisions:

"The best place for competitive intelligence is on a par with top management".

1. Ownership of the competitive intelligence competency at the highest level in the organisation. In most cases this will be a Member of the Board or General Manager;
2. Creation of a drivers team. Depending on the size of the company, division or business unit, a key driver will be needed and around 6-8 co-drivers supported by an external navigator/facilitator;
3. Training. The drivers team needs an in-depth understanding of competitive intelligence: awareness, objectives and strategies, achievements and deliverables;
4. Budget. The only commitment to implementing competitive intelligence is budget allocation. Then commitment becomes reality to let it happen;
5. Systems support. The creation of a competitive intelligence portal is a transparent and easy solution to establishing this kind of platform for information sharing, communication, storage and distribution.
6. Having the director of intelligence placed on the Management Team. Intelligence creates value if the director of intelligence sits at the table where future decisions will be made.

"By doing it this way the senior management creates its own "intelligence staff" in preparing the organisation to be part of the future. In the military or in wartime this is called "chief of staff" to the President or Prime Minister".

"CEOs or Senior Management desperately need such a chief of staff".

Success in responding to the 20 questions above is the way that management is able to manage the intangible assets of the organisation. This is the key differentiator for almost every organisational function as it is with competitive intelligence.

The success of a competitive intelligence competency is related to the intangible assets of the organisation. You can't see, touch or quantify the intangible assets but they make all the difference when it comes to market value. Part I chapter 8 of the present describes competitive intelligence at Cisco. The market capitalization changed, from 2001 at the start of Cisco's competitive intelligence capability, from US$ 135 billion to US$ 182 billion in 2005. Over the same period the market capitalization of the key competitors decreased from US$ 156 to US$ 93 billion, thanks to competitive intelligence!

Key intangible assets are:

▶ The collective skills, abilities, expertise in the way of doing business;

- The outcome of investments in staffing, training, compensation, communication and other areas of human resources;
- The way people and resources are brought together;
- The identity and personality of the organisation;
- Stable overtime: then it is very difficult to copy capital market access, product and services strategies and technology;
- Very difficult to measure;
- Tangible investments in assets receive far more attention than intangible assets.

This listing of the key intangible assets determines important conditions in setting up a competitive intelligence competency. Specific conditions in addition are:

- Talent: intelligence professionals must be able to question current and future strategies;
- Speed: intelligence professionals need to move quickly to deliver the answers on important topics fast;
- Shared mindset: intelligence professionals must create a culture including what they stand for, how they work and how they share operations across the organisation;
- Accountability: high performance does matter;
- Collaboration: the way the intelligence professionals work, gaining efficiency, effectiveness and leverage across the organisation;
- Learning: intelligence professionals must be seen as change agents and must educate others about how intelligence can improve job performance;
- Leadership: intelligence professionals must become part of organisational leadership;
- Connectivity: intelligence professionals must forge enduring relationships of trust with the targeted internal customers; directors, senior management and the Board;
- Strategic unity: sharing of intellectual behaviour amongst colleagues;
- Innovation: intelligence must become an important driver of innovation from the external business perspective;
- Efficiency: intelligence professionals must operate cost efficiently in managing the intelligence processes, colleagues and projects.

The competitive intelligence context of the intangible assets and the specific conditions provide a sound foundation for the establishment of a competitive intelligence competency.

Case: Infineon
A good example of positioning competitive intelligence within the organisation is Infineon. Infineon is the German-based semiconductor company with a top

ten position within the sector. The company has in place a small competitive intelligence team of around 6-7 people.

Competitive intelligence is fully integrated within the "Corporate Strategy Group". This group has three key focus areas: strategic management, mergers and acquisitions and competitive intelligence. The competitive intelligence efforts consist of three key directions, all essential for survival within the semiconductor sector:

▶ Market intelligence; continuous monitoring of changes in the market place;
▶ Competitor intelligence; continuous watch on competitor moves;
▶ Economic intelligence; continuous monitoring of the worldwide and regional economic climate and foreseeing planned investments and divestments by customers.

The competitive intelligence efforts are organised inter-departmentally and have a strong early warning focus. Each quarter the competitive intelligence team spends one day with the executive board.

In other sections of this book I have described how well the competitive intelligence capability operates within IBM, Cisco, Boeing and many other companies.

Case: Agfa Gevaert

Agfa, Aktien Gesellschaft fuer Anilin-Fabrikation, was funded in 1897. In 1936 Agfa introduced the first colour film. In 1964 Agfa merged with Belgian Gevaert. In November 2004, Agfa Gevaert sold the photographic business to the management for Euros 175.5 under the new name of "AgfaPhoto", representing annual sales of 700 million. In March 2005, the company even produced a new company logo representing the change of the company with the theme "the way to the digital age". The company wanted to focus on traditional photographic materials, but also on the digital storage of photos. In addition they wanted to make more use of the Internet as the new consumer channel for the development of photos.

Unfortunately, AgfaPhoto was unable to free itself from analogue technology and went into bankruptcy by the end of May 2005.

Case: We have been asleep

Young Dutch people no longer wish to work in industry. Since the report of Dekker in 1987 it is known what the problems are, but nothing has been done.

1. Technical education is not popular. The number of new students has been decreasing for many years.
2. Employers say: "we pay taxes and the government should take care of education"
3. The result of this is that the educational sector believes that the business world should not interfere with education.

4. In addition there is a lack of cooperation between the middle and high professional educational sector and the universities.
5. Education must be agreeable and fun. But if this type of education doesn't
   produce opportunities for employment within the sector, something is fundamentally wrong.
6. Technical education is seen as neither agreeable nor fun. This image must
   change.

It will take another 5 -7 years before the Netherlands has sufficient numbers of
skilled people again.

Case: Fortis

Fortis is the Benelux-based bank insurance company. Fortis ASR suffers from
price competition on the Dutch mortgage market and they have lost a substantial
market share.

In 2005, Fortis integrated the brands Amev, Woudsend and Stad Rotterdam
into Fortis ASR, the new insurance brand of Fortis. In 2001, Fortis had a share of
market of 13 percent of the mortgage market, which dropped in 2005 to 7.5 percent. The other key players developed as follows:

Rabobank: 24.6 percent share of market in 2005 from 25.2 percent in 2004.

ING: with Postbank the group gained a market share of 22.7 percent from 21.4
percent in 2004.

ABN Amro: including MNF and Bouwfonds 14.3 percent in 2005 from 12.6 percent in 2004.

In cases of mergers and acquisitions, companies develop a strong internal focus.
For competitors this should be an important signal inviting an attack on the
merged company.

The four biggest bank groups in the Netherlands have in total around 70 percent of the mortgage market. The market leader is still de Hypotheker. Fierce
competition from new foreign entrants resulted in a price war in 2006.

Case: EdF France

Electricite de France was listed on the stock exchange in November 2005.
The listing generated Euros 7 billion and around 5 million shareholders. The
introduction share price was Euros 33, which meant a market capitalization of
Euros 60 billion. German-based Eon and Italian Enel have a market capitalization
of 60 and 42 billion Euros. The listing was highly successful, but there are also
serious concerns about EdF, firstly, the lack of the necessary capital to dismantle
the 58 nuclear reactors – 26 billion Euros. Secondly, there is a structural deficit of
14 billion Euros in the pension funds. Thirdly, there is another debt of 19 billion
Euros, caused by the acquisitions during the second half of the 1990s. The total

deficit amounts to 59 billion Euros, only one billion difference from the total market capitalisation of 60 billion Euros. The French state still owns 86.2 percent of the shares and is legally obliged to retain a minimum stake of 70 percent. These figures indicate that the future of EdF is certainly less rosy than at first appears.

II.17   Strategic War Mapping

"If the WHY is big enough, the How is easy".
(Jim Rawn)

The aim of competitive intelligence is to obtain business foresights about the future developments organisations will face. Competitive intelligence is future-oriented. I have explained in the previous chapters about scenario planning and about strategy under uncertainty.

Strategic War Mapping is another solution for the identification of future developments. However, in strategic war mapping three important elements are different. The first is the word "war", which means that the direct competitors of the organisation play a vital role in strategic war mapping. The second is much emphasis on the future moves of direct competitors, which are supported by assumptions based on specific analysis tools. The third is the limited time frame in which the strategic war mapping takes place: two days. This means that strategic war mapping is a perfect solution for the remote strategic management of events that take place in organisations throughout the year. Strategic war mapping is an adaptation of military tactics to the business world.

The reason for executing strategic war mapping can be as follows: a contribution to the organisation's success by preparing the management to deal much more effectively with the future dynamics of customers, competitors, markets, technologies, legislation and other potential developments; it can help management with strategic, tactical and operational planning and execution; it can educate the participants in the strategic war mapping about the future realities and dynamics of the organisation's external business environment; it helps to avoid the danger of extrapolation and other spreadsheet forecasts, based on past successes projected into the future.

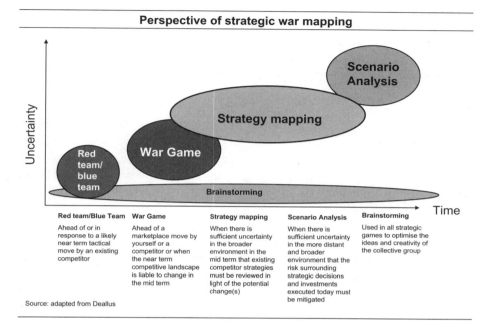

Perspective of strategic war mapping

Red team/Blue Team	War Game	Strategy mapping	Scenario Analysis	Brainstorming
Ahead of or in response to a likely near term tactical move by an existing competitor	Ahead of a marketplace move by yourself or a competitor or when the near term competitive landscape is liable to change in the mid term	When there is sufficient uncertainty in the broader environment in the mid term that existing competitor strategies must be reviewed in light of the potential change(s)	When there is sufficient uncertainty in the more distant and broader environment that the risk surrounding strategic decisions and investments executed today must be mitigated	Used in all strategic games to optimise the ideas and creativity of the collective group

Source: adapted from Deallus

There are many recommendations for running a strategic war mapping. The most important recommendation is to create a joint effort in the future success of the organisation, because during the two days of execution 5-6 teams of each 6-8 participants work closely together. This makes strategic war mapping and strategic management less elite, and generates much greater support throughout the organisation: 30-40 participants maximum can be involved per company, division or business unit. Other recommendations to be considered could be:

1. The organisation's business environment is changing fast;
2. The organisation is facing new ways of competition or major new direct competitors, especially those who do not play by the traditional rules, make up new rules or set new standards;
3. The strategies that contributed to the company's success in the past are uninspired and no longer seem to work;
4. Getting new passion into the organisation with the aim of meeting new challenges;
5. There is a critical lack of consensus about what the company's new strategic direction should be;
6. The organisation's executive team is complacent, arrogant, over-confident and desperately need new challenges and renewal;
7. The organisation has large amounts of data and information about customers, markets and competition but struggles to gain the right intelligence from it.

In such cases many organisations sit on a treasure of information and knowledge, but don't know what to do with it;

8. The organisation suffers from the silo structure. The various departments
and units do not communicate with each other or operate in ways that optimise only their own performance but limit the progress of others;

The outcome of strategic war mapping can be to define the organisation's strategy, make new strategic choices, improve the inter-departmental decision-making
process, challenge and drive for actions, obtain better insights and foresights into
the fast changes in the dynamics of the competitive landscape, better teamwork,
more inspiration, real passion and strong motivation. Another result can be better
monitoring of competitors' future movements so as to be well prepared for the
battle to win customers.

One of the analysis tools, in addition to at least five other analysis tools useful
for strategic war mapping, is Michael Porter's Four Corners Analysis. During the
four corners analysis the different teams must give the following answers: imagine that each team is playing the role of one of the organisation's direct competitors. You can imagine how powerful and dynamic such an analysis can be for
the company. The first issue to be covered is future goals, which give a clue as to
their level of satisfaction with existing strategies and current performance. What
are the other expectations? A second very important issue is the making of the
assumptions. What is the company's history/legacy in the marketplace and where
does its leadership come from? How do the assumptions look like both from the
competitor's perspective and the sector as a whole? The third issue is to identify
precisely the current strategies and how they compete and what the key differentiating factors are. The fourth issue is to find out about their capabilities. How
capable are they of reacting to change? The fifth issue is trying to identify the
offensive capabilities of competitors. What potential moves can be identified and
what will be the gains from these potential moves? The final issue is to identify
the competitor's defensive capabilities. Making realistic assumptions about the
changes to which competitors are most vulnerable and identifying where possible
how they will react when under attack.

> "Nobody can really guarantee the future. The best we can do is size up the chances,
> calculate the risks involved, estimate our ability to deal with them and then make our
> plans with confidence".
> (Henry Ford II)

Strategic war mapping takes on average two days for its execution. The preparation phase is the most important part of the strategic war mapping process
and counts for almost 90 percent of the effort, the reason being that the participants need to be extremely well prepared. They have to do their homework, gather

the relevant information and knowledge about the organisation's business environment – markets, customers, competitors, technologies and other key aspects, which influence the future position of the organisation. This makes strategic war mapping like the tip of the iceberg, which as the visible part represents only about 10 percent of the total effort involved in strategic war mapping.

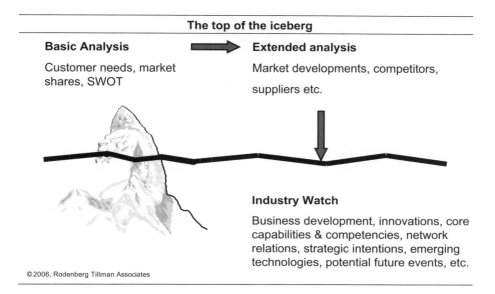

The top of the iceberg

Basic Analysis ➡ **Extended analysis**

Customer needs, market shares, SWOT

Market developments, competitors, suppliers etc.

Industry Watch

Business development, innovations, core capabilities & competencies, network relations, strategic intentions, emerging technologies, potential future events, etc.

© 2006, Rodenberg Tillman Associates

The steps in executing strategic war mapping are:
1. Detailed briefing from the organisation involved – about one half day;
2. Initial proposal for the strategic war mapping event;
3. Preparation of the content, planning, work formats and analysis tools;
4. Pre-strategic war mapping briefing of all participants;
5. The actual strategic war mapping: two days, preferably in a remote area;
6. The after-action report AAR.

The deliverables and results of strategic war mapping can be divided into two kinds of deliverables: the hard deliverables and the soft deliverables. Both are of equally high importance because executing strategic war mapping means action. The actions between the hard and the soft deliverables might be the following:
Hard deliverables:
▶ Probability impact grids such as outlines of competitive moves, relevant events and trends as well as the probability that each move will occur;

▶ Specific recommendations and actions for the exploitation of new opportunities, the blocking or neutralization of competitive moves, reducing risks and threats identified during the strategic war mapping event;

▶ The development of the appropriate contingency plans which might be significant;

▶ Defining current and future intelligence gaps and strategies for closing these gaps;

▶ The listing of the more immediate and near-term tactical lessons learned during the strategic war-mapping event.

Soft deliverables:

▶ The identification of new ways of competition which the organisation is not yet prepared to handle or react to;

▶ The commitment to increasing the effectiveness of internal communication and teamwork between the participants and the elimination of the functional and organisational silos;

▶ Recognition of the need to take short term decisions in order to ensure long term strategic successes;

▶ Generating the appreciation and commitment to implement competitive intelligence across the organisation as a pre-condition for long-term success;

▶ An in depth understanding of the need to watch constantly and consistently in a structured way the ever-changing dynamics in the organisation's external business environment from the perspectives of markets, customers, competitors, technologies, legislation and network relations of all kinds which influence the future performance of the organisation. Porter's five forces model might be the supporting tool for assessing the competitive landscape both now and in the future.

The execution of strategic war mapping is, in my experience of numerous organisations throughout the world, a perfect solution for the yearly reviews and new directions of the strategic management process. It forces the management to think beyond their own expertise and knowledge of the company and the sector it operates in. It gives management new perspectives beyond their industry boundaries and equips the organisation not to become part of the undesirable commercial conflict. Sun Tzu said: "know your enemies and know yourself and in a hundred battles you will never be in danger". This means that strategic management processes must become much more intelligence or evidence-based. Intelligence-based management is not best conducted by know-it-alls, but by managers and business leaders who seriously appreciate how much they don't know.

> *"Competitive intelligence involves breaking out of established patterns with the aim of looking at things in a different way".*

II.18   Analysis tools

"The best analysis is a whiteboard, a marker, brains and creativity. Analysis tools just provide support".
(Jan Herring)

In the information-gathering phase of the cycle of competitive intelligence, involving the interpretation, analysis and dissemination and delivering "actionable intelligence" to the key decision-makers, the most important part is analysis. In management we now have available a wide range of analysis tools to support our intelligence efforts. However, I fully concur with the above statement by Jan Herring: to break out of the established patterns by looking at things in a different way, the best analysis tool is a whiteboard, a marker, brains and creativity. Analysis in many organisations faces increasing difficulties. Key problem is the widening gap in information management: the volume of information in the world doubles every 18 months, whilst the availability of analytical personnel like researchers and analysts is decreasing. Since 2001 hundreds of thousands people have been fired by thousands of companies. Not only intellectual and social capital has walked out of the door but also highly knowledgeable professionals who were operating in the heart of the business world.

This is the first problem we currently face in analysis.

The second problem is the fact that people in key positions in such areas as marketing hate research, planning and analysis. Over 60 percent of marketers dislike analysis, according to an extensive international survey in 2006. And we have a lot of marketers in our organisations!

The third problem is that the majority of organisations embrace easy-to-use analysis tools. Just think of the spreadsheet projections, the famous SWOT approaches and last but not least the technique of extrapolation, in my opinion the worst analysis tool in business today, because it presupposes that next year's market will be almost identical to the current market.Such projections are utterly erroneous, unrealistic and certainly not intelligence or evidence-based. Yet far too many organisations still use this technique.

"Budgeting in the real world. Although the process still needs a lot of work, more and more companies are writing budgets that reflect strategy and reduce frustration".

What kind of personality does your company have in dealing with these kinds of analysis tools? Then we have, of course, the many internal analysis tools which are the outcome of balance score cards, performance management, financial analysis statements and the wide range of data-crunching tools from our IT-based business intelligence solutions. They don't bring any intelligence, just structure and access to data and information. It is only human intelligence that counts: having access to the right information, interpretation, analysis and transforming this into "actionable intelligence". Based on thorough analysis, I always recommend the format below: "The Intelligence Based Executive Decision Model".

Intelligence based Executive Decision Model	
Executive Decision Model	**Tips for Successful use**
1. Situation Description (facts/data): _____ _____ 2. Analysis/Explanation/Interpretation (impact): _____ _____ 3. Options (pathways to a solution): _____ _____ 4. Recommendations (If I were you, here's what I'd do.) _____ _____ 5. Negative unintended consequences: _____	1. Keep it one page, one side. 2. Use positive, direct, power language. 3. Provide at least three options, one being doing nothing. 4. Put yourself in the boss' shoes when you decide which of the options you're going to select as your recommendation. 5. Forecast collateral damage.

Source: James Lukaszewski

This intelligence-based executive decision model is my ultimate model for making real life intelligence based decisions because it has all the elements top management likes. Decision-making is the most difficult part of modern management, so the best tools are required. This decision model occupies only one page; it contains all the real strategic aspects. This model is unbiased, because at point 5 the intelligence professional writes down the negative unintended consequences such as the forecast of collateral damage. This means that potential decisions are really lively and dynamic and the reverse of static. From my own experience in competitive intelligence I have so often heard how much top management really likes this kind of "all-in-one" decision-based format.

> *"Around 75 percent of the mistakes a man makes are made because he does not really know the things he thinks he knows".*
> (James Bryce)

Another frequently-used model for decision-making is the format of the AAR, After Action Review. This model has been created by the Pentagon and is currently used in many organisations. I know organisations who have these AARs easy accessible within their competitive intelligence portals. The aim of the AAR is to learn and capture information from successful decisions as well as from failures. There are only four questions to be answered. The challenge here is to limit the format to one page.

After Action Reviews - AAR's

For individuals and teams to learn and capture knowledge & intelligence from both successes and failures.

Four key questions

1. What was supposed to happen?

2. What actually happened?

3. What were the differences and WHY?

4. What can we learn from it?

Source: Pentagon

Several research studies by SCIP, the Society of Competitive Intelligence Professionals, USA, show that the most frequently-used analysis tools are competitor analysis and SWOT. I do not believe either of these is the best in-depth tools for use in competitive intelligence: there are many other tools that are better suited to the task.

I will show several analysis tools such as those I frequently use in our competitive intelligence practices. Most of these tools are used frequently throughout the year, because dynamics are important for the identification of change and different patterns. However, let's first look at the Advanced Analysis Techniques which support the baseline assessments at IBM.

Advanced Analysis Techniques by IBM

IBM uses five key analysis techniques: I will describe here:
1. Scenario Planning: identifying the vulnerabilities or testing new identified strategic moves;
2. War Gaming: multi-player dynamics
3. Financial Forensics: generating deeper insights from cash flow, balance sheets and customer data;

4. Assumptions Testing: examining validity, breadth, consistency, dispersion and endurance;
5. Relationships Mapping: people-to-people, people-to-company, company-to-company and value-net-to-value-net.

Nine Baseline Assessments used by IBM in competitive intelligence: Company strategies: business strategy, marketing strategy and the product/services strategy; Ecosystems participation: alliances and value nets; Client-level data: client lists and profiling, share of wallet analysis; Marketing: brands and images, market positioning and communications and messaging; Go-to-market: channels and programmes, direct sales, teleweb coverage, customer-geographic-industry segmentation and coverage; Financials: quarterly results and shares, revenues and profit shares and modelling; Organisation: executives, organisation structures and employment services; Future directions: upcoming events, projected moves, reactions to IBM and offering roadmaps; Vulnerabilities: SWOT analysis, critical dependencies, ways IBM can gain advantages, identifying repeatable sales opportunities for IBM and its partners.

The advanced analysis techniques and baseline assessments of IBM listed above give a good impression of the tools used. The tools are a perfect combination of in-depth analysis from history and presence into the future. Scenario planning, war gaming, relationship mapping and future directions are excellent techniques for predicting future events. The other tools and techniques are mainly useful at the tactical and operational level.

Analysis tools used in competitive intelligence. An overview of applicable formats

This overview is not complete. Competitive intelligence is the outcome of an analytical and intellectual process, creativity and analysis. The supportive analysis towards actionable intelligence for decision-makers is a matter of assessing the possible relevance of these tools and how they fit into the organisational personality of the company. Some companies have very extensive procedures, others prefer the highest impact formats. I will list the analysis tool formats we often use in our competitive intelligence practices.

I have already described the supportive tools Scenario Planning (chapter 12), Strategy under Uncertainty (chapter 13) and Strategic War Mapping (chapter 17).

In the next few pages I shall show:

▶ Model of Freedom of Action: 31 business relationships elements outside-in, which influence the organisation's future level of freedom of action (see diagram at page 85);
▶ Key Intelligence Topic Format: the structured approach to the different phases towards action-based decision-making (see diagram at page 166);

► Competitive Position Analysis: based on the identified key success factors, identifying the future dynamic company position with the emphasis on the allocation of future management focus and management resources;

► Olympic Metal Focus Strategy Format: linking customer segmentation to market segmentation strategies;

► The shadow-marketing plan of competition: plans are made by people and not by companies. Marketing plans of competition can be developed combining intelligence gathering, making assumptions and analysis;

► SWOT Issues Matrix: the matrix gives the clusters of the confrontation matrix relating the strengths, weaknesses, opportunities and threats to each other. Results are the strategic issues for actions;

► Strategic Options Matrix: management can combine the future desired company activities based on the industry structure to be seen as stable or in change;

► GE Growth Matrix: good tool to combine the company's business strengths with the attractiveness of the different industry sectors, with the aim of identifying where to invest, divest, hold or harvest;

► BCG Matrix: frequently-used matrix for portfolio management with the four quadrants cash cows, stars, problem child and dogs;

► Competitor Profile Format: the complete one-page format; the important competitive elements for key competitors;

► Positioning Statement: a positioning statement of the dynamics in a competitive landscape;

► Technology Based Intelligence Cycle: one-page format positioning the current and future technology life cycle;

► The Competitive Assessment Model: a qualitative inter-departmental visual assessment model of eight factors that influence the power of competitors, suppliers and other network relationships;

► SPACE: the strategic positioning and action evaluation model of positioning the own company versus rivals in respect of financial power, competitive edge, strengths of the industry sector and turbulence in the external business environment.

> *"Great opportunities come to all, but many do not know they have met them. The only preparation to take advantage of them is to watch what each day brings".*
> (Albert E. Dunning)

Competitive Position Analysis

KSF's	Weighting Now	Weighting 2008	Our Company	Competitor A	Competitor B	Management Focus	Management Resources
Raw materials	20	15	3	4	2		
Productivity	15	10	2	3	3	●●	●●●
Overhead Control	10	10	3	3	5		
Quality	15	10	4	4	3		
Cash Flow	10	15	3	4	4	●●	●
Strategy & control	15	20	2	3	3	●●●	●●●
Support for customers	15	20	4	4	2	●●	●
Total	100	100	3.0	3.6	3.0		

Olympic Metal Focus Strategy

Strategic Options: Attack, Defend and/or Consolidate

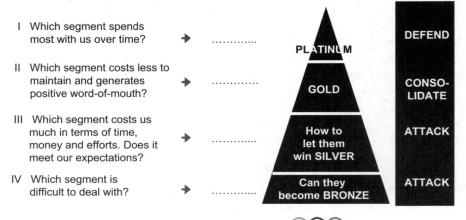

I   Which segment spends most with us over time?   ➜ ....

II   Which segment costs less to maintain and generates positive word-of-mouth?   ➜ ....

III   Which segment costs us much in terms of time, money and efforts. Does it meet our expectations?   ➜ ....

IV   Which segment is difficult to deal with?   ➜ ....

PLATINUM — DEFEND

GOLD — CONSOLIDATE

How to let them win SILVER — ATTACK

Can they become BRONZE — ATTACK

The shadow marketing plan of competition

• Executive summary	• A brief overview of the competitor's plan for a quick review by management
• Current marketing situation	• Relevant background data on the market, product, distribution, macro-environment and competitor's competition
• 'SWOTI' analysis	• A summary of the competitor's Strengths, Weaknesses, Opportunities, Threats and Issues that the product/service must address
• Objectives	• A presentation of the competitor likely product/service objectives, outlining volume, revenue, market share, profit and return on investment objectives
	• A presentation of the broad approach that will be used to address the plan's objectives: identifying target markets, positioning, technology, product, promotion, pricing, distribution, service, people's network
• Marketing strategies	• Answers the questions: What will the competitor do?
	• How much will they spend?
	• When will they meet the objectives?
• Implementation	• What will be the key success factors?
	• Who will do the work?
• Estimated income statement	• Profit-and-loss statement estimated

ISSUES

OPPORTUNITIES	THREATS
1. AAA 2. DDD 3. CCC 4. BBB	1. FFF 2. GGG 3. EEE 4. JJJ 5. III

		1	2	3	4	1	2	3	4	5
Strenghts										
PPP	1	0	+ +	+ +	0	0	0	+	0/-	+ +
RRR	2	0	0	0	0	0	0	+	0	0
MMM	3	+ /0	0	-	0	0	-	0	--	+
OOO	4	+	0	0	+	0	0	0	-	+
NNN	5	0	-	+	0	0	+ +	-	0	-
Weaknesses										
SSS	1	-	-	--	-	0	--	--	--	--
TTT	2	+	0	0/-	+	0	--	+	0	0
ZZZ	3	0	-	+	-	0	+ +	-	0	0
WWW	4	0	0	-	0	0	0	+	0	0

STRATEGIC OPTIONS MATRIX

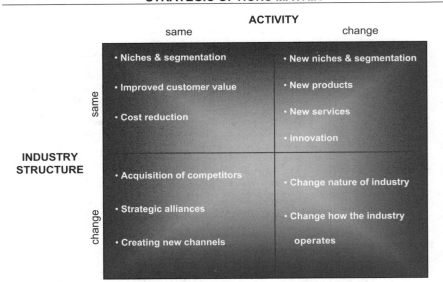

ACTIVITY

	same	change
same	• Niches & segmentation • Improved customer value • Cost reduction	• New niches & segmentation • New products • New services • Innovation
change	• Acquisition of competitors • Strategic alliances • Creating new channels	• Change nature of industry • Change how the industry operates

INDUSTRY STRUCTURE

Source: Hussey 1994

GE GROWTH MATRIX

Business Strength

Industry Attractiveness		Strong	Average	Weak
	High	Invest/ Grow	Invest/ Grow	Hold
	Medium	Invest/ Grow	Hold	Harvest or Divest
	Low	Hold	Harvest or Divest	Harvest or Divest

Confirming corporate strategy with a BCG-matrix

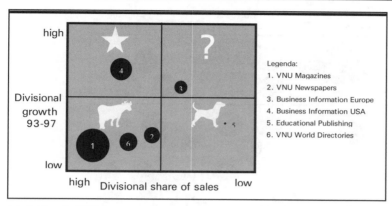

Legenda:
1. VNU Magazines
2. VNU Newspapers
3. Business Information Europe
4. Business Information USA
5. Educational Publishing
6. VNU World Directories

Adapted from the BCG

COMPETITOR PROFILE

Financial performance

	Group			Division			Unit	
	YR	YR	YR	YR	YR	YR	YR	YR
Sales								
PBT								
PAT								
ROA								
ROS								
Sales growth								
EPS								

Product portfolio

	Sales		Direct costs		Contribution		Market share		
Products/service s 1	YR	YR	YR	YR	YR	YR	YR	YR	YR
2									
3									
4									
5									
6									
7									
8									

Marketing & sales activity

Importance of activity to group

Scope of international operations

Sources of competitive advantage	
SOURCE	NOTES
Infrastructure	
R&D	
HRM	
Procurement	
Logistics in	
Operations	
Logistics out	
Marketing	
Sales	
Services	
E-business	

Key success factors

Strengths   **Weaknesses**

Implications   Implications

Critical success factor ratings

Factor	Competitor	Own	Index

Notes: Access each factor 0-10

Index is competitor score divided by own score

Apparent strategy

Organization philosophy

Personnel policies

Example positioning statement

Management consultancy ——— Business consultancy ——— Software vendor

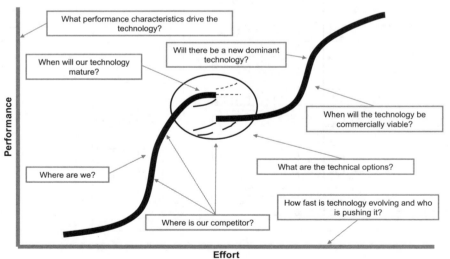

© 2006, Rodenberg Tillman Associates

Technology Based Intelligence

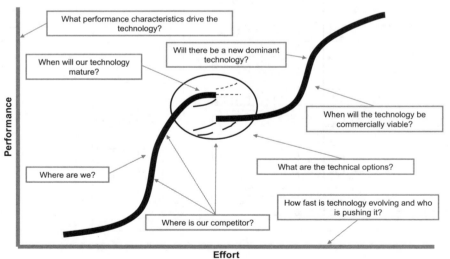

What performance characteristics drive the technology?

Will there be a new dominant technology?

When will our technology mature?

When will the technology be commercially viable?

Where are we?

What are the technical options?

Where is our competitor?

How fast is technology evolving and who is pushing it?

Performance

Effort

Source: SCIP US 1999

The Competitive Assessment Model

Fierceness level of competitive threat

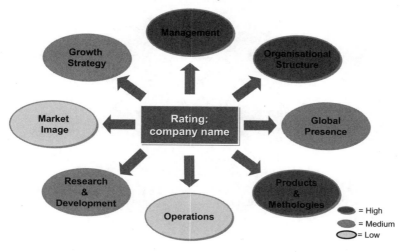

Source: M. Settecase in CIR 3/1999

STRATEGIC POSITION AND ACTION EVALUATION:
SPACE

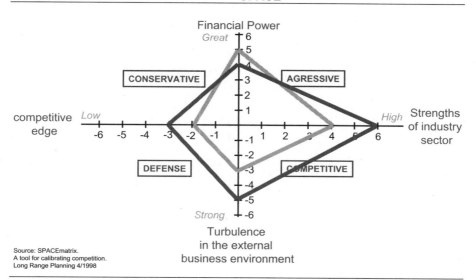

Source: SPACEmatrix.
A tool for calibrating competition.
Long Range Planning 4/1998

PART III

Epilogue

III

Epilogue

"Most of us never recognize opportunity until it goes to work in our competitor's business".
(P.L.Andarr)

1. Do you buy competitive intelligence as a pre-condition for future business success?
2. Do you see competitive intelligence as the differentiating factor for staying ahead of competition?
3. Do you see competitive intelligence as the potential driver of innovation?
4. Do you see competitive intelligence as able to identify future uncertainties?
5. Do you see competitive intelligence as able to monitor future developments?

If so, don't wait much longer before implementing competitive intelligence in your organisation. Establishing competitive intelligence in your organisation is a challenge but the rewards are immense. It's not a matter of asking yourself if competitive intelligence will be valuable to your organisation, but ask yourself how to make competitive intelligence valuable. Competitive intelligence is of no interest if you are not competing.

"Success is not to be measured by the position someone has reached in life, but by the obstacles he or she has overcome while trying to succeed".

Competitive intelligence can overcome all kinds of obstacles faced by management every day, and can identify potential threats, opportunities, emerging and future events in time. It's the ultimate driver for staying ahead of the competition by identifying the business foresights of changes that occur in your organisation's competitive landscape. Competitive intelligence is about avoiding surprises in the market place, eliminating blind spots in your own strategies and in the strategies of your counterparts, counteracting complacency and arrogance; it is the new art of being able to compete anyway. It's about making mergers and acquisitions more successful, it's a driver for business development and innovation and it feeds the strategic management processes. It feeds into scenario planning and analysis, strategies under uncertainty and strategic war mapping.

"Look ahead for opportunities. Forget the past. No one becomes successful in the past".

Why competitive intelligence, you may ask? I have a simple answer: enriched information and action. If you agree that information is the lifeblood of the organisation, why does management in most organisations still struggle so much with the management of information. Management is still managed by information rather than being able to manage information so as to take the best decisions. OK, you will answer that you have optimal solutions in place: many information technology-driven information systems such as business intelligence solutions, management information systems, balance score cards, the numerous performance management solutions and all the wonderful visually-based management cockpit solutions. So why would you need competitive intelligence as well? I have some simple questions for you. Do all these solutions deliver you intelligence? Do they deliver you the actionable intelligence for making the best imaginable decisions? Are you able to see in time the dramatic changes in the external business environment? Do you have a monitoring radar in place to foresee those changes? Do you agree with me that the most important decisions are taken not inside organisations, but outside organisations? Competitive intelligence has all of this, enables your organisation to compete successfully and is a pre-condition for existence and long-term company survival.

> *"Almost all men are intelligent. It is method they lack".*
> (F.W. Nichol)

Methods are the masters of masters. Competitive intelligence is such a method but above all another way of doing business. Employees make organisations intelligent and alert. Not information technology, in which management has invested and will keep investing for many hundreds of billions.

Year by year, 50 percent of all these investments still fail. It's people that make the difference in organisations. Change your priorities: invest in people. Make information and knowledge-sharing finally happen, if you agree with me that information is the lifeblood of every organisation. Competitive intelligence makes it happen. Now you will ask what level of investment should be made in competitive intelligence? The cost is peanuts compared to the benefits; it pays dividends.

The average investment in building a competitive intelligence competency is around 50,000 – 100,000 Euros for medium-sized organisations and around 100,000 – 200,000 Euros for large organisations. These are small amounts of investment compared to all the other investments organisations make in IT, performance management solutions, balance scorecards and all the other systems for measuring the control of the many departments in the organisation and above all control of your employees. One result of this is that it stifles creativity and kills entrepreneurship among your people, and destroys above all inspiration and passion to do things differently.

If you decide to implement competitive intelligence in your organisation, I recommend that you place the competency not in some department like marketing, nor in the middle-management layer. Of course, this is the practice area of competitive intelligence. No, you must place competitive intelligence at the top of the organisation, as the military and governments do; you might regard it as your organisation's chief of staff. Competitive intelligence starts with the guys at the top. This leaves only one possible place to position competitive intelligence within the organisation: on a par with the other functions which report directly to the Board of Management, Executive Committee or General Management.

> *"The best solution to where to place the office of competitive intelligence is on a par with functions that report directly to the Board".*

Sources

Newspapers: numerous publications from the Dutch newspapers Financieele Dagblad, Telegraaf, NRC Handelsblad, Volkskrant, Next and the international newspapers Financial Times and Wall Street Journal Europe, International Herald Tribune. Information from these sources combined with knowledge creates new knowledge and new business insights

Magazines: some publications in EuropeanCEO, FEM, Trends, Chief Information Officer, Management Team, Management Development, CFO

Management publications: Harvard Business Review, Competitive Intelligence Magazine

Business & Competitive Intelligence, management discipline in the 21st Century by Joseph H.A.M. Rodenberg. ISBN 9014063334. Samsom Management Selection, 2000

Enterprise Intelligence, creating the intelligent and alert organisation by Joseph H.A.M. Rodenberg. ISBN 905972013X. Eburon Publishers, 2004

The International Master Classes Competitive Intelligence of Rodenberg Tillman & Associates, 2003-2007, The Netherlands

The Business Intelligence Institute of Rodenberg Tillman & Associates, the Netherlands. Course materials from The Intelligence Specialist, The Intelligence Professional, The Intelligence Strategist, the Two Day International Master Class Competitive Intelligence

United Business Institutes Brussels, Belgium. Numerous case studies as part of Final MBA Graduation Programs 2003-2006

University of Novi Sad, Serbia. Numerous case studies as part of Final MBA Graduation Programs 2003-2006

University of Hanoi, Vietnam. Input of case based human & organisational intelligence 2004

American National Science Foundation. Research on the migration of R&D. FD April 6 2006

Nyenrode University. Professor P.K. Wagenaar. Research on migration of R&D. FD April 6 2006

Professor Steven Brakman of Groningen University and Maikel Batelaan at the National Congress of VSB 2005. FD April 21 2006

The world most innovative companies / BCG. Business Week April 24 2006

Dominique Moïsi of the French Institute of International Affairs. NRC April 28 2006

Hollandse Overmoed(Dutch Overconfidence) by Mathijs Bouman ISBN 9050186998

Straight From the Gut, by Jack Welch, 2001 ISBN 9027424349

Leadership in the 21st Century, Jack Welch. Management Team May 2006

Airbus Ambitions. Philips Semiconductors. Management Team May 2006

Harvard Business Review May 2006. Are leaders portable? 20 former GE executives

Harvard Business Review November 2005. Scanning the Periphery by George Day and Paul Schoemaker.

Missions of SCIP 1986, 2003, 2005. Publication in CIM March-April 2006 by Cliff Kalb.

Schaduwen over de woestijn, J.J. Brouwer, ISBN 90-808109-1-6

Seeing what's next, Clayton Christensen, ISBN 1-59139-185-7

The secret language of competitive intelligence, Leonard M. Fuld, ISBN 978-0-609-61089-3

The 33 Strategies of War, Robert Greene, ISBN 0-670-03457-6

Harvard Business Review July/August 2005. Manage your Human Sigma

Competitive intelligence research study 2005-2006 by SCIP Foundation & Cipher Systems

Code of Ethics of SCIP; www.scip.org

Key Intelligence Topics: created by Jan Herring for the CI Society

Key Intelligence Topic Analysis Iraq. Information gathered from the FT February 2004

Strategy as Active Waiting. HBR September 2005

Information Audit. Rodenberg Tillman & Associates

Strategic Audit. Rodenberg Tillman & Associates

SMP Portfolio Management. BCG/Insead in FT August 8 1998

Forecasting Emerging Technologies. Business case Automotive Study Rodenberg Tillman & Associates, July 2006

Competitive Impact Mapping and Current Technology Position Mapping. Arthur D. Little 2003

Technology Play Mapping, Shell, SCIP Benelux June 2003

Trade Show Intelligence. CIM 2/2005

Strategy Flexibility. CIM 1/2004

Organizational capabilities assessment. HBR July 2004

Scenario Planning. Royal Dutch Shell and GIA

Whitepaper Competitive Intelligence in the Netherlands. Dutch Strategy Forum VSB. January 2007 by Arnold van der Post and Joseph Rodenberg

Tom Peters on Management. Seminar Nyenrode University December 19 2006

Why mergers & acquisitions fail? Publication of a study by KPMG in FD January 2 2007

Case STMicroelectronics. CFO July/August 2007

Trophy of the new Russia. FD December 23 2006

Case EADS. Wall Street Journal October 27-29 2006

China's supply chain risk. CFO Global Outlook 2007

Connect + Develop by Procter&Gamble's new way of building of building external relationships. www.pg.com

Case Ford. Wall Street Journal December 2006

Ten recommendations for surprising attacks at Boards of Directors. FD October 7 2006

Good to Great. Jim Collins 2001

The Baseline Revolution. Hans Johnsson and per Erik Kihlstedt. 2003. Chapter V and VI have been based on this publication combined with two seminars on these topics in Sweden in 2004 and 2005. In 2004 and 2005 two whitepapers have been written by Joseph H.A.M. Rodenberg on the key topics based on the concept of The Baseline Revolution and have been adapted and fine tuned in this book

Strategy under Uncertainty. Case Rodenberg Tillman & Associates and based on the McKinsey model in HBR 1997

Breakthrough technologies. Publication How to deal with breakthrough innovations. SMO December 2006

Managing your Human Sigma. HBR J/A 2005. This publication has been partly adapted to the chapter on customer intelligence

Thomas Jonsson. Managing director/Founder of Enertio Sweden. Customer intelligence related to ClientIndicator

Case IBM. International Conference DCIF in Dresden, November 2006

Case Infineon. International Conference DCIF in Dresden, November 2006

Advanced Analysis Techniques and Baseline Assessment IBM. International Conference DCIF, Dresden, November 2006

The US Army Leadership Field Manual. McGraw-Hill. 2004

The Marine Corps Way. Jason Santamaria, Vincent Martino and Eric Clemons. 2004

The Art of War. Sun Tzu

Case Corus. Based on the publication in NRC Handelsblad October 25 2002

CFO Global Outlook 2007. January 2007

The Rise of the Rogue Executive. Leonard Sayles and Cynthia Smith. 2006

Key Intelligence Topics. Concept developed by Jan Herring.

Intelligence Economique. The Martre and Carayon Reports in 1993 and 2003. Presentation of Jamie Smith, Professor at Rennes International School of Business, Rennes, France

Twelve steps of scenario planning. GIA and CIM